Lifting the Covers

Also by Glenn Turner

My Way, 1975

Glenn Turner's Century of Centuries, with Ray Cairns, 1983

Opening Up, with Brian Turner, 1987

Lifting the Covers

by

GLENN TURNER

IN COLLABORATION WITH

Brian Turner

Longacre Press

ISBN 1 877135 19 4

First published 1998 by Longacre Press Ltd.,
P.O. Box 5340, Dunedin, New Zealand.

Reprinted 1998

Cover and book design by Jenny Cooper.
Front cover photograph by Reg Graham.
Printed by GP Print, Wellington, New Zealand.

Contents

DEDICATION

To New Zealand cricket's
genuine lovers of the game

The search for truth, 'It's about acquiring the courage of one's own thought, and if it's impossible to have courage without convictions, it's equally impossible to have convictions without knowledge and understanding.'

– Lewis H. Lapham

ACKNOWLEDGEMENTS

I couldn't have produced this book without the help of many people, most of whom have a considerable interest in the game of cricket.

Particular thanks to Gren Alabaster, Lee Germon, and Mark Plummer for their important contribution in support of a New Zealand cricket management team which was put through some very difficult hoops; to Brian Talbot for his friendship and help with work on contracts and job descriptions; to Richard Redgrove for his photographs and for putting up with me during the filming of TV pitch reports, and to Jimmy Biggam for the good times we shared when he was on the TVNZ Outside Broadcast team.

Thanks to Deek Rose for his photographs; to Peter Ingham of Unisys for wagon-wheel charts, and to Peter Marriott for his assistance in providing statistics. Acknowledgements too, to Shell and Hodder Moa Beckett – the editors and publishers of recent editions of the *Shell Cricket Almanack* of New Zealand, which was very useful for both reference and statistical information.

To my fellow TV commentators, and other members of the production unit, for their cooperation; and particular thanks to John Morrison, Ian Smith, and John Wright, for regular debate and exchanges of ideas.

Many thanks to Roger Dodd, John Howells, Erkin Bairam, and others for numerous philosophical discussions over a pint of beer in the university staff club in Dunedin. And similar thanks to the proprietor Pat McCarrigan, his family and staff, and the Friday night Guinness school at The Rover's Return in Caversham where sport in general and a great deal else gets a fair hammering.

Thanks to Toni Germon for information and opinions; to Peter Haig for his thoughts on one-day cricket; to Molly Anderson for her sentiments, and to H.C. (Peter) Hildreth for support and copies of his correspondence with Christopher Doig of NZC.

Thanks to lawyers Garth Gallaway, Diccon Sim, and David Howman; to Professor of Law John Smillie, to photographer Reg Graham, to Glenda Hughes for gifting me one of Murray Webb's caricatures, and to Paula Boock, Barbara Larson, Annette Riley, and Jenny Cooper of Longacre Press for editorial, marketing and design work.

Thanks to Jeremy Coney for his 'Foreword', and to various journalists – Ron Palenski, Richard Boock, Jo Romanos, John Campbell, Roy Colbert and Don Cameron among them – for useful observations and information.

Apart from the individuals named above, I want to thank collectively all those people who sent me letters and other messages of support and goodwill after I was sacked.

I want to acknowledge the support of my family, and to apologise to them for all the hassles I've caused by exposing myself to the negative political forces of the organisation known as New Zealand Cricket.

I thank, too, a number of present and former New Zealand players who talked to me or my brother Brian, and provided us with useful observations and information. For obvious reasons they asked that they not be named. Such is the climate of New Zealand cricket.

G.M.T

Foreword

by Jeremy Coney

I don't read many sports books. They're too predictable and banal. Some should be consigned to the book graveyard instantly. Cricket has played a part in pushing the boundaries of ill-feeling, bad blood and controversy here. From outside it seems a minefield landscape of conspiratorial whispers, subterfuge and lies.

So it will come as little surprise to learn that I haven't read *Lifting the Covers*, yet – just the first thirty or so pages. This leaves me – and you – at a disadvantage, but what I can do is suggest what kind of reading glasses you might wear; the contextual focus to your thinking; the sorts of things I'll be looking for (yeah, okay – I'll be reading it).

It's been a curious alliance, Glenn Turner and me. In 1973 he was injured so I got the chance to tour. He redamaged his hand before the second test enabling me to play my first. Then in 1985 he was confirmed as cricket manager and became (for me) a shoulder and a library. I gleaned (Glenned?) all I could from his experience. He was a key resource. And how absurd it is, when New Zealand Cricket is desperate for knowledge, that Glenn Turner is lost to them.

As a player he let his bat do the talking. But it was his talking and thinking that attracted controversy. He wasn't easy to get to know. His friendship wasn't the mateship kind. Well – we all know people like that. People respected his cricket skills but mumbled about coldness, unyielding obstinacy and an inability to let the human parts out. Often this meant he'd challenged, or made them feel embarrassed.

One charge you could never level at Glenn Turner was he didn't take what he was doing seriously. Yes, he might be difficult to shift once a decision was made, but in arriving at the decision he was a meticulous planner. He analysed issues by asking questions others decided to avoid. I'm not talking so much about his conclusions here but the process involved. I've always found Glenn Turner principled and forthright. These may be an uncomfortable combination at times but they can also lead to the wellsprings of improvement.

There will be those who won't be looking forward to this book. Readers should be aware that I am acting in the role of substitute – I've accepted this only after New Zealand Cricket declined to write the Foreword!

It's my guess (knowing Turner as I do) that in the course of its contours, this narrative will turn its filtering eye on key problems facing New Zealand Cricket's future. The real issues that prevent and hinder progress.

My advice to you is, discard past reputations, one-dimensional talkback opinions and third-hand bar gossip. And read smart.

If it's good, it'll raise more questions than answers – and we need a good sports book.

Introduction

Who'd want to take on the shambles that was New Zealand cricket after the South African tour debacle in 1994? Take on the job of restoring the game in the eyes of the public which had lost respect for the team and many of the players, saw them as ill-disciplined both on and off the field, lacking in skills, strategy, and resolve? Saw them as unprofessional, spoilt, deluded? Well, I did. But I'd hardly got started before I got the chop. This book is partly about that; it is also about why I took on the job, what I found after earnest enquiry, what I was trying to achieve with my co-selectors, captain and manager. It's about what we did as a New Zealand cricket team, and why. It's also about what I had in mind for the future, and it concludes with some observations about what has happened since.

From the outset I was very much interested in seeing New Zealand cricket's performance improve in every respect. Both team management and the players generally were keen to see New Zealand teams play good cricket; intelligent and inventive cricket whenever possible. Attacking cricket, cricket that's enjoyable to play and to watch. We wanted and were determined to be competitive; we wanted to help players improve their knowledge, their skills, their overall performance. We wanted to be seen as a truly professional unit, one that regained the respect of the cricketing public. I think we achieved quite a lot in those regards. But we had some problems obtaining the cooperation of a few players, some of whom had been a thorn in the side of previous management, and who, our team management can see now, were never going to change.

At times in this book I refer to instances involving certain players as examples of how and why teams go wrong, or for the purpose of discussing issues. Normally I wouldn't publicly disclose the less appealing antics of some players. But because of the way a few publicly and behind the scenes undermined and attacked me and other members of our management team, depicted us as intolerant, inflexible, unreasonable people – ogres, even – I think the cricketing public will be interested in the sorts of behaviour and attitudes we were dealing with. I've had enough of being vilified by people in support of their own interests. And what is more, unless certain behaviour is exposed it is likely to continue in New Zealand cricket.

While I am naturally concerned about what happened to us – particularly Germon, Alabaster and me – all along my greater concern has been for the messages given to cricketers, and for the nature, style, reputation and future of the superb game of cricket as it is played and administrated in this country.

I hope, too, that some people might find it interesting to observe the parallels between what has been going on in New Zealand cricket in recent years and what has been happening in New Zealand society as a whole. Here I think of what a former chairman of the Worcestershire County Cricket Club once said to me: 'Cricket is not a game, it is a culture', and he went on to say that the game was like an extension of what was occurring in the society of the time.

Chapter 1

The Wrong Culture

In 1994 I was in India working as a TV commentator for World Tel covering a tri-series of one-day internationals between India, New Zealand and the West Indies. The general feeling in India was that New Zealand had performed abysmally in that tournament. When New Zealand had finished its last game in Delhi, and been trounced again, I was sitting with the cans – headphones – on awaiting instructions when I overheard the TV director Gary Frances say, 'Well, thank Christ that's the last we'll see of the New Zealanders.' That struck a chord with me, an unwanted and discordant one. Then, because I'd had so much involvement with New Zealand cricket over a long period of time, I thought that rather than just sit up in the commentary box and suffer sub-standard performances, and have to comment on them, I would like to try to do something about it. (As an aside, until you actually give up playing you don't often realise just how important the game is to so many people. It matters a lot to cricket-lovers.)

I found when I got home that I still had the urge to get involved again in coaching the national side. I thought I could make a difference and, with help from the right people, go a fair way towards turning things round. It is our national team, and it is good when its performance gives one's countrymen and women pleasure. I saw the coach's job as a privilege and a chance to start to build a team that cricket-lovers would respect and therefore support. I was certainly grateful for, and felt honoured to be given the opportunity to work for the betterment of New Zealand cricket.

A number of people have remarked that only a fool or a brave person would take on the job of coaching or managing the New Zealand men's cricket team in the nineties. I know what they mean.

My background in cricket generally, and New Zealand cricket specifically, meant I had no illusions: I realised that I was taking on a tough job. I knew that the amount of travelling would be difficult – getting back on the jet-touring trail which I'd done for perhaps too many years as a player was not something to be relished. I knew, too, that I would have to deal with some awkward buggers, but felt that eventually, by getting the team to set up good routines and systems, things would become easier.

And because I had been professionally involved in cricket for the last 30 years, and had very likely played and seen more first-class cricket than any other New Zealander, I thought it was worth a try. After all, in the course of my career I played in many internationally diverse sides throughout the cricketing world, and I had been New Zealand coach before, in the eighties. From the time I stopped playing first-class cricket in 1984 I have continued to be involved with the game, coaching and commentating.

Add to that 10 years of managing a sports trust which greatly improved my skills in organisation, reporting, running meetings and co-ordinating the efforts of committees and other groups of people. This was important because as a player one doesn't acquire a very broad perspective of the game – a question of not seeing the wood for the trees. My overall knowledge of the game has improved immeasurably in the years since I stopped playing.

So I was by no means heading into the unknown, or so I thought.

* * *

I had been the 'cricket manager', as the coach was called then, in the 1980s when Jeremy Coney had been captain, Dave Elder the manager, and we'd enjoyed a successful campaign in Australia. But in the nineties the wrong culture – to use a vogue term – developed in the national team. The rot was clearly evident prior to the 1992 World Cup in which New Zealand performed very well. Our very commendable results in the competition attracted excessive attention, actually served to mask New Zealand cricket's deeper problems rather than rectify them. This view is shared by many others, including one of the most senior members of the 1992 World Cup team, who said he noted a marked and off-putting change in the attitude of several of the players around that period. He said many players embraced and believed all the advertising and media hype promoting them as superstars. They were given too much rope. Senior players were left to lead and educate the less experienced. That's fine, if the players concerned are strong, sensible and truly professional. They weren't, unfortunately.

The Board which appointed me in 1995 had come to realise this only too well. The climate in New Zealand cricket was awful. Management had had a gutsful of the players, and their antics; but the players had also had a gutsful of management. Look for trust and mutual respect and it was hard to find any. I wanted to establish respect and trust, bring both sides together.

Apprehending Realities

Within a few weeks of taking over I had read several reports to New Zealand Cricket (NZC) which backed up many of my own observations, which were that our key senior players hadn't measured up, were not highly regarded as role models. On top of this, management appeared to have been lenient and to have worked on the assumption that if players were happy they would perform well. But except for the super-heated few weeks during the World Cup the team was no more nor less happy than teams usually are.

Prior to my appointment John F. Reid had spent three months as an interim New Zealand coach after the departure of Geoff Howarth. He hadn't liked what he'd found. He saw: a lack of self-esteem and confidence amongst the players; poor personal standards of dress, grooming and lack of respect for people around the team; poor standards of personal and team preparation for matches (both practice and mental); some major technical problems with some players; a lack of strong decisive leadership within the unit; a lack of respect for NZC administration and the game; a team culture that promoted over-use of alcohol and lack of adequate rest/sleep by many players; concern regarding financial remuneration and the future directions of the 'contract' scheme; a lack of respect for the role of sports science and the academy in terms of performance enhancement; an inappropriate mixing of team/coaching management and selectorial roles; confused communication lines within NZC.

Not much that I wanted to disagree with there.

He said that both he and the manager, Gren Alabaster, had to focus on building standards and that 'Personal responsibility for preparation, planning and performance must be drummed into our developing players.' He also wanted 'to see the development of more player responsibility rather than rely on [the] coach to constantly check that work is done.'

All this seemed to square with my own observations on the state of the national team. So it was pretty clear, I thought, what NZC expected of me and the incoming management team. We – by that I mean Alabaster, captain Lee Germon, physiotherapist Mark Plummer and I – wanted to create an environment and routines whereby the players didn't feel, and couldn't say, that there was an 'us and them' situation. We all knew and accepted that we would have to be careful, fair and thorough if we were to alleviate the problems and develop fairness and trust. We also knew that it would take time to develop this, perhaps more than a year, given the nature of a few of the players in the team.

Further, we also knew that whatever structures we put in place could easily be dismantled by those who followed. We realised – or I did – that we might well end up being seen to have wasted our time. Nevertheless I felt that we needed to try to assist in the development of a group of senior players – or those that had been there for a while – and some new ones, who were keen to create a different culture from that which had grown up. A culture that was strong, that was underpinned by a much better tactical approach to cricket.

We needed a group at the top who were able to play and behave like true professionals and lead by example. Then, at the very least, you would have an overall culture – attitude, approach, discipline, skill – that would last for the length of their playing time. With luck that might be up to 10 years or more.

I'm a great believer in the dictum that eventually things have to come from the players because management personnel change more rapidly – in most cases – than the bulk of the team members. We were keen to set up a system whereby players became more self-sufficient, well-organised and truly professional. Something that would endure and help players survive the rigours of travelling and everything else that goes with playing international cricket. I had hopes of establishing a culture that would be carried on long after I'd gone, led by a group of players who had faith in each other, respect for the game, and were part of a team which the cricketing public admired. Players who'd earned respect. That's the sort of quiet pride I was seeking to instil and elicit. A pipedream? Of course, but worth trying. Cricket teams cannot function properly if one or two self-appointed leading lights expect to be deferred to most of the time, and their irrational or unreasonable behaviour tolerated because 'we're all individuals'. In the parlance of the day, New Zealand cricket was suffering from an overdose of those who talk the talk but won't, or can't, walk the walk.

A New Administration

I was employed by the tail-end of one administration which was fed-up and at the end of its tether with the conduct and performance of the national team. They wanted me to work to re-establish high standards both on and off the field. Then along came a new lot of administrators.

In sport as in business – and it's sometimes difficult to separate the two – the tone, the practice, the culture is often set by CEOs. In my view today's so-called corporate model provides CEOs with an unhealthy amount of power.

To me the new CEO of NZC, Chris Doig, who arrived, unfortunately, just after I took over as coach, brought some good and a lot of bad to our cricket. Since then I have often wondered how an organisation that employed me as coach could also have appointed a CEO, Chris Doig, whose views and approach are so diametrically opposed to mine.

The more I think of it the more bemused I become. The administration had identified severe problems in our cricket. They felt I was the person to put in place procedures that would, in a year or two, go a fair way towards rectifying things and set our cricket up for the future. So what did they do? They appointed a CEO determined to take them down a path that could only lead to a perpetuation of the sorts of problems I was employed to fix. Of course, Doig did say when interviewed for his job – so I'm told – that he was a great admirer of mine and was looking forward to working with me. Doig initially said to me that he didn't know a lot about cricket but he was 'a bloody good administrator'. I thought that meant he would leave the cricket to me. I soon found that this was not to be the case.

A Management Philosophy

When I got the job it was clear I wasn't going to be every player's cup of tea. But no one is. Nor was I the first choice of John F. Reid or Rod Fulton, then Director of New Zealand Cricket, and subsequently sacked from his job for allegedly leaking 'sensitive' information and speaking out of turn. I was disappointed when Rod was sacked because we were developing a very good working relationship.

I had the support of then Board member Cran Bull and All Black coach John Hart. (Hart subsequently told my brother Greg that he'd thought that rugby politics were complicated and full of intrigue but that cricket's outstripped rugby's by far. Hart's observation is similar to that of a prominent member of the New Zealand Sports Foundation who said that cricket was the 'soft underbelly of New Zealand sport'.)

When the then Board gave me the coach's job they said that they were well aware of the usual raft of criticisms of me that issued from the same people each time: uncompromising, inflexible, not good on man-management, etcetera. But they felt that the team needed a 'hard nosed... type of person at the moment.' It was thought, however, that my so-called tempered-steel hardness, and alleged inability to be sensitive enough towards the needs of tender individuals, could 'be addressed by the appointment of the right manager.' I'll discuss these things in due course, but for now suffice to say that I was well aware that certain people saw me as a determined and autocratic coot. But the way we set up management structures and procedures ('protocols' is the buzz term) showed that critics didn't know how we operated, or didn't want to.

I believe in a democratic approach. I was determined that my approach, and that of management overall, would be constructive and a whole lot softer than critics assumed. I was determined, too, to see that our system of management ensured that natural justice – by that I mean the right to a fair hearing and the opportunity to present one's case to a group rather than one individual – would prevail. There's nothing special about this, it's fundamental. This, I thought, would head them off at the pass, surely.

From the outset I expected that a few players would have difficulty with the sort of approach I hoped to establish. I had no illusions in that respect for the trend in so many areas is to encourage individualism and downplay our responsibilities towards the team and society as a whole. I knew certain players would not be willing to put the team's interest ahead of their own. When challenged some would try to undermine management, as they'd done previously, if they thought their position was threatened; you could say it's human nature.

Remember that we are talking about cricket at the highest level, so it is very demanding. Having experienced the pressures of playing and touring for years myself, the response of some players when asked to lift their performance and standards all round wasn't unexpected.

I did not and have never set myself up as the sort of coach who says, 'Do it for me, boys.' Coaches who look to have players do it for them are often more concerned with having their own egos bolstered. Unless an individual player is strong, has his own act together, then he's in no position to do very much for others.

Players have to want to succeed in order to have a clear conscience, for their own self-respect. That has to be a key motivation. The other key one, which runs alongside that, is wanting to perform well for and with the team.

Some are motivated by a wish to succeed for King (or Queen) and Country; some want to do it for family, others for friends, or for themselves. I don't see it as a coach's job to tell people which of such things to embrace, but for me the key ones are those I mentioned first: conscience – which includes meeting certain standards – and self-respect. I appreciate that patriotic feeling moves a lot of people and I respect that, but in my case I have always regarded myself as a human being first and a New Zealander second as a means of keeping things in better perspective. This helps develop a respect for other cultures and increases one's tolerance of difference.

I put together a 'Management Philosophy' for the national team. This worked on the assumption, 'That individual team members have their own motivational, psychological and physical make-up.' The philosophy or mission of team management was, 'To create an environment that promotes excellence and develops maturity, discipline, order, self-sufficiency and strength of character, whilst accommodating individual differences.' Most coaches, I suppose, have a similar end in mind. In my case it was to develop the team into a professional and consistently successful unit at both test and one-day international levels. I thought it would take a couple of years but didn't say so at the time. This aim was written into my contract with NZC. In the contract NZC required me to ensure that 'the individuals and the team play to the best of their ability... and that they are technically, physically and mentally prepared to the highest possible standard.' I was also required to ensure that 'appropriate team culture and individual attitudes are developed and maintained.'

While all this was discussed by team members and agreed to in what is sometimes called a workshop environment, some players don't think seriously about what's required and entailed. Sometimes the will or intelligence just isn't there; with some it comes down to a battle of wills, a fear that the individual might be unfairly subjugated and have to conform to the unfeeling might of the group. Mindful of that, management was at great pains to ensure that everything we agreed to contained a lot of flexibility.

Take the matter of the consumption of alcohol. The guidelines here referred to an amount 'appropriate to a professional athlete'. To me that's pretty open-ended.

My contract noted that as a member of the management team I was 'To develop and foster pride in playing for New Zealand and ensure that all the players represent the nation with credit both on and off the field.' I was also required 'To be proactive (along with the Tour Management Team) in ensuring that the strongest possible disciplines exist within the teams at all times,' and to see that as well as 'dressing smartly/tidily' all behaved 'in a manner appropriate to the status of the national team'. I didn't have a problem with that although it is fairly obvious that a few players did and have done for some time.

From time to time players will do things contrary to the team's agreed policy. You can find that they not only won't debate the issue, often they can't.

An example is when a player loses form and decides he will no longer play in accordance with the team's style, deliberately departs from the team's game plan, and refuses to discuss the matter. No matter how many discussions and team meetings are held, no matter how often you encourage debate, invite players to come and talk to you, they seldom will. It's easy for a player to say a policy is 'inflexible' without ever being willing to discuss the issue. So what tends to happen with some individuals, especially those who crumble under pressure and have difficulty coping, is that they ignore the fact that a management *team* is making decisions and instead prefer to point the bone at an individual. 'It's *his* fault, it's not me.'

I was accused of refusing to accommodate individual differences. I refute that. Of course people are different, have differing needs;

nevertheless if a team is going to function properly then there needs to be a framework within which people operate, otherwise things fall apart. Our framework was readily able to accommodate individual differences, of that I have no doubt.

The team aimed to ensure that individual needs were catered for while laying the foundation for 'collective unity and harmony'. The aim was to reach agreed goals 'through mutual communication, consultation, honesty and dedication.' I know, words and more words, but you can't do without them as a basis.

Overall there was quite enough communication and consultation for most players. A few thought there was too damned much. A few, the same few each time, speak of a lack of communication. Usually what they mean is that they would prefer to have a license to do what they please.

Team Management and the Nature of Teams

Team management and administration need to confer and co-operate when it comes to the make-up and management of teams. I'm not averse to reviews, and a case can possibly be made for using consultants. But reports should be the starting-, not the end-point. After returning from the West Indies, team management and the players had a right to have had a proper debriefing and brainstorming session. I am sure fair, reasoned and helpful conclusions and decisions – not to mention resolutions and accommodations – would have resulted. It never happened.

As management we tried to avoid springing things on players out of the blue, or changing tack willy-nilly. We looked for as much consistency and rationality as possible both on and off the field. Before we went on tour all players participated in a workshop at which we discussed such things as behaviour, lifestyle, timekeeping, media protocol, sponsorship obligations, wives/partners on tour, and so on. As a group we agreed to a set of standards. The players had 'ownership' of them.

It's worth emphasising that a touring professional cricketer's lifestyle is stressful and unnatural. We are talking about our international team; we are talking about the highest level of cricket, the highest level of a high-profile profession. We're talking about the requirements needed to perform at the highest level in the sport, and about what is required to prepare and perform at that level. We're talking about what's needed to optimise one's chances of success regularly.

To perform at a high level players have to prepare carefully and thoroughly in every way. The psychological pressures alone are difficult to overcome, and it's not enough for some to say that they'll do it their way thank you very much when it's pretty clear from their performance and behaviour in the past that it has not worked well enough for them. In itself the amount of time spent away from home is a major problem. Cricketers are away from home for far more extended periods than is common in other games. For example, in September 1995 we went to Darwin for two weeks. We returned to New Zealand for just a few days before going to India for about 8 weeks in October and November. No sooner were we back in New Zealand than we had to meet Pakistan in a test on 8 December. Pakistan was here until late December, then we had a series against Zimbabwe beginning early January. A few days after that series ended, in early February 1996 we took off for the World Cup one-day competition in India and Pakistan. No sooner was that over – there was no time to return to New Zealand – than we flew off to the West Indies where our first match in Jamaica was on 23 March. We finished with games in Bermuda on 11 May. Ponder and sweat over all that. Is it not a wonder the team and its performances held up as well as they did?

Compare this schedule with the All Blacks; compare it with the hours on the field, the size of the touring party, the back-up entourage, and so on. Consider, too, that the All Blacks tend normally to go only to western-style countries, not developing countries as cricketers often do, and you'll see that for the rugby players cultural and other differences are not so pronounced. In non-western countries players don't have the same number of options for easy socialising and the like when they leave their hotel. This forces players to spend even more time together and rely more on each other for support. It can become very inward-looking. Compare all that and imagine the stresses on cricketers.

Cricketers are constantly in the public eye, on and off the field. If you snore or pick your nose the public get to hear or see it. Players have to room with others and have hardly any real privacy. They train or play virtually every day, and for long periods of time. It's all-consuming; if a batsman's having a bad trot, wondering where the next run's going to come from can prey on your mind. If you're not in the first line-up it's tough mentally trying to keep up the fitness level and practise properly. Then there's the demand for media interviews on radio, TV, and for newspapers; and there's the official functions, the autograph sessions... no cakewalk.

To me it's no wonder there are occasional clashes between players and management; the wonder is that there aren't more. Which is a way of saying that I sympathise with players' difficulties: I was one, remember! The lifestyle of an international cricketer and the nature of the game can drive you close to insanity at times. It's a rare person who doesn't throw a wobbly. The constant travel and changing environment is very stressful.

Somewhere Sean Connery is reported as saying that 'Discipline is always worthwhile.' This doesn't mean that there is no room for fun, humour, socialising, relaxation, and so on. Quite the contrary. But it does mean getting one's priorities right. All my experience convinces me that players must become hardened and self-sufficient, self-reliant if they are to succeed in international cricket. They have to be able to look in the mirror and be honest with themselves, otherwise they won't succeed. There aren't too many cricketers of real note who have not been strong mentally. I can think of a small number, but they are few and far between.

Alabaster, Germon, Plummer and I tried to create an environment which would lift players to the level required to perform with the skill and discipline international cricket demands. There's no sadistic pleasure in this. But the great thing about cricket is that when you do well you gain terrific satisfaction from your performance because of the relentless demands of the game itself.

Happy Families: Praise that's Meaningful

A vocal few have accused me of not being caring and kind enough, not giving enough praise – or loud praise. I am not demonstrative when it comes to giving praise, but I make a particular point of acknowledging players' strengths as well as their weaknesses in order to develop and refine their art. Some coaches are liberal with their praise; a few are over-demonstrative to the point whereby it becomes indiscriminate and largely meaningless. They seem unaware that command performers become figures of fun.

I like to think that in my case a quiet word here or there comes to mean a good deal more. It is important for a coach to remind players of their strengths so that they don't diminish them while working to eradicate or mitigate weaknesses. The weaknesses are what hold you back. I would frequently say to guys, 'Don't take this as a criticism, but think of it as an area for improvement. I'm providing information. I'm offering technical, mental and tactical advice which may help you improve your game and the thought-processes involved.'

Nathan Astle told Lee Germon that once he got used to my approach he had no trouble with it and a quiet word from me meant a lot. Gavin Larsen said that on one occasion in the West Indies he'd bowled 10 overs for next to nothing and taken a couple of wickets. We'd won the game. When he came into the dressing room he remembered me sitting there and giving him a wink. 'That was enough for me,' he said.

Some say that when dealing with younger players, or those with little experience of top level cricket, one needs a more nurturing, softer approach to mine. I've never accepted this criticism because I don't rant, grandstand or raise my voice. I don't bawl at players when they perform badly. My approach has always been a soft and reasoned one. Having said that, I never soften the words; they are always to the point, as I see it, and I don't beat around the bush. I expect players to give of their best. If they fail in the effort when giving their all, then as a coach I'm not in the least bit tempted to upbraid them.

It's been said to me that a lot of the players are young, not much more than kids, and that they need to be treated accordingly. This is patronising and disrespectful to the majority who see the sense in a sound, consistent, considered approach to cricket both on and off the field. I'll admit that at times it can seem as if one's involved in a corrective training for boys exercise, but that's with a minority only.

The sporting public, and a number of officials, like teams to appear like happy families, and any sign of discord scares them. This group includes people who believe it's possible to find a coach who is all things to all players, or damned near it. Only if the coach is devious and dishonest. In time the chickens come home to roost with such coaches.

It's management's job to try to get team members to cooperate and be tolerant, and to work together for the good of the team. But you can't make people like each other, or necessarily have much respect for every member of the team. You should, though, insist they treat others with respect. Personalities and interests differ; some members of a team will never, at best, do more than abide some of their teammates. Take them away from cricket and they wouldn't want to even so much as pass the time of day with them. Of course it's better to have a happy unit, and one strives to achieve that, but in most cases success on the field enhances the chances of unity off it. I don't think it works the other way round to anywhere near the same degree.

There are exceptions of course. One is when a coach doesn't insist on high standards of conduct on and off the field, is prepared to tolerate poor behaviour. Players can quite quickly feel comfortable knowing that very little is deemed unacceptable. Another exception is when a coach, instead of upsetting a few players – which is the usual case – succeeds in offending just about all of them. This can have a bonding effect within a team. They're still playing for New Zealand, still getting all the attention that comes with it, irrespective of the quality of their performance.

For some reason cricket is a game in which enthusiastic amateurs come to believe that their knowledge and experience is the equal of top professionals. It doesn't appear to happen to the same degree in other major sports, in golf for example. In my dealings with John F. Reid of NZC I came to the conclusion that he was a romantic when it came to cricket, dreamed of some idealised team state where captain, manager, coach and team are one big happy family, united by mutual love, goodwill and understanding. He will ever be questing for that magic combination. Evidence suggests he'll have to look outside of human society.

Reid had been a member of the New Zealand side when I was coach in the eighties. Many of his teammates saw him as something of a softy, forever looking to the stands for acknowledgement and encouragement. Even the normally circumspect Richard Hadlee, sitting in the stand, sometimes took the piss out of Reid, saying things like, 'Look, there's Reido at it again. Yeah, we're watching Reido,' and then give him a wave. Reid was seen by many of the players as lacking a bit of bottle. The irony for me now is that I defended him in that regard, in an effort to keep him confident and positive about facing quick bowlers. It's significant that Reid cut short his own career, in part because he found the professional side of the lifestyle, especially touring, and the rigours of playing day after day, did not suit one of his temperament.

When I think back I'm not sure that a team needs to be happy to succeed. To be successful and happy is the ideal, of course. But in fact, some of the more successful teams that I've played for or been involved with weren't particularly happy. There can be all manner of differences off the field but the important thing is whether you can play in a professional manner on the park, and that involves the discipline and courage to follow intelligent game plans for instance.

It can even be argued that it's better not to keep the players too happy, in the sense that if they are contented then they're probably not stretching themselves enough.

International cricket is not a cosy environment, is not a normal workplace. When I began playing for Worcestershire in the 1960s Tom Graveney was our finest and highest-profile player. I found, to my surprise and disappointment, because I admired Tom both as a person and as a player, and thought that others were bound to, too, that he wasn't very popular with many of the players. In time I learned that most of those who weren't keen on him were simply jealous of his ability. I found Tom a very fair and considered individual.

When Bevan Congdon was captain of New Zealand he was not liked by most of the players. Bevan was so uncompromising, so unaccepting of failure – a dropped catch off his bowling for instance resulted in very terse words indeed – that the players actually hoped he would get whacked around when he was bowling. But one thing you could never say about Congdon was that he gave it away, gave less than everything he had for both himself and the team.

Looking for Consistency

To get consistency of performance you have to have a team of adults. International cricketers need to be mature if they are to survive in the game and develop the strength and ability which results in consistency. New Zealand cricket has gone round and round on this issue and tends to have harshly judged management and coaches, but not the players. Or *some* players.

When looking to achieve greater consistency and excellence of performance it is important to have a consistent team selection policy. It's also important that batsmen get accustomed to following the strategy needed for them to play particular roles. For this reason, generally it doesn't help to switch the batting order round, especially at the top of the order. The middle order is different and those there can expect more changes in response to altered or altering circumstances during a game. This is where tactical nous, astuteness and an ability to read a game comes in. Here it obviously helps to have a coach who has both played and seen a great deal of one-day and test cricket.

All players, along with their coach, need to go through the various scenarios that develop in a game. In time they then develop the instinct which enables them to intuit and respond to the moment. The coach and the players get to know the game so well that they'll say, 'Ah, such and such is happening, so we will put this plan into action to counter it or, conversely, take advantage of it.' This requires a high level of cricketing intelligence and ability from all concerned, and that is what must be striven for. A love of cricket does not give you that, a deep knowledge of it can.

If you have that knowledge you will not be taken by surprise by the way a game turns. You will be able to diagnose and recognise when a certain stage in the game has been reached. An example might be after the first 15 overs, say around 20 overs, when a batsman comes in and plays as if it's over 48 of 50. The bowling side quickly has to alter its approach, perhaps start bowling block-holers. Or the situation may be that a side's lost several wickets and because lower-order batsmen have come in, block-holers are inappropriate, that type of bowling is not the best tactic. Knowledge of the sort of flexibility required comes with experience but also with guidance from astute, informed people.

It helps bowlers to know that generally they will bowl at certain stages of an innings. But they must be willing to make adjustments when required as a consequence of tactical changes or circumstances in a game. Diagnosis is a critical part of the roles of both the coach and the captain, and the process is ongoing. A good team will develop consistency through working on basic strategies and an attractive style of play. But the captain and coach must remain alert and, when circumstances change, be prepared to react and alter their approach. That's where flexibility is needed. Also, team selection must reflect the style of play adopted. As an example I would cite our case where, having decided to attack from the start of the innings in one-day games, we chose sides that batted right down to number nine or ten in the order. But you also have to jiggle things so that the side has at least five front-line bowlers plus two five-tenthers to provide cover in case it's one of those days when one of the top five isn't on-song. New Zealand – and most other sides too, for that matter – still finds that to be the case quite often.

The need for flexibility is therefore a given. But so, and probably more so, is the need for a side to adopt a style of play, and strategies that go with it, and stick to it for some time. In other words, practise it on the field of play. That way you refine it and get better at playing it. The big danger is that some players, and coaches, get cold feet too quickly and chop and change their style and strategies from game to game. That isn't smart; it's scatterbrained, indicative of a loss of nerve and a lack of confidence in their knowledge of the game.

International cricketers and coaches have to be able to keep their nerve. They have to have thought long and hard about their theories and practise them before they are introduced. I understand why some players start to have their doubts, especially when they have got out a couple of times playing loose shots. Then there's a tendency for them to feel that they are risking their position in the side if they continue to play freely. But once they get accustomed to striving to extend themselves, stretch their boundaries both technically and mentally, the rewards can be very great and satisfying. They learn and go up a level. In 1995 Lee Germon and I were very conscious of the fact that some of our players had strike-rates in the sixties per hundred balls and that for them and the side to become more competitive we had to push them to lift their rates into the seventies. They did.

Bowlers, too, have to recognise when a batsman has been lucky and has taken runs from a loose or risky shot. Or has played a good shot to a loose ball. A bowler has to guard against insisting the field be changed whenever this happens, has to maintain his faith in his ability not to bowl many of the bad balls that allow batsmen to put him away.

Much of the above is specific to one-day cricket. In three- to five-day games batsmen can get used to batting in the one position in the order, and therefore psychologically attuned to that. This is helpful. Nevertheless, limited-over cricket strategies are being applied to the longer form of the game more and more. One result is that players who have been getting a preponderance of limited-overs cricket, which requires more flexibility, actually find that this adds a dimension to their play in tests and the like.

Characteristics more than Characters

Most people have no idea just how difficult and uncooperative some cricketers can be. Ask the captain. Time and again certain players try to get him to bat or bowl according to their preference should he win the toss. And when they don't succeed in getting their way, they are openly critical. That's irritating and creates negativity and uncertainty in the team. Then there are the problems that occur when individuals want to decide whether they practise or not, and when; whether the practice balls are new enough, or too new, and so on. It gets to a point where unless someone tells them to just get on with it chaos ensues.

My point is that one needs firm direction and a stable environment. We didn't have it all the time, of course, but we were determined to have it in the end. Or as far as you can reasonably expect from a disparate group of individuals.

From time to time it is suggested that today's cricketers are a lot different, implying that the current crop won't put up with attitudes and styles prevalent during my playing career which spanned the sixties to the eighties. Well, the way you play a cover drive has never changed, and there are certain values and basic courtesies that ought not be neglected. A few, just a few, of the current players fall short in this regard. But the fundamentals of cricket, and the requirements which go towards making a top cricketer remain the same. It is therefore puzzling and regrettable to find that some players have a lack of respect for the knowledge and experience of cricketers of their parents' generation. No one in my time would have said that people in their forties or fifties were 'too old' to coach or manage a national team. To my mind this is indicative of an erosion of respect for the middle-aged and elderly in our society, and NZC's administrators are exacerbating it by promoting cricket in ways that are off-putting to large numbers of more mature people. The so-called 'entertainment package' set up for one-day cricket is aimed at a very young audience. This invites several questions, among them, Are they coming for the cricket or is it a mere distraction? Does the whole presentation enhance or detract from the cricket itself? I know many of cricket's longer-term and most loyal supporters don't like it, feel alienated. In cricket as in society at large we have to ask, Who is setting the standard?

One thing that has changed and greatly influenced the behaviour, attitudes and standards of our cricketers is that many of them have never had to get up every day and go to work at eight or thereabouts in the morning. Our efforts to instil a proper work ethic came as a shock to a few.

Perhaps the point needs to be made in relation to team and playing standards, that as management we never had any expectation or intention of setting out to produce clones of ourselves. As former long-term Board and Life Member of NZC John Heslop said after sitting in on discussions between Alabaster, Germon and myself in the West Indies, 'Anyone who thinks that they were always of a similar mind and didn't have differences of opinion isn't very perceptive.'

Getting on with the Job

I officially took over as coach on 15 May 1995. NZC's then Director of Cricket, Rod Fulton, had been reviewing the state of New Zealand cricket and events of the previous year or two. That a thorough review was necessary was clear given the fiascos culminating in the indulgences of the tour of South Africa. I found Fulton to be an extremely hard worker, a determined burrower for information. He seemed genuinely concerned and dismayed about the overall state of New Zealand cricket both on and off the field. I felt Fulton and I struck up a rapport, held similar views on what was required. We worked together closely until he got fired; then it was my turn to feel dismayed.

I found that Rod and others in and around New Zealand cricket actually had stricter views or opinions than I did, particularly in relation to standards of dress, alcohol consumption, curfews and so forth. I saw my role more in terms of following through once views had been canvassed and policy established.

At the time I did not know that Fulton had been in favour of appointing the Australian Jeff Hammond as coach. Subsequently he told me that his views of me were largely based on hearsay and that to an extent he had been influenced by John Reid's opinion of me.

Fulton said that after working with me he didn't find me inflexible at all, he found me open to ideas and prepared to bend and change my approach. He felt that my reputation as a difficult bugger was grossly overstated and went back to the days when I was New Zealand's only genuine full-time professional and was trying to negotiate acceptable terms for myself with the New Zealand Board. Fulton thought that the stigma surrounding my spat with the New Zealand Board in the seventies remains and has continued to be used against me by my detractors whenever convenient.

I was keen to seek the establishment of an executive management group which ideally would include the CEO, the Director of Cricket (Fulton), and myself. The idea was that we would co-opt others when it came to looking in detail at specific areas of our cricket. But about the time I got my job the then CEO Graham Dowling resigned. This left Rod Fulton, me, and the Deputy-Chairman Cran Bull. It was Bull's casting vote that got me the coach's job, although I wasn't aware of it at the time. Fulton and I got on with our work.

I saw the job as going through several stages: first a thorough analysis of players' strengths and weaknesses, then giving the incumbent players an opportunity to prove themselves under what I hoped would be a fair, better-organised and consistent regime (and to give them ample time to adjust). From the time I took over we were looking ahead to almost seven months of international cricket, a great deal of it touring. Our team management and the national selectors saw this as a chance to identify and develop emerging players, and improve the standard of some of the incumbents. As selectors we were keen to see the emerging players get as much cricket as possible in the domestic series in New Zealand, so a lot of work was to be done in the background, with age-group tours and refinement at the cricket academy. Together we were looking to put in place strategies that would enable us to have new players of sufficient standard if we felt some of the older hands needed replacing.

I resolved to have a thorough look at all the leading players' records. That meant getting up-to-date statistics, and canvassing the opinions of coaches and selectors all over New Zealand. I was determined to garner the views of others and set them alongside mine before making decisions.

You don't have to be around cricket long to realise that some players have reputations not always justified by the quality of their records. Occasional outstanding performances have been enough for them to have acquired 'star' status in the eyes of some. This hasn't helped them or our cricket.

I set about gathering information. I read manager's and coach's reports from the previous two years; I obtained full statistical information on all of the players in contention for national selection (this included detailed stats on bowlers and batsmen for the most recent one-dayers and tests, about 35 matches in all, that had been played in the previous 12-18 months); I asked the Unisys man Peter Ingham to give me wagon-wheel charts showing the bowling and batting performances of several of the players in international matches in the previous season; I also went to TVNZ and got hours and hours of video tape of all the matches played during NZC's Centenary year, plus Shell Cup matches. My father Alf Turner went through the tapes and made a detailed list of times when various players featured on them. This meant that I was able to go quickly to the tapes and have a good look, frame by frame if need be, at just about all of our leading players.

I also went travelling, all over New Zealand, initially, and met with 16 coaches/selectors, six medical people, and four others including Dave Gerrard and Chris Ineson, head of the New Zealand Sports Foundation. I went and sounded out players, including Martin Crowe, Mark Greatbatch, Dipak Patel, Gavin Larsen, Adam Parore and Stephen Fleming. I got reports on the physical and mental capabilities of players and started developing short-, medium- and long-term plans for our cricket.

From the start I was determined to consult widely because I wanted to get a broad overall picture before I firmed anything up, and also because I had three roles to fulfil: selector, coach, and a consultant's role in the choice of the manager and other selectors. Before long it was clear we would have to look at setting up a tour management team (TMT) and discuss how it might operate. At the time I had more responsibilities than I would have liked but, because of Dowling's departure and the fact that we were in between administrations, so to speak, basically there was only me and Rod Fulton to get on with such work. When Fulton was removed I was left pretty much in isolation and tended to use NZC's general manager Tim Murdoch as a reference point. I thought Tim Murdoch and I worked closely and well together and had a decent understanding.

Cran Bull was helpful at the time and presented a report to the Board for me early on when I was overseas briefly.

At this time NZC's administration was in limbo, about to be reorganised and taken in a new direction in the playing area – which was where I came in – and also administratively. We were waiting on a report from the New Zealand Cricket Review Committee which was produced in August 1995 and entitled 'A Path to Superior Performance'.

Before I went off to talk to selectors and coaches I sent them all a letter. I said that I had put together a draft 'New Zealand Cricket Selector's Plan' which would be developed by the incoming panel after I'd gathered information and opinion on leading players. When seeking others' opinions on players' worth and abilities, it's not just a question of asking if somebody can play and how good they are. You need detail on how they'd assessed players and why they'd chosen them. I had a whole bunch of questions to put to them on batsmen and bowlers, and on their fielding. For batsmen I wanted them to list players' technical strengths and weaknesses by analysing defensive and attacking skills off the front and back foot on both sides of the wicket. I also wanted their views on players' theoretical knowledge and understanding of shot selection; I enquired about players' acceptance of game plans and their ability to adjust them to changing conditions and circumstances; I had questions about players' knowledge of when and how to attack and when to defend; skill at pacing a performance and their ability to identify strengths and weaknesses in their play.

I had questions on bowlers' actions and their ability to swing and/or seam the ball; I wanted opinions on their accuracy and the amount of bounce they obtained, and on their command of flight and spin. I wanted to know how the selectors and coaches assessed their bowlers' knowledge of bowling over and round the wicket; use of the crease; variation of pace and use of flight; how they planned an over, spell, session, day; consistency of line and length; and so on.

I wanted their views on the psychological performance, and the fitness and physiological make-up of their players in respect to every aspect of the game.

My hope in asking these questions was to encourage coaches and selectors throughout New Zealand to think even harder about their choices and generally increase the standards of player assessment nationally. I saw the process, too, as an exchange of ideas which would help to build more unity of purpose nationwide.

I think it's important to collect specific data on players. However, I did say to the coaches and selectors that I didn't expect answers to all questions, and added that I accepted that, 'There will always be limitations in accurately assessing the ability of players from questionnaires alone, particularly when it comes to weighting the importance of one area of skill against another.'

It's a pain in the proverbial gathering such information but unless you make the effort players too often get picked by instinct or on whim. At this point I can hear the voices saying that it's pointless getting too theoretical, too technical and that cricket's all or mostly in the mind. Not so, you have to have a good theoretical understanding and very sound technique or you are unlikely to succeed consistently. These things underpin and provide the basis upon which to apply a rigorous, disciplined mental approach to the game. Natural ability is obviously very important, and natural ability alone will sometimes carry players past most others, but by developing other areas players add considerably to their talents. I am aware of the fear of paralysis by analysis but a player should never be afraid of or averse to information. Occasionally people also trot out the cliche 'a little knowledge is a dangerous thing', and it's true that I have known players who decided not to delve too deeply into things and had a damned good attitude to their cricket, just got on with it. But it's my belief that one shouldn't be afraid of knowledge and information.

The more you learn about the game of cricket and the more you learn about yourself, the better you become at analysing your own game. Then, as you become more self-sufficient, you don't need to rely so much on others. To me, the best coaches are those who provide information and expertise that is so good that in time they in effect do themselves out of a job.

While the main purpose of my tour of the provinces was talent identification and talking with coaches and the like, there was also a need to talk to Martin Crowe and discuss his contractual arrangements, his knee and other physical problems, and his future availability. Adam Parore heard that I was going to be in Auckland and asked me and Rod Fulton to talk to him and his agent. Also, Martin Snedden, a lawyer and former New Zealand player, wanted to talk to me about the future of fast bowler Danny Morrison and the medium-pacer Chris Pringle, for whom he was acting as agent. There are a lot of areas where interests and responsibilities overlap, or conflict, with people involved in New Zealand cricket. No wonder the politics is so intricate and hard to fathom.

Parore told us he thought he was captaincy material, that he should be vice-captain, that he assumed Martin Crowe would be taking over from Ken Rutherford, and that when Crowe departed – because he couldn't see him lasting much longer – he was the natural successor. Adam was sure the players respected him and that he was generally held in high regard. He also felt that NZC ought to pay him a good retainer as it did with the likes of Crowe, Morrison, Greatbatch, Rutherford and Andrew Jones. He said that his performances had warranted similar arrangements. He also told us that he didn't want NZC to assume that he should be bound by any sponsorship agreements made by the national body, and that he should receive a fee whenever his photograph was used to promote cricket; he didn't want NZC to place any restrictions on sponsorship deals he and his agent might negotiate. I simply listened but not without feelings of some astonishment. I wanted to hear what he and others thought before conferring with whoever the other selectors might be.

The meeting with Parore left me feeling a bit shell-shocked. Rod Fulton seemed unfazed. He said he'd heard a lot of that sort of thing before. I remember standing in the shower later that day and feeling a bit nervous about some of the things that I'd been hearing and learning about the attitudes and expectations of some of the leading lights of New Zealand cricket.

While touring the country I got hold of Mike Dolden who was in charge of NZC's sponsorship arrangements to get his thoughts and find out about sponsors' concerns and expectations.

In Wellington, after talking to Gavin Larsen, Bruce Morrison and Robbie Smith, I had a session with Lyn McConnnell, sports editor of the *Evening Post*. I'd put together a draft media plan, looking at how to deal with media requirements in the future, and I wanted to get his reaction to it. I then met with another journalist, Kip Brook, to get a second opinion about this.

I met NZC's then medical team in order to be briefed on players' physical condition and psychological characteristics. So I met the exercise physiologist Paul Carpinter, sports psychologist Gilbert Enoka, Richard Edmond (a general practitioner who'd also been a physiotherapist on a tour of India), and the fitness trainer Graham Nuttridge. All of these men were based in Christchurch. I wanted to know their views on where we should be going and the areas in which they thought we should be aiming for improvement.

When it comes to physical fitness and training a lot more is required of players today than in my playing days. I freely admit, for example, that at times I drank more than I should have. On the arduous tour of the West Indies in 1972, a tour on which I made four double centuries, there were times when I couldn't sleep at night. On a few occasions I was not out at stumps and wasn't able to switch off my mind, so early in the evening I took to having a few gins in the hope that they would knock me out. All that happened was that I woke up in the early hours and couldn't get back to sleep. Few of us had any real knowledge of fitness training and relaxation techniques which was the reason why, in desperation, one turned to alcohol. All the alcohol did was ensure that I became more dehydrated at the crease.

In today's sporting world far more time, money and effort is put into providing professional support and advice when it comes to fitness training, exercise physiology, nutrition, psychology and medical matters generally. So if a sport is going to use people with expertise in those areas, then it has to respect their professional knowledge and, in most cases, go with their advice. It should also be noted that in my day there wasn't the same amount of media coverage and exposure, so our activities weren't so visible publicly. When Chris Doig was asked if he thought the Australian spinner Shane Warne was too fat, his response was to refer to the opera singer Pavarotti, no midget in any company, and comment, 'Who's to say that it affects his singing?' Doig's response was the sort that completely undermines the work of everyone involved in sports fitness training and medicine.

My approach to those in the sports sciences is to listen to them all and take from them, given my knowledge and experience of cricket's requirements, what seems helpful and enhancing. This is understood and accepted by them also. Care needs to be taken here because it would be easy for a coach and team to spend most of their time endeavouring to accommodate the total wishes of each area of science, and then have no time left to practise the skills of the game.

My interest in and grasp of sports science areas came through having been closely associated with the University of Otago's Physical Education Department and its High Performance Centre during my years as Director of Sport Otago. I ran many coaching courses and discussed sports science generally with prominent academics, so while I can't claim academic qualifications in the sports sciences my knowledge there is greater than that of most of those involved in

NZC. On several occasions I was asked to give lectures on sports psychology to sports groups and to students at Otago University, and to outline how I saw it applying to the game of cricket. In 1997 I learned that few in NZC's administration, including the Board, were aware of the extent of my knowledge in the sports psych area. And it is pretty clear from their utterances that those within NZC tend to think of sports psych as mainly involving motivation when that is but a part of it.

The Vexed Issue of Player Contracts

Martin Crowe's availability or otherwise was of major interest and concern. Did he want to continue to play international, or any, cricket? Was he going to be fit enough? There was a feeling that Martin was getting paid, by NZC's standards, quite a lot of money without actually being required to come to work. I was being told that Martin ought to be doing more to earn his pay, and that several current New Zealand players felt he was getting special treatment. Whatever the situation it was a source of friction and division and it needed to be addressed.

Rod Fulton and I thought that the best thing was to talk with Martin and air the various concerns. We felt it best to rely on an innate sense of reasonableness and put it to him that it was not reasonable for NZC to pay him a substantial retainer unless he was able and willing to actually play. We needed some assurance that he would be ready by a certain date. Under the old agreement it looked as if Martin was going to earn double, and in many cases more than double, what other players were getting. Some guaranteed singing for supper was required. To give Crowe his due, he agreed with us, agreed that he felt a bit uncomfortable about being paid quite a lot of money without having to do much to earn it. He was more than happy to go along with what we suggested he do by way of work for NZC, and that his retainer money be built into appearance fees.

By reaching an agreement with Martin we thought it would do something for his image and at the same time show the rest of the players that we were intent on treating everyone fairly and justly.

Andrew Jones was being paid a generous basic amount by way of a retainer and was required to do very little to draw it. Not his fault, of course. (On top of that he was to be guaranteed sizeable fees for tests and one-dayers, plus an extra amount per week when touring overseas. Then there was the likelihood of a share of prize-monies.) Again, as with Crowe, Jones would have been getting double what most of the rest of the players were getting. There seemed to be a degree of distortion here and a feeling that what had evolved wasn't fair to the majority of the players.

Of course it wasn't over to me to determine payments, but I clearly had a recommendatory role, and most people I spoke to were adamant the player payments system needed a proper overhaul. We expect you to do something about it, they said.

Mark Greatbatch was also thought to be doing quite nicely with a basic payment from NZC and from Central Districts. And Danny Morrison and Ken Rutherford were on retainers, too. The message I was picking up all over the place was, 'Shouldn't these guys be required to do something, or a bit more, for their money?' Well, it was intended that they do some coaching and other things for NZC, but there didn't appear to have been anything written into the budget to provide for this. So it wasn't the players' fault. We found that the players supported retainers but rather than have one on $60,000, say, and two others getting nothing, there was a school of thought that felt such an amount would be better spent spread among three of them.

Fulton was as concerned to clarify and sort out the contracts issue as I was, perhaps more so. We didn't think the existing system was equitable or specific enough – again, not the fault of the individual players. Just about everybody agreed with the policy that pay should be based on the quality of performance, but having said that, both Fulton and I thought that while in the long-term retainers should be provided, they ought to go to more players and in smaller amounts.

But at the time no one seemed to have answered such questions as: Should NZC require players on retainers of, say, $30,000 or more, to undertake courses at tertiary educational institutions to broaden their education, and/or do some work for NZC? If so, then which courses, and should NZC pay the costs, and how many days' work? There was talk of looking to see if some players might be given work with sponsoring companies for part of a year, and NZC paying half of an appropriate salary. This way we would be helping players prepare for the rather different reality of life after cricket.

Another question was, How do we compare and equate a player

playing overseas for an English County 1st XI with a player back in New Zealand?

We were also asking, What would happen to leading players over the winter if NZC decided to move to a non-retainer system at the end of the tour to the West Indies in 1996?

I am not opposed to players receiving generous payments, nor to improving their conditions in every respect. But it seemed to me and Fulton, and others, that there was too big a disparity between the money being paid to contracted players and the rest. The disharmony was audible and obvious. I felt we had to sort out the contracts issue because it was clear that any widening of the disparity which existed over payments between players would, (a) encourage more players to demand unreasonable retainers then and in the future, (b) negatively affect team morale, and, (c) indicate the NZC administration was not prepared to take a fair, reasonable and more equitable approach to player payments.

Some of our better players were based in England in our off season, and some of them were being paid reasonably well there. Sponsorships and endorsements could also be picked up by players playing overseas. This was also the case with a few at home in New Zealand. The point at issue here was, should NZC pay a retainer to those playing overseas on other contracts, as well as to those at home who were doing some coaching for NZC or were being subsidised into jobs?

Regarding endorsements and the like, when it comes to TV commercials it's not always the best players – some say sadly – who get to do these. The shape of the butt can be deemed more important than cricketing ability and the quality of the brain. Irrespective, Fulton and I had to work with the size of the budget NZC then had and that was that.

NZC had a budget for all players of just over $1M, and five players were receiving about a quarter of it as retainers. There was no guarantee that their form would ensure future selection, nor that they would be fit enough to play international cricket. But if they were all playing at the same time then there was the likelihood that together they would have been drawing perhaps two-thirds of the budget.

I was for a system that guaranteed players a reasonably good basic wage, appearance money, and generous bonuses based on performance in tests and one-day internationals. As far as I was concerned sorting the payments issue out was a priority so that all of us could get on with concentrating on the prime task, improving New Zealand's cricket performance.

But from the time the team went on tour to Darwin and India in 1995, until I was sacked in 1996, I had virtually no say in the nature or offering of future contracts. Chris Doig and, possibly, others took complete control.

Chapter 2

Who to Pick, How and Why?

I had read player and tour reports relating to recent tours and series in which many of the then current players had been involved. I compared the contents of these reports with my own impressions, and then with the results of interviews with a large number of selectors, coaches and players around New Zealand. As coach and convener of selectors, one of the first things I and the other selectors had to do was consider whether we wanted to retain Ken Rutherford as captain of the national team.

Rutherford was well-known to me. I'd seen him play a lot and I knew his personality. Management's reports on Ken gave him the thumbs down in important areas, and I didn't find many people who felt that Ken was the sort of captain and player needed to restore New Zealand cricket's fortunes and set the appropriate example.

Prior to our team selections Rod Fulton and I met with Rutherford at Carisbrook in Dunedin. We discussed general matters relating to the New Zealand team and its recent performance. I couldn't tell Ken he was going to be dropped because that was a decision for the selection panel, which had yet to meet.

In the New Zealand context Ken had his merits as a player but he'd had a great many opportunities. Basically I didn't think that Rutherford had the all-round qualities and ability to do the job New Zealand cricket needed in 1995. When the time came, the other selectors agreed.

When Rick Pickard, Mike Shrimpton and I chose our first team, NZC's Board initially wouldn't accept it because Rutherford wasn't in it. Obviously many administrators think they know who ought to be in the national team. That being the case, one feels like asking them, Why bother to have selectors? Ken played about 120 one-day internationals for New Zealand and averaged just under 30 per innings. He often played attractive shots but in between times he wasn't very good at working the ball around and therefore his strike-rate wasn't quite good enough, 64 per100 balls. Rutherford's test average from 99 innings was 27.08. There seemed to be a perception that Rutherford's statistics had been badly marred by performances early in his career. However his most recent figures leading up to his non-selection spoke for themselves. Against Pakistan in 1993-94 he averaged 20.33 in six test innings, and 26.80 from five one-day innings. Against the West Indies in 1994-95 he made 55 runs from four innings at an average of 18.00. He batted three times in one-dayers for 63 runs at 23.00. As selectors we thought it time to try new players.

Late in 1995 Francis Payne, cricket author and statistician, provided me with statistics which mostly confirmed what we had known before we picked our first New Zealand team. Payne contends that a knowledge of batsmen's strike-rates is 'essential'. I agree. Payne said that by the end of 1995 New Zealand had 'played in 20 one-day international tournaments (i.e. with more than one other team) without winning a single one.' Looking at the overall strike-rates of New Zealand's leading batsmen he said that, 'Quite clearly... NZ has scored too little *(sic)* and/or too slowly.' To become more competitive we needed to do something about that.

In 1995 the strike-rates of most of our best one-day players were lower than those of most of the better players in other international sides. In December 1995 Payne gave me a list of both current and former New Zealand players showing their averages and strike-rates in one-day internationals over the years – prior to the 1995-96 season. Martin Crowe ave. 38, strike-rate 72; Fleming 28, 77; Greatbatch 28, 72; Chris Harris 23, 62; Howarth 23, 59; Jones 35, 58; Parore 35, 69; J.F. Reid 27, 58; Rutherford 29, 64; Thomson 22, 67; Turner 47, 72; Young 23, 58; Wright 26, 57. The New Zealanders' strike-rates in internationals for the 1995-96 period improved: Fleming, Twose, Astle, Parore and Germon were all in the 70s; Harris, Cairns, Spearman and Patel were in the 80s.

Regarding players, I think it worth emphasising that one needs to consider a good deal more than just a player's on-field results. That said, I'm pleased that we have a number of very good players who practise hard and accept the need for direction and for maintaining reasonable standards all round. But for some time New Zealand hasn't had anyone whose playing ability is so superior to others' that his absence from the team would be seriously felt. And, frankly, if the player or players chosen to replace a couple of our 'stars' weren't able to do better than those so-called stars, then it's unlikely that we'd become a significant cricketing force internationally. The reality, in 1995-96, was that none of our more troublesome players were in the truly top rank internationally. That is still the case.

At the time I took over the one exception was Martin Crowe, but he was, due to injury, struggling to play at all. Crowe was a fine player whose shortcomings were more openly visible to all and sundry than are most players'. Partly this was because he hungered for attention. Public emotional outbursts left many doubting whether his influence was as valuable as it might have been; others felt that he asked for too much special treatment – conditions, favours, privileges. At one time, for example, he didn't want to go to India and Pakistan because he felt he couldn't cope with conditions there; on another occasion, he asked for special nets and pre-tour arrangements in South Africa. My view is that, in the main, special treatment for individuals goes down like a lead balloon with most players. It's always been so and it remains so today. What is more, it doesn't help the performance of the player concerned either. Taking short-cuts is a recipe for under-achieving.

* * *

In late June of 1995 in Christchurch we had a debriefing and planning workshop for a group of players who were uppermost in our minds as candidates for a couple of weeks in Darwin, then the tour of India as a prelude to the World Cup. Eleven players were asked to attend: Bryan Young, Martin Crowe, Dipak Patel, Justin Vaughan, Adam Parore, Danny Morrison, Mark Greatbatch, Matthew Hart, Shane Thomson, Stephen Fleming, and Gavin Larsen. Vaughan was brought down because he was felt to have a good brain and would contribute usefully to our planning for the future even though he wasn't, at that time, seen as a front-runner for the tour to India. I actually told him that before he arrived, and although he was obviously disappointed he still came. (We didn't take Vaughan to India or the World Cup, but later called on him to join us in the West Indies. His omission was a mistake. I wish, now, that we'd picked Vaughan from the outset.)

At the workshop in Christchurch we discussed almost everything pertaining to the playing of cricket both at home and abroad: playing philosophy, practice routines, discipline and order, media protocols, payments, sponsorship arrangements, and the always vexed and contentious issue of wives or partners on tour. Each player was interviewed by the medical team, fitness programmes were reviewed, and testing carried out. They were put on new or revised fitness programmes for the remainder of the winter.

Several players were based overseas, namely Lee Germon, Darrin Murray, Kerry Walmsley, Simon Doull, Aaron Gale, Roger Twose, Chris Cairns and Dion Nash. I planned to go and see them individually in the UK and Holland in early August.

One or two omissions surprised some of the pundits. Andrew Jones's absence was one. Naturally he wasn't pleased and after I'd had a discussion with him on the phone he wrote to me and told me what he thought. Fair enough. I had a lot of respect for Jones's efforts and record for New Zealand. He seldom gave away his wicket without a fight and made the very most of his abilities. He was tenacious and showed himself able to concentrate when at the crease for far longer than virtually anyone else in the New Zealand team. So we didn't lightly exclude Andrew. We thought that he'd had a very good and long innings and that his abilities were in decline. Against the West Indies in 1994-95 he'd made 24 runs in four innings, and in the one-dayers he batted three times for a total of 45 runs. And while against Pakistan in 1993-94 he'd done well in tests – 298 runs in six innings at 49.66, in the one-dayers he'd managed only 76 runs in five knocks. As selectors we had to be thinking about the six one-dayers we were down to play against India, and then the World Cup one-day competition. Andrew was told that he needed to get back to scoring well again in our domestic competition. In the 1995-96 season, when New Zealand was mostly away on tour, at home in the Shell Trophy he had 6 innings, totalling 117 runs, highest score of 55, for an average of 19.5 per innings. In the one-day Shell Cup competition he made 195 runs in 10 innings at 19.5, highest score of 80. His run-rate in recent times, especially in limited-overs games, had usually been fairly low. We didn't think that Andrew's range of shots was wide enough and he was not at that stage of his career one of the better fielders. We doubted that he would help us win one-day games. In fact it could be argued that if he played a substantial one-day innings he was more likely to play us into a hole.

In late 1995 Francis Payne pointed out that while Andrew's average and run-rate for New Zealand in one-day matches had been quite good for a fair proportion of his career, 'his last five series have brought him a total of 266 runs at a strike rate of just 38 (and average of just 13)'.

Jones said that he'd only learned of his omission from the squad by phoning NZC himself, otherwise the first he'd have heard would have been through phone calls from the media. He said he'd have credited me with more courtesy. I understand his annoyance and regret the manner of his finding out that he had been dropped. I'd been told that the Chairman of NZC Peter McDermott wanted to inform Jones himself. Unfortunately he didn't.

At the time Jones felt he could recover his form and was saddened not to have been given the chance. He said that when he'd returned to the New Zealand side in January 1995 the team was extremely disharmonious, that players had lost respect and trust for each other, and were 'looking sideways for excuses not inwards for answers'. Others, including Rod Fulton, reported similar concerns. Jones's assessment struck me as right on the button.

Despite his disappointment and irritation Jones said that he wished me the best and that NZC 'desperately needs somebody hard and honest to drive the national side'. It was generous of Jones to end on that note. It's not easy to drop players who have given good service and there were times when we would have valued a few more players with Jones's disciplined determination.

Apart from Jones, there was the issue of Ken Rutherford. Again, Peter McDermott said – insisted, in fact – that he wanted to break the news to Ken. McDermott said he'd like to tell Rutherford himself. When he rang Rutherford he told him he was no longer captain but for some reason – he later told me he couldn't bring himself to give Rutherford a double dose of bad news at the one time – he failed to say that Rutherford wasn't in the team either. It got messy. In the course of the afternoon Rod Fulton discovered that Peter hadn't told Ken the full story. Fulton immediately got hold of me and I straight away faxed McDermott and re-iterated what I'd told him earlier, that I was prepared to tell Ken the whole story. A little later Peter rang and admitted that he hadn't passed on all the bad news. I thought, lovely, bloody lovely. I immediately tried to get through to Rutherford on his cellphone but he was somewhere in the Bay of Islands and had switched it off, understandably because he'd sooner not field a number of calls from the media.

It was unfortunate that Ken ended up finding out about being dropped through the media. Ironically we both felt let down and annoyed by what had happened. Ken made some capital out of it. I might have been more sympathetic if he'd not publicly claimed some time beforehand that he'd never seen hide nor hair of me even though we lived in the same town. This was untrue; it was only a few days after Rod Fulton and I had visited him in Dunedin that he spoke to the members of the St Clair Golf Club and told them he'd not seen me. A very short memory, in that instance anyway. My feelings about this weren't helped when I agreed to be interviewed by Paul Holmes and caught him at his snide worst.

* * *

Before I went off to the UK to visit Germon, Cairns and others, John Howell, the coaching director of NZC held a level 3 elite coaching clinic in Christchurch for selectors and coaches of provincial associations. On the fourth and final day the chairmen of provincial associations also came along to discuss the future playing and selection style of NZC. There was a feeling that New Zealand cricket needed to be more cohesive and I certainly thought it would be useful to get general agreement over the way we would try to play cricket throughout the country. In advance I had circulated brief papers discussing possible ways of arriving at a philosophy to guide the playing, coaching and selecting of our cricket, and I posed several questions related to planning our future approach to the game here. I had many questions on batting and bowling, and also on how to find the ingredients for a winning tactical formula in limited-over games. For example, there's often disagreement over the value of wickets in hand versus runs on the board. One needs to ask, At what stage, if any, does a team attack, collect or defend? Do conditions influence the approach and if so, why?

I thought it would be interesting, too, to discuss what sort of pitches we would like to produce, and then consider outfields to see whether there was a preferred boundary length, should grounds be rolled, and was there an ideal length of grass? We weren't out to enforce or impose uniformity of style – there must always be room for coaches and players to try something different, provided it's not clearly off the wall – but we felt it wouldn't hurt to have a bit more unity and common purpose nationally.

On 20 July I met with Gren Alabaster. Prior to that I'd sent him a draft manager's job description so that he'd have a chance to comment on it. I wanted input from him in respect to the jobs it would be appropriate to ask of players on tour. Gren had been called in as manager for the period in between Geoff Howarth's departure and my arrival and he had a pretty good idea of what had and had not been working. I'd been asked to approach people with a view to inviting them to apply for the manager's job. Unsurprisingly, given previous events and the widespread low opinion of New Zealand cricket's all-round performance, people weren't queuing up for the job. At the time the most likely candidates were seen to come from people out of a job, retired persons, or those who ran their own businesses and were prepared to depute someone else to run it while they went off to manage a cricket team. Another approached was former New Zealand captain John (J.R.) Reid, but he was already involved as an international referee in a series in England and felt that he had a good chance of picking up more work of that type, so he chose to stick with that.

The outgoing NZC Board had been very happy with Gren's performance so it seemed to make sense to look to him again. He'd also had experience in the New Zealand coaching job. Add that to his 20-odd years as a player in first-class cricket – he'd also played for New Zealand – and he clearly had a solid background in cricket. I'd detected a strong lobby was in favour of appointing a manager with a strong cricketing background, someone who knew how to run team meetings, and who might be able to help with technical advice as well. To me Gren seemed like a person who you could bounce ideas off and was likely to come back with intelligent input. I indicated that I was quite happy to work alongside Gren and the Board pushed for him.

There hadn't been much opportunity to cast a wide net for selectors. But Rod Fulton said that Rick Pickard of Northern Districts had expressed a desire to become a national selector. I met Pickard and was impressed by how organised he was, and by the detailed information and player-performance breakdowns and assessments he'd gathered. While I was overseas we were going to need someone in New Zealand who was prepared to put in the time, and document material in such a way as to be an efficient and informed *de facto* convenor in my absence. When talking to Ian Smith he said he would be keen to be a selector, so I put his name into the hat. I thought he would add to the mix for he hadn't long stopped playing and was right in touch there, but NZC wouldn't wear Smithy. Mike Shrimpton was chosen as the third selector which gave us continuity with the previous panel.

Ross Dykes, the previous panel's convenor, had rung me to see if I thought there was a place for him on the new panel. I said I thought he'd had a fair trot and that, one way or another, things hadn't been working all that well. I said I thought Mike Shrimpton would give us the continuity needed and that there didn't seem much point in having four selectors. Another point in Shrimpton's favour was that he'd had considerable experience with age-group players at the academy and thus had a good knowledge of emerging players. Dykes announced that he and I had philosophical differences which meant he wouldn't be putting his name forward. Interesting that within a year, before I was relieved of my job, he was happy to put his name forward again.

On 22-23 July Pickard, Shrimpton and I met in Christchurch. I produced the video tapes which I'd obtained from TVNZ and had closely examined. To my mind it's the best way to go when considering the relative abilities of players. You can have all the stats and wagon-wheels you like – they are of some help – but video tape is best, much better than turning up at grounds and watching players. Video tape allows you to analyse techniques and isolate various parts of them. You can decide to watch a batsman's feet, then go back and look at how he picks up his bat; you can concentrate on a player's head position, and so on. In other words you can have a very careful look at all aspects of a player's technique, be he a bowler or a batsman. Rick Pickard made the comment that it was the first time he'd been able to use video tapes and make such a considered assessment of players. It's time-consuming but it does give you a far more accurate picture of players' abilities.

The video tapes were helpful too in enabling us to get away from the perceived need for selectors to front up to so many matches around the country. That is time-consuming, it eats up lots of money, and looking at players from a hundred metres or more away isn't the best way to carefully scrutinise their abilities. The PR side of this was being covered by consulting with other selectors and coaches in the provincial associations. It was a useful and needful exercise and one we didn't see as a chore.

At this meeting I also tabled a draft selection and management plan that I'd put together in 1992-93 and presented to the then cricket committee of NZC. The committee was like a think-tank on the future of the game here. Whatever was resolved then hadn't seemed to have worked very well. Pickard, Shrimpton and I went through that draft which I'd hoped would enable NZC's selection policy to become thoroughly professional. I felt we needed sensible guidelines to help draw up a short-list of players and to plan properly for the short-, medium- and long-term. In order to carefully assess the relative merits of players selectors need to ask a whole heap of important questions. I wasn't convinced we'd been thorough enough in the past.

We looked at drawing up a short-list of probables, say 11-12 of those, (the usual combination, two openers, three seamers, one or two spinners, a wicketkeeper, an all-rounder and two or three other batsmen), then a possibles group of about nine, and an emerging group of 13-14 of the more promising of the crop nationally.

Although it was winter we still had to pick a team for New Zealand's tour of India to start early in October. We felt able to do this because we'd collectively gone to some pains to try to ensure that all areas had been covered, in respect to activities both on and off the field, so that no one would be able to say, 'Oh, we never discussed that,' or, 'Hang on, I never agreed to this,' and so on. Management felt that we wanted to cut down on the likelihood of argy-bargy and complaint once we were on tour, so that all the energy would go into the playing and performing. Well, that was the theory anyway.

I discussed with each player their fitness programmes, and the aspects of their game that they should be working on specifically in the period prior to leaving New Zealand. At the June workshop I'd put it to the players that everyone should have a vision, to successfully reach their full potential, and that they should be looking to improve their life through cricket. I emphasised the need to improve skills – mental, physical, technical, sociological – and to advance their theoretical knowledge and understanding of cricket. Among the desired outcomes was for players to reach their full potential, help the team to win and to gain satisfactory monetary rewards.

In the short-term we planned to improve the performance of the more experienced players while working to raise the level of those on the next tier. By creating greater depth we'd have a stronger all-round national team, for there would be more players in contention putting pressure on the more experienced incumbents.

I took video tapes with me and sat down with each player and discussed strengths and weaknesses with them. I encouraged self-analysis as an important part of effecting improvements and setting goals. All players were asked to bring draft copies of their own personal performance plans with them to the next camp which was to be held in August in Auckland.

A New Captain, a New Approach, and Codes of Practice

I was keeping in touch with Martin Crowe over his fitness and had been since first meeting him back in May. We were keen to give him as much lead-time as possible in which to get back to the level of fitness required. A fit Crowe was going to be a great asset to the side. I also talked with him in some detail about Lee Germon. I wanted to get as much information and opinion on Lee as I could, not just views on his character as an individual, but others' assessment of his cricketing skills, leadership ability and knowledge. I wasn't fully aware of the assessments of his wicketkeeping ability. I felt that Crowe's view of the comparative abilities of Parore and Germon would be worth having. Crowe rated Germon as better than Parore with the gloves – interesting in light of subsequent events. I talked with the Canterbury coach Denis Aberhart, and two of New Zealand's better former 'keepers in Barry Milburn and Ian Smith. I had them assess the various wicketkeepers in New Zealand at the time and compare their skills for me. They both considered Germon to be the best gloveman in New Zealand cricket at that time.

I'd seen quite a bit of Germon at the cricket academy over the years – he was the only player who'd actually approached me and arranged to see me on a one-to-one basis. He had a whole list of questions to put to me about captaincy. Lee searched for information; he was organised, questioning and eager to learn. Several others told me that they thought Germon was intelligent, that he could express himself well, and that he had the sort of mental toughness that was going to be required over the next few months. And although he didn't have international playing experience his success-rate while captaining Canterbury was very good. Germon took over as Canterbury captain in 1990-91. Under him the team won the Shell Cup one-day competition five times, in 1991-92, 1992-93, 1993-94, 1995-96 and 1996-97. The Shell Trophy competition for three- and then four-day matches was won in 1993-94, 1996-97 and 1997-98.

Between 1987 and 1995 Germon had played 69 first-class games for Canterbury, making 2037 runs at an average of 30.86. He was Canterbury's all-time leading wicketkeeper in terms of dismissals with 190 catches and 21 stumpings. Next best was John Ward with 136 and 17. I noted that on the 1994-95 season tour of South Africa and India Germon was given only 6 hours of cricket when the general assessment of Parore's 'keeping on tour was that it was 'poor'. Written reports of the tour said that the 'dirt-trackers' – Germon, Harris, Su'a and Hartland – didn't get a look in but maintained their standards of behaviour and were diligent in continuing to practise. I was impressed by that.

Germon's record with the Canterbury side was superior to that of any of the other provincial captains of his time; he had effected more dismissals as a 'keeper than all other provincial glovemen in New Zealand first-class cricket other than Ervin McSweeney of Wellington and Warren Lees of Otago, and he was very handy with the bat, being able to strike the ball cleanly and with power. Germon's first-class average by the end of the 1995-96 season was 31.91.

Lee undoubtedly had a cutting tongue, at times, and didn't suffer fools gladly. He demanded high standards. As they sometimes say in the UK, 'he had a bit about him'. We believed Lee had the sort of leadership qualities and intelligence required to redevelop respect for the New Zealand cricket side. As selectors we felt it imperative that we take steps to pick up the team's reputation and performance both on and off the field. We wanted New Zealand players to attract support and be admired as the right sort of role models.

With the exception of Rutherford and Jones we had decided to stick with most of the incumbents, for the time being anyway. There obviously wasn't a great depth of talent available, and we felt we ought to give incumbents the chance to perform under a new management and culture. It was a decision which provided yet another chance for some players.

Some people were surprised and disappointed by the exclusion of the young left-arm spinner Matthew Hart. He had not been bowling well when the players had gathered in Christchurch in June. It was pretty clear to me from watching him, and by looking at video tape, why he had lost accuracy and control. He was bowling too much across his body; his right foot was going right out into the box between the return crease and the popping crease. One effect was that his left arm was too low and he was undercutting the ball. He was also going sideways away from his target and wasn't able to come over the top of his front foot enough to be able to get the necessary amount of purchase and overspin on the ball. I asked John Bracewell to add his expertise and to take over the supervision of Matthew's work. Bracewell had worked with Hart in the past. We told Matthew what he had to do in the next few weeks and recommended that he work on his bowling daily. Hart is a good all-round cricketer, very useful with the bat, so there was some dismay when we found that his bowling had deteriorated. We said that unless he could show us he'd got back to somewhere close to his best we couldn't pick him. This was disappointing for there was a dearth of top class spinners. We left it to Bracewell to see if he could help Hart reconstitute his bowling.

Hairstyles, Earrings, and other important things

The overseas players weren't yet aware that they had been chosen for the tour of India, so I got on a plane and flew to the UK to see and tell them. I wanted to fully inform them of our plans, explain what decisions had been made, how they'd been arrived at, why, and what would be expected of all players. I wanted to stimulate their interest, check on their commitment to New Zealand cricket, and give all players a chance to express their concerns. It was their chance to discuss the issues and declare their unavailability if they weren't happy. I knew that Cairns had on a previous occasion stated his dissatisfaction with the management of a New Zealand team and had declined to play under it. Everybody saw Cairns as tricky.

In London I saw Chris Cairns and Dion Nash together. We went over the protocols worked out by the players at our debriefing in Christchurch in June. I wanted feedback from them. They raised no objections except in respect to what's known as sledging (a term used to describe verbally abusing your opposition, individually or collectively). We were proposing to cut that out, preferring to put our energies into playing and performing well without resorting to mouthing at the opposition. Cairns said he was prepared to go along with it as long as he could chip Tendulkar. He wasn't really asking permission to 'sledge' Tendulkar, but wanted to glare at him, engage in significant eye contact. This, he said, would unsettle Tendulkar and help get him out. I said Okay, if that's what you want, for if he thought Tendulkar would fail as a result of that treatment I wasn't going to interfere.

Nash suggested we run our team meetings along the lines of those then practised by Middlesex. According to him the players were free to have a go at each other – verbally only, one assumes – and show no mercy. He said that although he'd found that disconcerting, especially as a new and young player, he got accustomed to it. Nothing was left unsaid and as a result it tended to do away with the back-biting that often occurs. He said it was a way of making players face up to their shortcomings.

I thought, This could be interesting, very interesting. So when I got back to New Zealand I brought up Nash's suggestion at the players' camp in Auckland. The group felt that there was no need to go to that extent. Nash's suggestion stuck in my mind, though, and I was later to adopt it, once, during the tour of the West Indies.

I went up to Lancashire to see Aaron Gale and Simon Doull. Doull at that time sported a Mohawk-ish hairstyle. I raised it with him, partly because I had already come under pressure to do something about the appearance of certain players. I wasn't making it an issue, it had become an issue. Subsequently Doull drew attention to this issue in the media on more than one occasion, saying I didn't like his appearance, and implying that I was trying to trample all over his personal rights. This was a wider issue than Doull seemed to recognise or allow. We all have rights which we are often quick to claim, but we are not always so keen to acknowledge our responsibilities. The two are indivisible. Both players and management have a responsibility towards New Zealand cricket and its supporters. A vexed issue, but one that has to be confronted. I recall, many years ago in the 1970s, defending Stephen Boock when the convenor of the Otago selectors told me that we ought to get Boock to remove some of his hair. My response was that we should make allowances for his youth, the fashion of the time, and that we should be primarily concerned about his cricket ability. I also recalled that for a time my hair was, by today's standards, quite long too.

I'd been told repeatedly that the national team too often appeared like a rag-tail lot and it wasn't good enough. Those who controlled the purse strings in companies – often persons of the baby-boomer vintage – had certain expectations in respect to appearance, as did and do the older cricket supporters. I hadn't made a recommendation to NZC on hairstyles, or earrings and the like, but I sure as hell got an earful from all manner of cricket-lovers who expected me to do something about the more exotic trends. Take sports columnist Bob South as an example. Writing in the New Zealand *Sunday Times* in October 1995, he fired a broadside at Gren Alabaster and me for being too tolerant: make that slack. He said – and I'm not saying I agree with everything he said – the team 'still lacks some discipline.' He went on, 'For a start, why is Chris Cairns' hair so darn long? Why does he need to wear a sweat band in his scalp to keep the hair out of his face when bowling? Why must he look like one of the Three Stooges? And while on the subject of hair, why is Shane Thomson trying to imitate General Custer, and why are any number of other Pop Guns growing cute lil' goatees?

'Discipline begins at home, each morning, in front of a mirror. If a player can't turn out for his country, or any team for that matter, suitably groomed – not half shaven, not untidy, not with hair out of shape and in your face – then how is that same player supposed to be disciplined enough to perform at his best? He can not and will not.'

My response was to say to NZC, your decision. Frankly, I'm more interested in behaviour than in appearance. Generally, it's over to individuals to determine what is or what is not acceptable in terms of dress. But in our case, both the players and management agreed to dress properly, tidily and appropriately when in public, according to the situation or function. That meant whites (a special loose-fitting pair if players wished) and other normal playing gear when in the nets, but shorts were fine for fielding and fitness work, along with an appropriate team-issue shirt. Official-issue floppy hats or caps were okay, too, but we asked that the peak be forward not at the back. This was partly because the sponsors' names were on the peak and they wanted their caps worn in the appropriate manner. Sponsors were keen for us to wear their T-shirts at fielding practice too. Reputable brands of sunglasses were allowable but they had to be the wrap-around blade plastic type and not too dark. We had been getting quite a lot of mail from cricket enthusiasts disapproving of players wearing sunglasses. Many were also concerned about the possibility of impaired performance. I had actually asked for professional advice on whether sunglasses caused visual distortion, and the opinion seemed to be that brands like Oakley, Adidas and Bolle were less likely to distort sight.

I have found that, generally, those who want to stand out from the group in terms of their appearance tend to be less concerned about a team's cause. Having said that, management is unwise to try to take away any added determination or spunk players might have, and one tries to encourage them to put that energy into their game.

* * *

Before Pickard, Shrimpton and I had made our selections I'd had a lengthy telephone chat with Phil Neale, a former captain of my old county Worcestershire. Neale is now Warwickshire coach having taken over from Bob Woolmer. I'd also spoken to Dennis Amiss, the former England and Warwickshire batsman. I had played against Dennis for 15 years during my county career and knew him well. We discussed Roger Twose, to try to get a better line on his abilities, potential and personality. Both Neale and Amiss gave Twose the green light and saw him as possible captaincy material in the future. They had one or two minor reservations – there are always one or two – but said that he had proved to be a good player of quick bowling the previous season. Warwickshire had had South Africa's White Lightning, Alan Donald, on the staff and had got their ground staff to prepare hard, green bouncy pitches. Twose had made a good hundred for them against the quick West Indian Franklin Stephenson and showed, Neale said, a willingness to stand up to the quicks. So the reports on Twose were favourable and I went and saw him too. Twose said he was more than happy to be a part of the team and the set-up we had worked through.

Although Kerry Walmsley, the young fast bowler, hadn't been selected for the Indian tour, we saw him as one of our most promising young quicks and I wanted to chat with him about his bowling action. Kerry had been reported to the International Cricket Council (ICC) who had viewed video tape and deemed him very 'suspect'. I told him that we'd like him and Heath Davis to go down to Christchurch for a few weeks to work with Dayle Hadlee, the exercise physiologist

Paul Carpinter and the fitness trainer Graham Nuttridge.

Tim Murdoch of NZC had been aware of the ICC's opinion, so I went back to him saying that we needed to be mindful of the possibility that the ICC might decide to expose Walmsley, and that if they did, Walmsley would be best advised to say nothing. In my letter to Murdoch I said that we must be prepared because the whole issue of throwing was one that 'will not go away easily'. I am amazed that this issue hasn't really boiled over in the last couple of years, so it must be something no one wants to face. The technology is available to determine just who does and doesn't throw as defined in the current 'laws of cricket'.

A sports scientist – a biomechanics expert from Australia, John Harmer – believed that every bowler with a front-on action can't avoid having a kink in the arm during delivery. He said it becomes more pronounced when bowlers put in a bit extra – letting go bouncers for example. In 1995 NZC brought Harmer across from Melbourne as a key-note speaker at the level 3 elite coaching clinic in Christchurch. His workshop sessions were impressive. Biomechanics has a significant role to play in injury-prevention for quick bowlers.

Later, on request, he produced some very useful technical analyses on the bowling actions of Heath Davis and Kerry Walmsley.

Under the laws of cricket, front-on bowlers often throw because the arm is bent then straightens. Harmer had video tape of several examples of the former Australian bowler Merv Hughes dismissing batsmen in this way. He also thought that the West Indians Ambrose and Walsh came into the same category as Hughes, and that they were just some of the better-known bowlers whose actions could be deemed 'suspect'. I said to Murdoch that it was 'interesting to note that the Aussies are coaching and encouraging the front-on action'.

Given what I'd heard and learned, I had a look at video tape of a one-day international between the West Indies and New Zealand at the Basin Reserve earlier in the year. I told Murdoch that I watched Curtly Ambrose and Courtenay Walsh with great interest. Even though they were not bowling bouncers as in a test match, and even without the assistance of all the angles and close-up shots produced in the Walmsley tape, it was obvious their actions were similar to those described as being of concern to the ICC. I hasten to add that I am not taking a shot at the bowlers mentioned above; they were just some of the better-known bowlers of their type being looked at at the time.

I said to Murdoch that I wasn't sure how we should approach this matter, but that if others were going to make an issue of the Walmsley tape, 'they should be very careful what they say. We can be sure it is only a matter of time before technology and sports science openly produces evidence of a whole host of things which will expose previous theories and assumptions and make it very uncomfortable for many people.'

When examining video tape of a bowler's action attention is usually focused mainly on the last frame before the arm reaches the vertical position. I'm not certain what effect the straightening after that point has. But the law as written would class this as a throw as it refers to an arm that 'bends and straightens'. One thing you can say is that the more side-on a bowler is the less likely he or she is to throw, but I don't like the chances of anyone trying to get everyone to bowl side-on. One can also say that this is not something that can usually be picked up reliably by the naked eye. The problems of adjudication are considerable. When a batsman's given out, should the umpires call for the third umpire and check to see that the bowler's action was fair and within the rules? There are already enough delays with replays as it is. The usual video film of matches runs at 25 frames per second. The really high speed cameras – referred to as 'the super slow-mos' – aren't numerous. Generally there are two and they are used to follow the flight of the ball, or for getting in close to see if a ball is spinning, or how it is coming out of the hand – that sort of detail. At the moment match referees don't even use one of these cameras for side-on replays for run-out decisions and stumpings. They need them for that purpose because the action is so fast. It's costly, but needed if third umpires are to be more accurate, or if bowling actions are to be properly scrutinised. If all this happens, of course, then people in their living rooms and third umpires are going to be seeing far more than the umpires in the middle. One result could be even more contention, possibly occasional turmoil.

Media and Mediation

The role of the sporting media, and the relationship between journalists, commentators, players and officials, is important, complex and interesting. Journalists tell me that their editors put on the pressure for them to get quotes from management and players. Nevertheless some of them appear unduly reliant upon player interviews and comments, and on selective information from administration.

Both players and management felt that too many people within the game had been saying too much to the media and the picture being painted was not flattering to New Zealand cricket. We felt that journalists and others ought to be doing more than stringing player or official quotes together, and that they'd become accustomed to a degree and frequency of access that was disrupting team and individual preparation. Most of the players were sick and tired of the number and extent of media requests. Also, a lot of administrators were telling me that too many players were reefing off to the media, that it wasn't good for the players, or the game, and that they were sick of it.

We never had any intention of muzzling the media or trying to direct what they said. It's their job to write or talk about what they see. But my personal view, and it was widely shared within cricket, was that many in the media had become used to taking the easy road. We didn't feel we should be writing their reports or columns, or quite such a large part of them.

The issue of media contact – the nature and frequency of it – aroused a lot of comment and predictably, some members of the media didn't like what we decided.

Some believe that there should be very few restrictions on media access to players and officials, and that the public has an insatiable appetite for players' opinions, irrespective of their value or relevance. I'm not convinced, but what I am sure of is that the public likes to think that cricket writers and broadcasters are well enough informed to present intelligent reports, analysis and commentary of their own.

Here's what Ron Palenski said in a column in *The Dominion* in October 1995. He said some might 'mutter angrily about the muzzling of the media' and others 'talk darkly about the cricketers being entertainers and public figures and their "duty" to the news media.

'But for others, who've been bored rigid by some of the least original, inarticulate talkers in the sports business or wasted hours standing around dressing room doors waiting for the pearls to drop from a great man's lips, usually to be told what they already know,' the 'decree will be as welcome as the first test victory of the summer.'

Palenski felt we 'could be doing us all a favour.'

My own view was that too many players had been spending too much time on peripheral matters and not enough time on preparing for and playing cricket. It was nice to read the comments from a straight-shooter like Palenski. If all media people are required to do is collect and record quotes from players and coaches, where's the security, or the need for independent-thinking, serious and thoughtful journalists?

The reason I had consulted with journalists Lyn McConnell, Kip Brook and others before we drew up the media protocol was to ensure that we worked out something mutually acceptable. Everyone accepts that the media are, together, an important part of the game.

The team and management decided that once the team had assembled pre-match they wouldn't agree to interviews during practices but that, of course, media were free to watch and take photographs. On the day before matches we undertook to make the captain, coach and manager available for media interviews at 12 noon, immediately following practice, or, if we'd practised in the afternoon, at 5 p.m.

During test matches we decided to leave media interviews until the end of the match rather than go through the ritual at the end of each day's play. Generally we didn't want players to engage in interviews during matches, but said that the coach or manager would consider special requests. If journalists wanted to do feature articles on players then we were happy with that, but said that material should be gathered between or before matches, and that it not be 'detrimental'.

That word crept in because it was used in player and management contracts with NZC. To us detrimental meant information or remarks that might set player against player, or generally stir up controversy between players and management and so disrupt a team. I don't think it is players' or management's job to provide journalists with contentious material. But the presence of the word detrimental in our contracts showed that we were required to protect both our backs and that of NZC. Despite that it was our intention to be far more open and honest with the media than most previous management and administration had been and I think we were. We told the players that we were not prepared to defend any acts of stupidity and wouldn't have done so.

We were quite willing to speak to the media straight away about any unusual or contentious events that occurred on the field of play, and answer any questions on matters that might be regarded as controversial or interesting.

If a player had taken a bag of wickets or made a big score then access would not be denied. We received quite a lot of requests and tended to bend in that area, but I concede we did have hopes of weaning some journalists off and hoped they would start doing more thinking for themselves. More recently our cricket administration has worked at persuading the media to say what it prefers the public to hear, and with some success. But where it hasn't succeeded the reaction from NZC has sometimes been sour to say the least.

It was in this area that I first got wind of a fundamental difference between Chris Doig and me. When some media interests said they weren't happy, a member of the media said they'd been told to ignore the media protocol, screw it up and throw it away. I said to Doig that before he behaved like that the least he could do was discuss the matter with us for, after all, the policy had been worked out by the players and team management, not by me. His response was to say that in the world he came from – I assume he meant opera – they sought exposure and publicity, actively encouraged it. I guess he was saying that restrictions antagonise the media and that it doesn't pay to get off-side with them. But there was more to it than that. In my view Doig wanted to see as many players as possible given a high profile through the media, and saw this as in the interests of both the players and NZC. But team management, and many of the players, were conscious that a high proportion of the cricketing public viewed them with some derision, as young guns become pop guns. We had a lot of catching up to do.

Further, we felt that the amount and the timing of media access had proved seriously detrimental to our cricketing performance in many ways.

Ironically, after I'd been sacked, Doig clearly became very unhappy about some of the media comment. Too much of it was 'negative', not 'positive', in his view, and he sought to get at least one commentator sacked from his job. He made threatening remarks to Don Cameron, warning him that he would cut out all the negative things Cameron had written about NZC and present them to Cameron's editor on the *New Zealand Herald*.

When NZC announced in 1998 that henceforth the national team would be known as the 'Black Caps', and Doig was invited to talk about it on radio, he said that he would, but not if John Morrison or I were invited to comment too. Woe betide anyone in the media who was insufficiently 'positive'. But one can only paper over so many cracks. In my view NZC since the advent of its present CEO is lucky not to have been even more closely scrutinised by the media.

Planning a New Approach in India

When teams travel to play in India and the like they have to pay a great deal of attention to things that are seldom a problem at home. For instance, fluid intake and dealings with crowds need to be watched carefully. Dehydration is a real danger, as is the likelihood of having to avoid objects thrown at you by the crowd. At times there is the threat of rioting, a threat which occasionally becomes a reality, and players can end up gathering in the middle fidgeting like a herd of highly apprehensive animals. Cricket fans there have long been excitable. More recently, though, things are better organised and controlled, and I think the influence of international match referees like Raman Subba Row, for instance, has helped. In New Zealand, unfortunately, we can't claim to be significantly better any more. In India the crowd behaviour is improving, here it's deteriorating. A lot more objects are thrown on to the field here than used to be the case.

When in India teams are not advised to simply walk off the ground when the crowd starts making more than the normal noise and fuss and creates a serious problem. In India and Pakistan events or encounters which seem innocent or innocuous at first can easily grow quickly into something extremely serious and volatile. When I'd been in India in 1994 doing some TV commentating the West Indies had walked off the ground during a test in Nagpur. This really aroused the crowd's ire. Subba Row was the match referee. He insisted that one thing the police should do to help prevent incidents was watch the crowd rather than the cricket. Walking off can undoubtedly create more problems than staying out there while the match referee and other authorities are consulted.

Nothing is straightforward in India and Pakistan – but neither is it anywhere these days. You have to be thoughtful and prepared to go along with local customs and courtesies. Take the signing of autographs: players shouldn't start signing autographs on the field of play. The team adopted a policy of only signing autographs when not actively involved in play – after batting, say, was a good time – and of always having a barrier between themselves and autograph hunters. Local kids will sometimes start to throw things purely to try to catch a player's attention. There's seldom time to sign autographs during one-day games for players really have to give what's happening on the field their complete attention.

Before we'd left New Zealand we had an interesting discussion when deciding on a policy relating to the drinking of alcohol and went round in circles for a while. One player felt we shouldn't drink at all; others said that what counted was one's performance on the field and the amount a player drank should be left to him. One said if he could drink 10 pints and make a hundred next day he should be allowed to have 10 pints. I said that he ought to consider that by cutting it down to 5 pints he might get 200. In the end we agreed to limit alcohol consumption to a 'level appropriate for an athlete'.

What we were really hoping to encourage was a habit of self-policing and arrive at a state whereby there wasn't an 'us' (being management) and 'them' situation. We felt that there was a perception that such a situation had developed in New Zealand cricket, although to me, and to others, it had seemed that the team was accustomed to running itself. The ideal situation is when team members take responsibility for not only their own behaviour but that of their teammates and gently pull them back into line when they start to overstep the mark. We've a way to go before that happens in New Zealand cricket.

Regarding the 'us and them' syndrome, I think there should always be a gap between management and players. One can't always be buddies together; management has its role, players another. But in the end both parties are striving for the same successful result.

One of the most interesting things about sorting out protocols with the players was that most of them had a lot more to say when it came to matters relating to social behaviour than they did about things specifically to do with cricket. There was little or no feedback on the style of cricket we wanted to play, or on strategy, tactics, and so on. I found this lack of input into the theory and practice of cricket surprising from a group of international sportsmen. But on the social side, a different matter.

We didn't set a curfew. Everyone agreed that the best thing to do was to agree to keep sensible hours in line with those most athletes follow. But we did decide to take a firm line to ensure that transport to grounds left at the stipulated times and that anyone who was late would have to arrange his own transport at his own cost. This applied to all members of the touring party. Anyone who has been on tours knows that the same one or two people tend to cut it fine – in fact, if you become too 'flexible' here, two minutes late becomes five, and so on – but we didn't have many problems in that area. Just occasionally it's been known for the captain or a manager to get left behind and this always delights a few in the party, and is one of those little games that has a slight edge to it. But no favourites. Often, at the appointed hour, players would start yelling in the bus, 'Time's up, let's go,' and it wouldn't matter who was late, they'd enjoy leaving one of their mates behind. As the timekeeper I'd be yelled at and encouraged to 'come on, let's go.'

We even had a policy under the titillating heading 'Dissolute Behaviour' which, put baldly, said no drugs, no betting, and no womanising; no acts unbecoming of a professional athlete representing his country.

Now some might say that grown men representing their country surely don't need to have all these things spelt out. Anyone who thinks that has never been on tour with groups of young men, or has forgotten what it was like to be a young man. The fact is that when you are on tour, in public you are seen as a New Zealand cricketer, not as an individual. Players are under far more scrutiny today, what with the extra media coverage, the greater number of reporters, and the greater likelihood of sleaze or transgressions being reported. We wanted players to act discreetly, with some decorum, and didn't want to see public displays of pawing, drooling, bum-pinching and the like. That's what was meant by no womanising. It didn't mean no women, or men for that matter.

We wanted to ensure that as a team we showed proper respect for the people and the culture of the countries we visited. Unless you spell this out there is a tendency for a few to take the mickey out of hosts and, sometimes, abuse them.

Then there was the perennial question concerning wives or partners being present on tour. It's always been a difficult issue and touring party after touring party has often left it in the too hard basket.

The general consensus was that it was probably better if wives weren't on tour with the team, but some said that they wanted flexibility, felt they had a right to have their partners along. You can't really ban partners even if you thought it desirable. If wives or partners turn up at a venue you can't shoo them away. In the end we had few if any restrictions on wives or partners except to say that NZC and management didn't have responsibility for them, weren't liable for their expenses, and so on. It can of course be mildly amusing and cloak-and-daggerish when players start whipping breakfast out of the dining room and carting it up to rooms. And anyone who happens to have a room on their own – often the captain for instance – occasionally comes under pressure to move. Transport for non-touring party members can be problematic on some tours, especially in England when sponsored cars are involved. And on match days players will be watching to see who their partners are sitting with, are the pants being bored off them, did they remember to give them tickets for lunch? And so on. Apart from the disruptions, it's seldom much fun for any of the parties involved. Wives generally find that their husbands are stressed out, pre-occupied with cricket and other related matters, tired and generally difficult to be around.

Sometimes players' friends are recently-acquired, are hardly partners at all in today's sense of the word. Then there's a greater likelihood of having to deal with the impact of bust-ups. In India a New Zealand actor turned up and she and the player she'd come to see had a falling out after only one night – then they both had to endure a couple of weeks before her departure.

I haven't got an answer except to say that tours shouldn't be long, and that there should be decent gaps between them. We were to experience a great deal of difficulty with the issue of wives and partners on tour because most of the players were away from home for all but a few weeks between late September 1995 and the middle of May 1996. I wonder if the CEO of NZC, Christopher Doig, really has much idea of the pressures that exerts. He had a much better idea after the West Indies tour in 1996.

Styles of Play, Especially for the One-day Game

As a group prior to touring we talked over the style of play we wished to adopt. One is always looking to be a jump ahead of other countries. We were very much against letting games meander along

Sukhi and I, Bombay, 1969.

Right: The wedding – Sukhi's parents putting on the garlands at the sikh ceremony in London, 1973.

My extended family at a gathering in Wanaka, January 1987.

This caricature by former fast bowler Murray Webb was a gift from staff and trustees when I left Sport Otago.

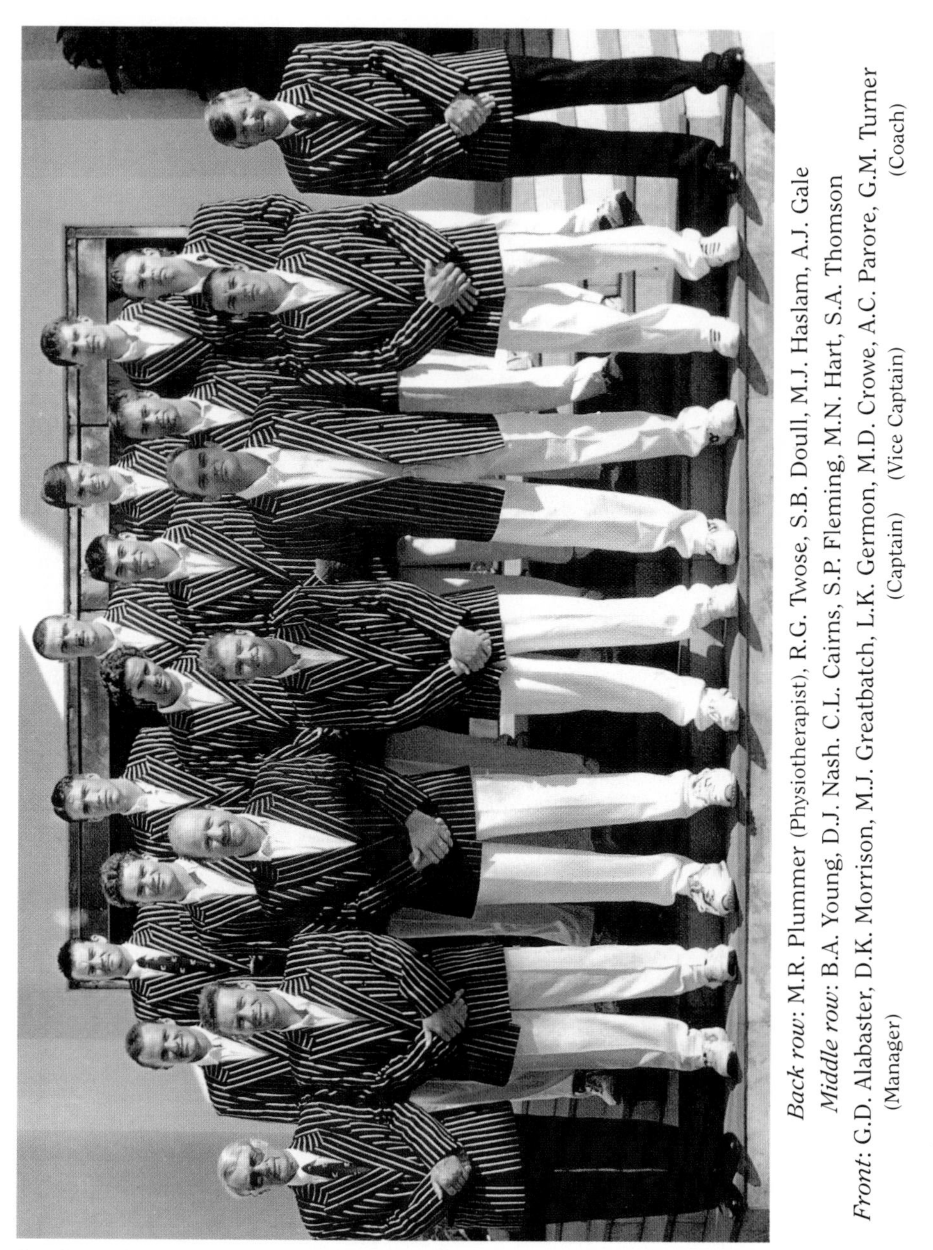

Back row: M.R. Plummer (Physiotherapist), R.G. Twose, S.B. Doull, M.J. Haslam, A.J. Gale

Middle row: B.A. Young, D.J. Nash. C.L. Cairns, S.P. Fleming, M.N. Hart, S.A. Thomson

Front: G.D. Alabaster (Manager), D.K. Morrison, M.J. Greatbatch, L.K. Germon (Captain), M.D. Crowe (Vice Captain), A.C. Parore, G.M. Turner (Coach)

Terry Baines Photo

The New Zealand Cricket Team
Tour to India 1995

Above: Homeless streetkids in Bombay outside the schoolroom where they are taught by aid agency volunteers and others.
Photo: Deek Rose

My friend, cameraman Deek Rose, introduced me to this young woman who, when younger, starred in a film about Bombay street-life. She and her family live and sleep under a tarpaulin beneath the trees in the background.
Photo: Deek Rose

and aimed always to look to win from the outset and only to go into defensive mode when it became obvious we couldn't win. In the past we felt that New Zealand teams were prone to adopt a wait and see, cautious approach from the start and not really go all out to win unless the opposition was in trouble. Our tendency had been to abuse the time available rather than optimise it. (New Zealand was not alone there, other teams did the same.) We felt we should be prepared to lose in an effort to win. We couldn't see anything wrong with making declarations which might let the other side back into a game provided it left us with the better chance of winning.

Urgency without indiscretion was an attitude that we wished to instil.

Look at each game as a self-contained unit and ignore the past and the future; play or bowl one ball at a time and set short-term goals, from the start of a session to drinks break, then to the end of the session.

Most sides, if they go one up in a series, for instance, tend to play conservatively from then on. We thought that New Zealand ought, if and when it got into that position, still go out looking to win.

I recall Martin Crowe saying, in respect to discussions about the style we wanted to play, words to the effect that, 'You just tell us the way you want to do it and we'll get in behind it, get stuck into it.' I was a little surprised to hear this because I'd been expecting, and hoping, that we might hear some ideas for fine-tuning.

In my view some players become overly-preoccupied with statistics, as do the media. I don't have a problem where players use them as motivation, but when they interfere with the team's plan, then there is a problem. Each player needs to find his way of best motivating himself, or be helped to find it. There are bound to be differences in this regard. Statistics are one means of motivation. The desire to improve one's statistics can be beneficial for a team, more so when the player is a bowler rather than a batsman. Bowlers almost always help their side by taking wickets – they don't look to take wickets slowly, whereas a batsman is more likely to spend too much time accumulating runs in a situation where the game plan calls for a faster rate. There's some merit in aiming, say, to take 15 wickets in a series, but once you've done that, you have to quickly set a new goal otherwise it's too easy to sit back and say, That's good enough.

One game at a time is the best way to approach one's cricket, in my opinion. It's helpful to have an overall performance goal. When batting a team should be looking to score 325 to 360 runs in a day, at a strike-rate no less than 66 per 100 balls. Bowlers should be aiming to restrict the opposition to 2.7 runs per over or less, under 250 runs per day. In the longer forms of the game these rates are achievable. And in the limited-overs games bowlers should try to achieve an economy rate of 4 runs or less per over.

We were also concerned to try to bowl say 100 instead of the required minimum of 90 overs per day. The more balls you bowl the more chance you have of winning. Of course, if it looks as if you might lose then there's no need to rush through the overs. When I played county cricket and captained Worcestershire we managed to bowl 18 to 19 overs an hour without too much bother – sometimes it was a doddle.

Batting: My message to the batsmen was that they should seek to master the fundamentals, begin by preparing to play every ball with a straight bat, adjusting the stroke according to the line and length of the ball. To some that may seem like oversimplification, but the art of batting generally hinges on playing with the full blade, especially in England, New Zealand, India, Pakistan and the West Indies. It's best for players to ensure that the need to play straight is firmly implanted and uppermost in their minds. Practising and simplifying thought-processes helps with concentration and consistency, particularly when it comes to the right shot-selection. They will still find that when a ball comes along that can be cut or hooked, they will naturally get into the right position to play the shot if they choose to. Batsmen who want to spend time at the crease do not set out with a pre-determined thought to cut and hook.

We were also concerned to see that batsmen looked to push each ball into a gap, that they avoid the habit of dead-batting. Angle the bat, propel the ball into a gap and take a run so that the score is kept ticking over. It is an art which most modern players seem to have lost, which is a pity because it is the difference between a good and a very good player. This practice often relieves the pressure and the temptation to attempt a risky boundary shot.

The fact that the limited-overs game is now a dominant part of cricket has undoubtedly increased batsmen's awareness of and ability to play the big shots. However, the art of picking up ones and twos has lost ground. All batsmen need to train themselves to collect runs between their boundary shots, and be looking to attack first and defend second.

Overall, my advice is to be positive and aggressive. I concede that in three-, four- and five-day games there are occasions, especially against the new ball, when survival comes first. It's then that you can positively let the ball go and think defend first and attack second.

If players feel they must play the ball to third man they should not run it with the open face of the bat. Too often, even though the slips or slip may be gone, fine nicks are taken by the 'keeper. There are ways of more safely playing a ball to third man: one is to get over the ball and play it a little late with virtually the full face of the bat. The pace of the ball will take it down to third man. But once you start playing with half the face or less the chances of nicking it are too great.

When discussing batting I always emphasise that there must be an overriding determination not to get out, and that each batsman should try not to be influenced by what's gone before him. A confident, aggressive approach must be pursued irrespective for a batsman is better to think that he can turn the game around in his team's favour. Any preoccupation with the need to rebuild after losing a couple of early wickets will not help a team's chances of winning most of its games. Nor is it likely to help the individual's performance, and it usually lessens the likelihood of a team getting a truly competitive total.

I should reiterate that in playing freely and aggressively you must still be determined not to get out. It is too easy to say, 'Oh, well, we needed quick runs,' or, 'It's a limited-overs game,' or, 'Bowler X came on and we needed to make hay and it gave me an excuse to get out.' A batsman has to sense when he's taking too big a risk, is being reckless. He has to take responsibility on his own shoulders and stretch himself as far as he can without giving it away. A player has to say to himself, 'I will make the difference.' Has to want to do that and not pass the buck.

Notwithstanding the above, the degree of risk taken by a batsman should be determined by the opposition tactics. If the batting side loses wickets early then the opposition captain will often bring back the opening bowlers during the middle stages in an effort to drive home an advantage and, if things go really well, mop up the innings. Both Younis and Akram have been used in this way by Pakistan. If this happens the batting side is justified in being more cautious in the middle stages in the knowledge that if the front-line bowlers are blunted the lesser bowlers will have to be used at the death. So of course one has to be flexible.

Bowling: Bowlers have to constantly work at mastering the fundamentals of line and length, accuracy and control. We just don't seem to have a high enough regard for the importance of line and length; selectors and commentators and others keep saying 'we must have wicket-takers' as though such are guys that run up and bowl quickly, or bang the ball in short, or bowl yorkers, or come up and bowl swinging wide half-volleys hoping batsmen will nick it, and so on.

Good bowling is very much about creating pressure through persistent control of line and length, and it's amazing what can be achieved with that. Attacking bowling is often tight bowling. The better the player you are bowling to – a good example is Brian Lara – the more important it is to tie him down. He gets irritated and impatient; he doesn't think ordinary-looking medium-pacers should be allowed to bowl and restrict him, so his response is to take chances. It's then that field placement becomes even more critical, and by careful positioning of boundary fielders the 'big' shots return only one run. Not only does that frustrate a batsman – the good shot brings a mere single – but it means that the best player loses the strike.

I emphasised the importance of bowling dot balls. Do that and wickets will follow in due course. Particularly when a wicket is doing a bit, if a bowler keeps putting it on or near the right spot, the percentages will work in the bowler's favour. And balls are not being wasted. The quicks can be gulled into wasting a lot of balls: a couple of short ones that fly harmlessly by, then one down the leg-side followed by a wide-ish delivery outside the off stump, and most of the over has been squandered.

I'm not saying we shouldn't use and look for quick bowlers, and I concede that on really flat tracks there is an argument for having a bowler who can tickle batsmen up and put them off their game by bowling a variety of deliveries. The quicks may go for a few extra runs, but if they are inducing false shots which result in the loss of wickets then the runs are not so important. But we need to be wary of encouraging the macho cricketer stuff at the expense of the skilful medium-pacer, particularly when one considers such medium-pacers are as scarce as hen's teeth.

Outswing bowlers in longer forms of cricket will sometimes bowl a full length and get the ball to swing in the hope that a batsman will, when trying to drive through the off-side, nick it into the slips. But in one-dayers the more likely result is four runs. The better course is to aim for a good length, thus giving the bowler more chance of delivering a dot ball. The new ball is always likely to take the edge because it does more from the pitch when the seam's still standing proud.

The current left-arm New Zealand opening bowler Shayne O'Connor is a good example. He tends to bowl too full, particularly to left-handers, because he backs himself to swing the ball away from them hoping for the nick to slips. If he pulled his length back a bit, he'd still entice batsmen to push forward with equally as good a chance of catches flying to slips, and he'd also very likely improve his economy-rate per over.

It's also vital to have the confidence to persevere with your strategy. Occasionally a batsman will attempt and pull off a high-risk shot, but such occasional success shouldn't disrupt one's plan of attack. In other words the captain, bowler and the fielders must keep their nerve. Sometimes, of course, it is obvious that a batsman has become very good at playing what is for most a high-risk shot. If that's the case then you have to change your strategy for *that player*, but generally, no.

Field placements are a critical attacking element associated with bowling. For example, when a spinner is bowling, rather than tossing the ball up to encourage a batsman to hit over the top, my belief is it is better to have the field in and bowl tightly. This tempts batsmen to try to hit good balls over the top and increases their chances of getting out. When an off-spinner is bowling to a right-hander, for instance, or a left-arm orthodox spinner to a left-hander, with the ball turning into the pads, it's a fairly simple shot to hit the ball over the infield. To me it is a good idea to position a fielder half- or two-thirds of the way to the boundary, or in such a position where it requires an excellent shot, except to the bad ball, to safely clear the field. I suppose an exception to what I've been saying here is when a real blocker is at the crease, one who won't be tempted, it's worth tossing the ball higher in the air. The extra bounce alone can help edges to carry to close-in fielders.

Nine times out of ten games are about restricting the number of runs the opposition scores, and particularly about suppressing their run-rate. What I am saying here is that it's worth striving to bowl dot balls in between the taking of wickets, in all cricket. Tight, accurate bowling restricts the runs in between the dismissals. I agree that taking wickets often slows down the run-rate, but in one-dayers it's the total runs scored that invariably counts for more than wickets lost.

One-day strategies: In cricket one has to operate with the fundamentals very much uppermost in the mind. My philosophy in respect to one-day games is that they are mainly about scoring as many runs as possible when batting first, and more than the opposition if batting second. Elementary of course, but it doesn't help to overcomplicate things or, as they say in golf, try to get 'too cute'.

Sometimes those directly involved in the game are not as smart as some members of the cricketing public. For instance, in 1994 I got a letter from a Wellington enthusiast Peter Haig. He reckoned that too many commentators, journalists and the like when discussing the one-day game, 'cling to the conventions of the traditional game.' I concurred. He said very pertinently that, 'a side which makes 210 all out in the 48th over wins if the opponents can manage only 209 in their 50 overs – even if they don't lose a single wicket!' He felt 'too much emphasis' was placed on 'preserving wickets, and too little on the need to get on with the run-making.' He also said that, 'a dot-ball is a mini-victory for the bowling side in the first over just as much as in the last.' Quite so, I thought, and quite again.

What is the point of having wickets in hand at the end of 50 overs if you don't have enough runs? Why save wickets for the final few overs when the opposition is able to use its best bowlers at a time when only the minimum restrictions on field placements apply?

Take, for example, the Pakistan pace duo Wasim Akram and Waqar Younis when in their pomp. I know that has passed, but they would usually return to the crease 'at the death' when they were able to get reverse swing, fire the ball in at yorker length, and set defensive fields. A team could easily end up facing the final eight overs from them having saved a bundle of wickets that turned out to be of limited use. Hoarding wickets in case you might need them is an undesirable form of conservatism. To my way of thinking a team is better, in most cases, to have built a good score by the time the final overs come round.

In our discussions on playing style we noted that individual form comes and goes, that concerns would likely emerge as to whether our strategy was right or wrong. We said that where necessary we would revisit things and would welcome players challenging the style we had adopted, but that no changes would be made without good reasons being advanced. We were mindful of the fact that a new strategy needs to be given time, and that the ups and downs of form have to be taken into account.

We decided to try to score at a fast clip in the first 15 overs of limited-overs matches, and our selections would reflect this. The teams we would select gave us batting down to number 10 in the order. Consequently we felt that we could lose three or even four wickets in the first 15 overs and still recover and post a good score.

The first 15 overs are a real opportunity to set up the foundation for high totals by scoring a lot of runs. We knew that it would take some players time to get used to not worrying about consolidating after the loss of a few early wickets, and instead bat in such a way that we went on to win the game.

We agreed that many sides waste opportunities to push on in the middle stages of their innings. We aimed to milk the middle overs with real urgency, through swift running and taking many singles and twos, for boundaries are often hard to get.

And we took the attitude that it is tactically unsound when batting first to assume that a particular score will be enough to win a game. A good score is as many runs as you can get. Sides that do well in the first 15 overs are tempted to tick along through the middle stages because they think that 250-260 runs, say, is probable, and that this will be enough. But a side isn't safe with such a score these days: we decided 300-plus must be the aim.

The Honourable Loss Syndrome: Too often New Zealand teams, and administrations, tell us that we should be heartened by 'honourable' losses, that we should applaud the 'positive signs', that we are 'learning'. I've never been quite sure what it is we are said to have been learning, but whatever it is we have become expert at forgetting.

Those who talk often about the need to be 'positive' are usually the same people who, in the next breath, tell us that we can't really be expected to 'beat the World Champions'. And so on. I disagree. I think that New Zealand has the players to, if well-tutored, regularly win far more matches than it loses. But tactically, technically and mentally we haven't been making the best use of our talent.

Incidentally, who are the World Champions? Usually Australia is the team referred to, by our hierarchy and cricket supporters, whether they are or are not. We seem to have been conned by the Australian cricket commentary teams with all their exaggerated waffle about the abilities of 'the great Australians'. Determined and continuing reverential nods in the direction of Australia has not done us much good. We overestimate their abilities, attribute to them a degree of cricketing perspicacity and wisdom they do not have, and relentlessly underestimate our own. What's positive about that?

It was true that, when we looked at the other international sides leading up to the 1996 World Cup, few would have said we were oozing with talent. Nevertheless we felt that by adopting an aggressive strategy and playing out of our skins, we had a chance of upsetting the pundits. We felt we could beat anyone, if we had the right tactics and resolve to follow through. It is possible, if a coach has the background knowledge, to look at the world's best players, focus on areas of weakness, then seek to exploit them. I am convinced that it is not difficult to persuade players that another international side is not very good – many of them are not. You do that by carefully deconstructing the opposition so that their flaws are revealed. This is very good for the confidence of our side. Many other international sides do not play to their potential. Unfortunately New Zealand continues to spend too much time pointing out how good others are. All that is, is making excuses prior to failure.

Chapter 3

Shaking-down in Darwin

At the players' camp in Auckland in mid-August 1995 we had to have another look at Matthew Hart to see if he'd made progress. We were definitely keen to have Hart but only if he was able to show that he'd returned to something close to his previous best, or what was perceived to be his best. I hadn't studied Hart's bowling before the camp in Christchurch and had to accept what others told me, that previously he had been a much better bowler.

During this camp we discussed the structure of team meetings and practice routines and how and when we would conduct them. In addition to having meetings on the eve of tests, we decided to meet regularly during the matches. Updates and assessments after each day's play. We split the team into two groups, batsmen and bowlers, with all-rounders Cairns and Thomson contributing to both. If we'd been batting that day, the batsmen's group would meet that night to discuss their performance. Likewise if the bowlers had been operating that day. The coach and captain naturally attended all meetings and helped set the agendas; the coach introduced each item and the captain acted as one of the group. The manager and the physiotherapist attended as observers. If one group felt there was a need for the entire team to meet then we would.

The idea behind having two groups was that individuals get more chance to contribute if a group is smaller. Bigger groups tend to be dominated by one or two people and we wanted to break away from that. We realised that there was a risk of a split, bowlers versus batsmen, but we felt that we would have enough whole group meetings to avoid most of that. I don't think I've ever been in a team where there isn't a bit of that, it's simply a matter of degree. If batsmen are not getting runs on flat pitches, and the bowlers get whacked for plenty because of the conditions, then they start to get grumpy. 'Jesus,' they say, 'the conditions suited the batsmen and ours let us down.' And vice versa. When a pitch is doing a bit and the bowlers don't take advantage, the batsmen are apt to grizzle. We didn't have a particular problem in this regard, although it was the case that the problem players tended to be bowlers rather than batsmen. What was it that the former England opening bowler John Snow said? I know, by his own admission he said he was too intelligent to be a fast bowler. Pounding away day after day like that is not really a natural act. Pick your conditions.

No doubt there are occasions in rugby when backs grumble about poor quality ball, or conversely, forwards bark about possession being frittered away by bumblers behind them. Updates during tests, looking at where you are and where you ought to be looking to go, are a means of easing such tension in cricket.

Apart from the special simulated match-type practices which we were to use in Darwin, we decided that during the normal practices those not bowling or batting in the nets, including the wicketkeeper, would practise a variety of fielding skills. This is a good way of ensuring that all players make good use of their time. It meant practices were more full-on and could be shortened. The players drew up their own practice routine. We started discussions on that with a blank page.

We explained the role of the tour management team, how we saw our role. We also outlined the respective roles and responsibilities of the coach and manager. With previous teams the manager had the authority to be all powerful, if he'd wanted to be, although it seemed that in more recent times managers had been reluctant to be assertive. I wanted things to be more democratic than usual, hence the inclusion of the captain, acting as the players' representative, and the physiotherapist Mark Plummer. Plums was reluctant to join the management team at first, partly because his closer physical involvement with players resulted in him hearing things that could prove awkward and compromise a kind of medical confidentiality. Also he'd experienced a situation with the previous New Zealand side where there was no respect for management. But we convinced him that our procedures would be so fair that it should not be seen as an issue.

As coach I could have assumed far more power in the party, but chose not to. I have found that the more you know about cricket the more there is to know (I imagine this is true of most things), so I required and encouraged input from others. That's why we sat down with the players and worked out protocols together. I don't like ad hoc decisions. But even more than that, I wanted fairness, and it seems to me that when it comes to matters like discipline and order, a group is more likely to dispense it fairly than one individual.

Although the English-based players, Cairns, Nash and Twose, weren't party to these discussions, I had gone through our proposed protocols when I met with them in the UK. I spent a good three hours with them going through the protocols and looking for feedback from them. Simon Doull, Aaron Gale and Lee Germon were others with whom I went through this process. We were also to have further team meetings before, and then during the early stages of the Indian tour, so that no one could be in any doubt as to what we were looking to achieve, and what my approach would be as coach.

I'd now engaged in a great deal of dialogue with all manner of people involved in New Zealand cricket. I can't recall ever having had so many meetings. But I welcomed them because I was very interested in what people had to say. I also made a point of talking to some of the older group – former New Zealand and Auckland opening bowler John Hayes, who had played 15 tests in the 1950s, was one with whom I had a couple of discussions, and Merv Wallace, who first played for New Zealand in 1936, and for the final time in 1953, was another. It was good to talk to the older men and get their thoughts and feelings about our cricket. Also, because talk is often loose and/or cheap, I wrote a lot of things down and handed them out to team and squad members.

While thinking about our aims and objectives, and what sort of a culture we needed to instil in New Zealand cricket, I'd come across and been quite taken by some of the thoughts of the famous American basketball coach John Wooden. (Coincidently, not long after this I was talking to John Wright and he too had read some of Wooden's thoughts and found them useful.)

To Wooden, it is said, dishonesty was unthinkable and he wasn't keen on flamboyance, gimmicks or tricks. He asserted that *success is a very personal matter* and felt only the individual can judge success for him or herself. Only individuals can know if they gave of their best, and didn't shirk, or take the easy way out. Wooden was fond of quoting Grantland Rice's poem 'How to Be a Champion' which says that the higher up the scale you go, and no matter where you 'look to see the knack', you find, 'The most of it is practice and the rest of it is work.' Wooden designed a pyramid of success, at the base of which are blocks called 'Industriousness', 'Friendship', 'Loyalty', 'Cooperation', and 'Enthusiasm'. The next tier up comprises 'Self-control', 'Alertness', 'Initiative' and 'Intentness'. At the top of the pyramid is 'Competitive greatness'. Wooden told his players that 'our team condition depends on two factors – how hard they work on the floor at practice and how well they behave between practices.' When observing Wooden at work and how he spoke to his team it was discovered that 'Instruction', described as 'verbal statements about what to do, or how to do it' made up 50.3 per cent of the total communications. 'Hustles', 'verbal statements to activate or intensify previously instructed behaviour', comprised 12.7 per cent of the whole. 'Praises', 'verbal compliments, encouragements', 6.9 per cent. Wooden must have been more of a 'Southern Man' than me.

I gave all members of the team a sheet which proffered definitions which might be useful in working towards our goals. I used some of Wooden's credos. For instance, 'Success' was deemed a very personal matter, and that only individuals, ultimately, could judge it and know whether they'd given of their best. It emphasised the need to keep one's self-respect, show 'Loyalty' to oneself and to those dependent on you, and to remain loyal to our agreed goals. Under 'Cooperation', 'Enthusiasm', and 'Self-control' it called for united effort, enjoyment of work and a willingness to stimulate others, good judgement, common sense and emotional control. There was a reference to the importance of physical and mental conditioning, of which two key factors are (a), how hard you practise, and (b), how well you behave between practices. Under 'Team Spirit' we had the following: 'Selflessness. An eagerness to sacrifice personal glory for the welfare of the group as a whole. Togetherness and consideration for others. **Note:** It is not necessary for everyone to particularly like each other to play well together, but you must **respect** each other.' We also noted the importance of preparation as a means of achieving 'inner motivation, with the main focus on the self not on the opponents' in order to find the 'confidence in your ability to play well'. If individuals and teams are to attain something approaching peace of mind it can only come with proper preparation. With that comes the knowledge that you are at your best and that the team will be too because you can all point to broadly similar preparation. It's then that teams collectively and individually will have gone a long way towards developing the strength to conquer outside pressures.

These thoughts were reminders, really, and I didn't dwell on them. If it helped a few become better cricketers and better people, well and good.

The issue of loyalty is and was terribly important. It was something we often talked about in the ensuing months. In the recent past in New Zealand teams it had seemed that loyalty had tended to mean little more than protecting one's mates and those around you. I saw that as blind loyalty and we made it plain that that wasn't the way we wanted to function, and that there had to be accountability. We made it clear that if someone did something daft in public then they couldn't expect to be protected. I hasten to add here, that when I went to England to see the league and county players, Cairns and others, I made a particular point of saying that it would be important that players be loyal to the policies and practices we'd agreed to. If things happened off the park which weren't in the team's and NZC's best interests we'd do our best to keep them in house, but when it came to behaviour on the park and in very public places then they would have to suffer the consequences of their own foolishness.

All a coach or a captain can fairly ask of a player is what that player can ask of himself, that he does his best as often as possible. Sometimes you fail; at times you play below your best and still come out on top; at times your opponents play better than you do and succeed. Keep it all in perspective. Success or failure is not always dependent on the result. In this regard you can't afford to take much notice of what the papers or the commentators say, for they will get it wrong sometimes and say that you performed well on a day when you know that you didn't do very well at all, and vice versa.

Emerging Players: At the end of August we had a meeting of the emerging players squad. I spoke to the whole group and outlined the philosophy and style which we'd worked through and were looking to develop for the future of New Zealand cricket. The players in the emerging squad had also been given the same questionnaire relating to their game which the senior squad had. In the emerging group were batsmen Aiken, Spearman, Howell, McMillan, Richard Jones, Parlane and Mather. We also included Stephen Fleming because the meet was being held in Christchurch and we wanted to give him the opportunity for additional practice. The seamers were

Allott, O'Connor, Penn and Hayes; the spinners Hart, Loveridge, Furlong, Wiseman and Spice. The 'keepers were Croy and Robbie Hart. We naturally couldn't call on a number of players then engaged overseas in various leagues. I'd already set up some specialised work for Kerry Walmsley, and for Heath Davis who was to go to Christchurch for work with Dayle Hadlee and sports science and fitness people like Paul Carpinter and Graham Nuttridge.

I had one-on-one sessions with several of the emerging players in order to discuss areas of their play that they should consider working on – I had video tape of many of them. Emerging players need more than merely an indication that you have your eye on them; they have to be put on programmes to develop both their fitness and their play.

To Darwin, with Optimism

From 11-26 September we were in Darwin in Australia's Northern Territory. It's a pretty gruelling place in which to play anything, let alone a game with the duration of cricket. We felt that this would be an ideal preparation prior to the tour of India, particularly taking into account we were coming from a New Zealand winter. In fact Darwin was hotter than any of the conditions we encountered in India.

In Darwin their club cricket season was about to finish as the rainy season was imminent – their climate is rather different to that of the dominant cricket-playing states of Australia. The pitches for both playing and practising were good – fairly placid by Australian standards but good preparation for India – and even though the outfields were a bit slow, it was still going to be excellent practice. We were able to practise against Australian state sides who were taking the opportunity to put in some early season work. We had games against South Australia, Victoria and the Northern Territory.

We chose the following team: Germon, Astle, Crowe, Doull, Fleming, Gale, Greatbatch, Hart, Loveridge, McMillan, Morrison, Parore, Thomson, and Young. Simon Doull asked to be allowed to remain in the UK to see his season out and was replaced by Allott. Loveridge got injured before the first game and he was replaced by Haslam. I was very sorry to see Loveridge badly damage a finger in the nets because he was extremely promising, a right-arm leg-break bowler who when batting could strike the ball well, and was an excellent mover with a very good arm in the field. It would have been nice to have played a part in the development of a top class leggie.

Having two two-day games against South Australia, two one-dayers against Victoria, and further one-dayers against both Northern Territory and South Australia was very useful. The matches were valuable because they got us into good habits combating heat and managing our water intake, and in developing the thinking needed to play genuinely competitive match cricket instead of spending most of one's time in nets. But what we did try to develop in the nets – and most found it very useful – was simulated game situations. Where possible we had batsmen in the nets batting in pairs for an hour, and two bowlers who would bowl alternate overs in five-over spells. Batsmen ran between the wickets so that the strike was changing, and I kept an eye open to ensure that they didn't just run the odd single but occasionally took three. It's good to puff and blow a bit and then have to collect yourself and concentrate again. All round this practice routine was a good mental and physical exercise to prepare for the real thing in the middle. It meant, too, that all players didn't have to go down to the nets at the same time, and we could stretch the practice out during the day. We did get some local bowlers in to help us out when we ran orthodox-type net sessions.

In his book *Boundary Hunter* Mark Greatbatch says that when we went to Darwin he and the team were 'immediately struck by the different level of organisation and discipline. Everything we did was purposeful, and we measured our performances at matches and at training. If we had 30 high catches, we recorded it, if we did 10 minutes of sprinting in our batting gear, we recorded it, so by tour end we had an accurate dossier on all the work we had put in and what our thoughts were on the innings we played.'

The games against the state sides enabled players to bat for longish periods in quite testing hot conditions. Nothing beats 3-4 hours at the wicket to help strike form early in a season. A similar gain for the bowlers was the opportunity to have concerted spells of 6-ball overs instead of the sometimes tedious 20-30 minutes or more, one ball after another sessions in nets. Net practice for batsmen is not nearly as useful as match-play. Twenty minutes is usually the maximum and you get a random selection of bowling: slow spin, medium to fast, then a dibbly-dobbly. Very much second-best in all respects.

During the Darwin trip I held a meeting to see if we could dilute the animosity which still existed among several of the players as a result of the dope-smoking fiasco in South Africa. The feeling was that one of their number, Danny Morrison, had dobbed-in the others. I didn't want lingering animosity so we had a meeting at which Morrison gave his side of the story and others were able to put questions to him. As I recall, Morrison said his main motivation was to try to expose and help oust the management at that time, not to dob-in players. It cleared the air a little but didn't completely resolve the issue. It was clear that for a number of the players it was going to take more than that for them to accept what had happened and let it go entirely. The Judas stain never faded completely.

We discovered that we'd inherited a number of players who had not been managed before. Perhaps one could say they had preferred not to be managed and had been allowed to go it alone, with sorry consequences. Alabaster, Germon and I were therefore a shock to some. We were appointed to manage and did. I recall after the Darwin trip Mark Plummer telling me that some of the more senior players were expecting us to 'join them' and were not pleased to find that this wasn't so.

The English-based Twose, Cairns, and Nash were not able to return to New Zealand in time to make the trip to Darwin. We weren't too concerned about their absence because they were still getting cricket, and the general feeling, which I shared, was that they would have been imbued with the best elements of professionalism, and would thus welcome a disciplined and sensibly-run professional set-up. Before too long I had to revise that view.

The Darwin trip was a success. (New Zealand's results against Australian state sides on the 1996-97 tour show that we went backwards a good distance in the ensuing two years.) For the record, in Darwin in 1995, New Zealand won 5 of the 6 games played. We had good playing conditions, good opposition and satisfying results. Allott had shown promise for the future; in fact he was our best bowler in Darwin. The work ethic and general attitude of the players was pleasing. A two-week tour should be a doddle, considering the absence of pressure created by international matches and the freshness within the players following a few months off.

Chapter 4

Bombay, Bangalore, and other parts of India

For several weeks prior to the tour of India I was involved in awkward discussions over the itinerary with the secretary of the Indian board, in particular over where we would start the tour, and what practice facilities would be available to us in the first few days. I didn't handle negotiations directly, that was Tim Murdoch of NZC's lot. We were keen to get up to Chandigarh in the north where I knew practice and other facilities were excellent. I also knew the man running cricket there, which would have been a great help. But the Indian board insisted we start in Rajkot, a decidedly 'rural' area. Reports from some other touring sides had not been favourable but many are overly-critical of conditions in India.

As a compromise it was agreed that we would arrive in Bombay on 1 October 1995 and stay there for four days before going up to Rajkot. Although we knew it would be stickier in Bombay, we were able to practise for four days in the nets at the Brabourne Stadium where the pitches did a bit but were good enough. It would have been better to go to a smaller centre, rather than a major one where things are far more social, and can divert players' attention at a time when the priority is to knuckle down and prepare for the tour.

The New Zealand team was Lee Germon (captain and wicketkeeper), Cairns, Crowe, Doull, Fleming, Gale, Greatbatch, Hart, Haslam, Morrison, Nash, Parore, Thomson, Twose, Young. Gren Alabaster was manager and the physiotherapist was Mark Plummer.

Originally we'd selected Dipak Patel but when he was injured before we left New Zealand we replaced him with Haslam. Later in the tour we replaced Gale and Hart with Nathan Astle and Gavin Larsen for the one-day series. In line with seeking to maintain continuity of selection where possible we had resisted making major changes to the side for the tour.

We flew up to Rajkot on the sixth and we found the place quite good. The hotel was fairly basic but the rooms were large and clean and things were more than adequate. The tour opener was against the Indian Cricket Board's President's XI the next day. We left out Hart and the guys who had virtually come straight from a season of county cricket in England – Twose, Cairns and Nash. It was hot and dry in Rajkot but as we had had time in Darwin, and then those few days of stickiness in Bombay, the team wasn't greatly stressed.

We scored 366 for 5 in 90 overs, with Greatbatch getting 138, Young 52, Parore 79, and Germon 29 not out, so we felt we'd started off well in the style we were aiming to play.

The wicket was flat and the seamers had no joy. The President's XI rattled up 399 for 6 off 99 overs, then we followed up with 251 for 5 off 64 overs with Crowe not out 101 and Fleming 72, so both sides' bowlers and batsmen had a good workout. Although it was encouraging to have a good run-rate, it wasn't my main concern at the start of a tour. What is important is time at the crease for the batsmen and decent spells of bowling for the bowlers, and the batsmen showed that they didn't have too much trouble scoring at the sort of run-rate required if a team is to win games rather than draw them.

* * *

When we got to Bombay I thought of asking the team if they'd be prepared to put in say 20-30 rupees a day (about NZ$1) out of the approximately 800 rupees they were each getting for food expenses. My idea was that we would donate the money to a fund for underprivileged in India; it might be to a group providing sports equipment in Bombay, or a home for street kids, or to needy families, and so on. I thought it might be nice to show some sort of collective humanitarian side, and, of course, it would also do our PR no harm. There was no denying that, and nor was there any denying that in a way I would have been attempting to encourage the team to support and share my own concerns and values. Having thought about it I decided against floating the idea.

But in Bombay I took Stephen Fleming and a couple of others to meet and chat with one or two of the people who live on the streets there. I'd taken a particular interest in one family near our hotel, the Taj Mahal in Bombay, and Flem and the others quite enjoyed the experience of meeting them.

When we returned to Bombay late in the tour I found that one of the street people we'd met was having trouble getting a license to sell flowers. This woman made about 30 rupees a day selling flowers and had to bring up three children. Her male partner, the father of her children, brought in about 30 rupees a day himself. The woman had told me that if she could get a license to sell flowers out in front of where they lived, she felt that she could treble her income. These people lived in a shop doorway, and there was an opportunity where, by moving a little further down the road, they could find a place with a roof over their head – if they could get together about 10,000 rupees, approximately $NZ400. Some of the guys were interested in putting in some money to help make this happen, which was pleasing because it showed how the attitude of most towards the local people had improved from earlier in the tour. It wasn't necessary to take a collection because I'd already given the money to the woman concerned.

* * *

Our second tour match, this time against Bombay at the Wankhede Stadium, was rather different as the pitch had a lot of life and sideways movement in it. By this time I'd had sessions with each player and discussed the records they were keeping as a means of charting their progress. All players had been issued with 'Performance Record' forms for each week of the tour.

We had instituted this record system in Darwin. By keeping records the players could see exactly what work they'd done and could better assess which areas needed more or less attention. It was also designed to encourage players to have some pride in their performance. The records were quite detailed – time spent on warm-ups, stretching, batting, bowling, catching, throwing, and warming down. We even broke things down into how long they spent facing spinners and seamers, whether they had throw-downs, and whether they batted with or without a partner. Bowlers recorded how long they bowled at a stump alone and at batsmen, and there was space to record time spent on close as opposed to long catching, medium or long throwing, and so on.

Players were encouraged to comment on their day's work. Some of the comments on Martin Crowe's record for the first week were, for example: 'Felt good first up. Good use of feet to spinners'; '15 mins knee strength work'; 'Great against spin. Need to keep still, trust movements against seamers'.

These records were mainly for the benefit of the players as a help in analysing and charting their progress. Management was keen to see that players did keep records of what they'd been working on. This had not been done with New Zealand teams before and we saw it not only as helpful in aiding with refinement, but also as a means of motivation, as a means of maintaining interest in practices as well as matches. Most players seemed happy enough to go along with the scheme and would have concurred with Mark Greatbatch's views as he expressed them in his book *Boundary Hunter*.

The ball nipped around in Bombay and it was always going to be a risk batting first, but we wanted to make sure that we had two bats if possible. We also decided to use the players we were hoping to include in the next game, the first test in Bangalore. This was disappointing for the back-up players but as a general rule it is best to give the test players as much play as possible when there is only a short lead-up period before test matches on tour. So the team included Twose, Cairns, Nash and Hart, the only notable exclusion was Crowe whose knee required rest and treatment.

Bombay was a strong side, as usual, and the Ranjit Trophy champions. Greatbatch batted well to score 100, but the rest struggled, especially against the seamer Mhambrey who took 4 wickets for 79, and we declared at 217 for 8 off 64 overs.

The home team's batting line-up was very strong with Manjrekar, Tendulkar and Kambli at 3,4, and 5, and Bombay made 360, those three batsmen making 79, 39, and 104 respectively. Muzumdar, one of Morrison's 3 wickets for 48, got 53. We made a point of bowling our spinners and Thomson got through 33 overs and Hart 20, both taking 2 wickets.

In our second innings we opened with Young and Twose who both went cheaply, but Parore (64), Fleming (79 no) and Thomson (45 no) batted well in our 192 for 3 off 51 overs.

We had gone from a real flat wicket at Rajkot to a seamer at Bombay and were reasonably happy with our preparation leading in to the first test at Chinnasawamy Stadium in Bangalore.

* * *

In Bangalore a group of us went to a Game Reserve (or park) and found that the animals were not in the slightest bit interested in us. At one point two tigers copulated mere metres away from ogling cricketers in a bus. A brisk performance, not much pawplay, and a moment of hindlegs, post-coital triumphant strutting.

The Indians are not afraid to charge tourists a fair old whack. Indian residents paid 5-10 rupees to enter the park (the exchange rate was about 25 rupees to the NZ dollar). We paid 150 rupees each. Perhaps, I thought, using this as an example, New Zealand could extract more from its visitors than it does.

Every team has its wheelers and dealers. With us, both Mark Greatbatch and Roger Twose come into that category. In Madras we noticed that in their spare time they were often preoccupied with looking at finding ways of buying Indian goods and importing them for sale in New Zealand. Good luck to them. It did mean that once they missed, or were late, for a social gathering the players had organised for themselves. That may have cost them a few rupees.

The Peninsula Hotel where we stayed in Madras had a top-class restaurant which offered a good standard of French cuisine. For about $NZ30 you could have a fine dinner, so we treated ourselves a couple of times when there. I was told the fillet was flown in especially from the USA. The Hindus aren't big on beef (cow and all that) so in most restaurants you get 'Indian beef', in reality water buffalo.

Naturally, as I am married to an Indian, I am much more familiar than most with Indian life and culture. I've played, toured and visited India quite a lot, perhaps as often as 20 times, and it never fails to fascinate me. India is not as hard a place for westerners to tour and play cricket in as it was 20-30 years and more ago. But there is still great colour, great confusion, the astonishing contrasts that make up the human condition. Great wealth, saddening poverty, amazing tolerance and, here and there, scary intolerance and burning, centuries-old enmity. India puts much of what passes for discomfort and deprivation elsewhere into perspective.

We had to get through the streets of a large slice of Calcutta in a bus. What an extraordinary passing parade there is. Talk about the variety of seething humanity. Enormous numbers of people have to concentrate on survival, have little time for pettiness, triviality, or envy. But the middle classes have been growing in India. Now it's said there could be as many as 300 million people in that broad category.

I first went to India on a cricket tour in 1969. Since then India has been opened up more and more to multi/trans-national business interests, there are more and more cars, pollution is getting worse. One sees it in the likes of Hyderabad and Bangalore where pollution was barely noticeable 30 years ago. Auto rickshaws certainly don't help. But the light in India is special for all that. I term it softer, tranquil, and no doubt partly determined by pollution, not harsh and hard like in the south of New Zealand.

Spirituality is ubiquitous, the number of languages and dialects dizzying. India sees itself as a highly multi-cultural society with a great many religions. It differs greatly from Pakistan in this regard, which is solely a Muslim society. You might not see many white faces but you can't help noticing the diversity for all that. Livestock wander the streets of cities and are fed by the passing multitude. Goats, cows, camels. Bullock carts. People defecate in the fields alongside the animals. I would advise people to go to India every five years or so just to remind themselves that a bit of humility is both a virtue and a necessity.

A great many people speak English sufficiently well to be able to converse adequately with mono-lingual cricketers. Street kids selling flowers or begging round the Taj Mahal Hotel in Bombay will have enough words in French, German and English, for example, to persuade tourists to give them something. Granted it's dog-eat-dog in the sense that people have to battle to eke out a living, but one consequence is that families are much closer than in New Zealand. And once you get to know people they are extremely hospitable. There is surprisingly little crime. I have not detected, either, quite as much envy as one finds here. Is that something to do with religious fatalism? Perhaps, but it is more than that.

Australia's Shane Warne may not like the food but it is far more varied than at first meets the eye. Tins of baked beans and spaghetti didn't help him bowl to Tendulkar in 1998 so perhaps he should have persevered with Indian food after all. I find it delicious. Down around Goa on the west coast, once a Portuguese outpost, fish is prominent on the menu. In Hyderabad, with its strong Muslim history, they eat differently – and there's quite a bit of Urdu spoken too.

To me India has everything, except a lack of people. It isn't a vast country physically – you can fly between the main centres in two to three hours, or less – but it's remarkably varied. You can go from the hot, dry, dusty plains to the Himalayas and the roofs of the world in the north. On the plains around Delhi and northwest up into the Punjab summers are hot and dry with temperatures into the 30s and

40s. In winter you can even get light frosts. One of my favourite places is up in Himachal Pradesh in the foothills of the Himalayas. Rhododendrons abound, and there are forests, still. There's a romance about going up to Simla (at about 2000 metres), the old English summer capital, where the temperatures are much more pleasant than on the hot dusty plains in summer.

The monsoons are of a different character on the west and east coasts and come at different times. The Punjab – flat, land of five rivers – is known as the bread-basket of India. The famous Basmati rice comes from the Punjab. Rivers are the lifeblood, the greatest geographical influence on life in India. Coastal areas are not nearly as significant in India as they are in New Zealand.

And when in Hyderabad in the central south I always like to have a look at the wonderful Golkunda Forta on the outskirts of the city. The barren, rocky outcropped landscape around the fort intrigues me, is a bit like parts of Central Otago.

There is corruption in India and often it's open. But there's corruption everywhere. In New Zealand ours takes slightly different forms and we work to hide it.

I suppose it's fair to say that I've always had a soft spot for the under-privileged, call it a social conscience. So one of the things that frustrates me about New Zealanders is that some who have been given a skill, a talent – international cricketers for example – can get carried away with themselves and abuse others in less fortunate circumstances or with different priorities. Part of the reason for this response from some Westerners is that India's infrastructure is under enormous pressure. Delays alone can cause a lot of frustration and stretch one's tolerance. So much seems forever under repair, and it's remarkable therefore how the country functions as well as it does. Indian mechanics must be among the best there are; the bottom line is they keep things going. Some of the vehicles look like objects from the film *Mad Max*. An irony lost on many Westerners is that Indians look upon many of us as uncultured, uncivilised and superficial.

* * *

It was interesting to note the response of the Indian media to the protocol we'd sorted out before leaving New Zealand, and which had miffed a few back home. In India, we actually gave the media a list of dates on which players would be available for the more lengthy interviews required for feature articles, and the Indian media greatly appreciated it. Guarantees of availability and certainty generally is very much appreciated by journalists in India – and most other places, too, for that matter – and some of them actually travelled long distances to see us, secure in the knowledge that they would get access and wouldn't have to spend hours or maybe days lurking and hanging around in the hope of snaffling a player.

The team's dress code proved mildly contentious for a time. We had agreed beforehand as a team that we would have number ones and number twos – ones for official functions requiring a tie and a jacket and team trousers, twos just a shirt and trousers. But we hadn't envisaged some players – Parore and Thomson are two who seem to like showing off the body beautiful – would want to roll up their trousers and display their enticing calves. They liked to wear shoes but no socks. Also there was the question of earrings and the like. We suggested it might be better if players put in 'keepers' or studs when playing, to avoid the danger of items catching in clothing and tearing an earlobe. Team management discussed this issue and Gren Alabaster, formerly a secondary school principal, said that such assertions of individuality tended to come and go, and that fads changed. It could be earrings for a month or two, shaved heads for another period and so on. A few players wanted to wear their shirts hanging out. Gren said, 'All right then, if that's what you want.'

All we were really concerned about was that the side presented an image when in public that satisfied most of cricket's supporters. For us it was a case of the too hard basket. We decided that it was over to the players' employer, NZC, to determine how it wanted its players to look.

Only two or three players saw this as an important issue. To me it was of little consequence when compared to everything else. But I am reminded of a discussion I had with Shane Thomson before we came away. He liked to wear a black singlet whenever he could. He'd done a lot of work pumping iron and fancied showing off his body. Shane was fond of wearing black leathers and was keen to ride his Harley Davidson motorbike to the ground in New Zealand.

It begs the question, should there be uniforms at all? But the fact is that NZC decrees that there will be blazers and ties and team-issue trousers, and so on, and requires they be worn. These things do highlight how some people are more suited to individual rather than team sports. At the time, trying to get a New Zealand cricket team to pull in the one direction was like setting out to herd cats.

* * *

Although we'd only had two matches in India prior to the first test, we had been working on fitness programmes for months; we'd had personal performance programmes in place, and briefings, and camps, and two good weeks in Darwin. We couldn't say we were underprepared. We thought we were getting into the right sort of groove.

We had our across the board code of conduct and were hopeful that before long that would become accepted and uncontentious. Of course onfield behaviour is always harder to control and in the heat of the moment lapses are to be expected and, occasionally, are understandable. But everyone was working hard and things seemed to be going nicely. The batsmen had all scored runs and the bowlers had put in good work.

But we had begun to grow concerned about Danny Morrison who appeared to look for short-cuts. It was difficult to get him to bowl more than a few overs in the nets and we felt he would be losing rather than gaining fitness. We had been warned before leaving New Zealand that Danny's level of fitness was well short of where it needed to be. Morrison looked to be saving himself for the next match a lot of the time. He admitted that he'd looked at New Zealand's schedule, saw that much of the next seven months would be taken up with cricket and therefore felt that if he was going to get through, he'd need to pace himself very carefully. Clearly Morrison was in conserve mode, and while we were prepared to accommodate him up to a point, he needed to be fully fit if he was going to do the job we required of him, which was to charge in and bowl at full pace in the crucial games.

According to fitness trainers – exercise physiologists and the like – what tends to happen on tours is that players are often fitter at the beginning than the end. The travel, the disruptions, the eating, the practice and the play often prevents players putting in enough time on their fitness work. In Danny's case, for a variety of reasons, and especially because of his unfortunate history of injuries, he wasn't fit enough at the start of the tour. We'd discussed this, and he made no secret of the fact. He knew that a habit of saving oneself for tomorrow is not really in a team's interest, nor in his own if he was to perform at his best. We were very conscious of not over-bowling our quicks in the nets, nevertheless there is a minimum amount of work that has to be done or bowlers are not able to turn it on when required.

But everything thus far on tour had been but a preliminary, and we were just about to start on the real tough stuff, cricket requiring strength of character both individually and collectively. The tests and one-day series were next.

A Clayton's Test Series

There had been quite a lot of talk about the state of the pitch at Chinnasawamy Stadium in Bangalore. The test started on 18 October, which is quite early in the cricket season. Bangalore, being in the south, catches late monsoons. Pitches are therefore likely to be crusty with little depth of hardness. It was clear to us that the pitch was indeed very crusty, the ball was likely to go through the top early in the match, and the surface would deteriorate rapidly. We felt that it would be a good toss to win and that neither side would want to bat last.

If you think the issue of what to do when winning the toss is straightforward and seldom contentious, think again. Normally, the coach and captain discuss this subject, pool their thoughts, and then it's over to the captain to decide whether to bat or bowl. He is mindful of conditions, the composition of his side and that of the opposition, the type of bowlers available, and so on. And of course he will have given some thought to the team's views and preferences. But in most teams, at all levels, players accept the captain's decision and get on with it. Not in the case of a few players in this New Zealand team.

Lee and I would look at a pitch, and so, occasionally, would Gren. His opinion, given his long playing experience, was also welcomed. We'd also done research on previous matches played at each ground, checked scores of sides batting first, or second, and so on. More recent history was given greater weight.

We usually left the choice of the twelfth man until the morning of a match because conditions can change a lot in the preceding 12-24 hours. I believe that in the end the decision on whether to bat or bowl must remain with the captain as he is the one who must live with it on the field.

The players were made aware of the procedure that we would adopt in regard to the toss. It was discussed at team meetings. Usually you find that bowlers wish to delay their task and so do the batsmen: bowlers want the side to bat first, batsmen want the side to bowl. We talked about how this is a psychological thing – this tendency to want to delay the inevitable – and that while it varies from individual to individual, it was something that collectively we had to overcome. We said that batsmen should look forward to the challenge of fronting up and performing their task from the outset, and the same attitude needed to develop among the bowlers. It hardly needs saying that approximately half the time a side doesn't have a choice anyway, because you lose the toss.

When Lee Germon won the toss we were pleased and thought that it would be an advantage to bat first. As it happened I don't think that in this instance it would have made a lot of difference either way. In my experience it's not always worse to have to bat last on an underprepared pitch. The pitch in Bangalore turned crispy very quickly, the ball went through the top and really bounced and gripped from the first delivery the spinners bowled. I think it was actually at its worst on the first day. After that, once a pitch dusts up it tends to turn more consistently and a batsman can better judge the amount of spin than is the case when only some of the balls are breaking the crust and leaping up. Pitches like this one were always going to make it difficult for us to bowl out other sides cheaply enough because we just didn't have the sort of spinners to take advantage of them. Raju and Kumble were more potent than Hart and Thomson, Kumble taking 9 wickets in the match.

We were concerned about Matthew Hart's bowling, for even though he'd been on remedial work prior to the tour, he was still having technical problems which were hampering his ability to return to his previous best.

New Zealand was bowled out for 145, only Crowe – who got a nasty one from Kumble that turned and bounced – and Germon, with 48, looked skilled against the turning ball.

When India batted, although we didn't have an attack equipped to exploit the conditions, our bowlers did well to restrict them to 228, Cairns taking four wickets, and Nash and Morrison three each. The trouble was India's 83-run lead was significant in the conditions. We battled in our second innings and lasted for 73 overs before being all out for 233. Fleming played well for 41, Hart was not out 27, and Germon again impressed with 41.

Martin Crowe got a bad decision, was hit very high by Kumble and given out LBW for 24. In retrospect I feel this may have been a turning point for Crowe. He found the decision extremely hard to accept. He made a great fuss in the pavilion and dressing room and the noise could be heard some distance away. He was raging while simultaneously apologising for his display and inability to control himself.

India knocked off the 150 required in 41 overs for the loss of only two wickets. I felt afterwards that this match was a good example of how the game of cricket requires that teams' and players' merits can only be judged over a fairly lengthy period of time. India had the players for the conditions, we didn't, and despite our good preparation we were humbled. And while we didn't realise it at the time, we were embarking on a Clayton's series, in that the next two tests were both to be ruined by rain.

An episode in Bangalore marked the beginning of Martin Crowe's unwillingness to cooperate fully, and to me it highlighted just how unusually and surprisingly delicate he has been throughout his career, both mentally and physically. Martin is one of the finest cricketers we have had, and one of the most sensitive and easily affronted. He is about as temperamental as a cricketer can be, and those who know cricket and cricketers will realise that I am talking about heights Himalayan.

I had spoken to a feature writer on *The Sportstar*, one of those burbly, wide-ranging interviews which occasionally get printed unedited and in full. At one point I was asked why I thought New Zealand cricket had declined since the 1992 World Cup. I said that I thought the decline had set in before that and that the good performance in the World Cup had been a bit of a blip. In my view the results in the 1992 World Cup hadn't meant that New Zealand had turned the corner. I said to the journalist that it seemed to me that some things had come about by accident – often they do in cricket as in all games – and that the much talked-about tactic of opening the bowling with the off-spinner Dipak Patel 'tended to be the last resort because they were trying to get him through before what I would like to call the "smack" overs. They were trying to fit him at a point where he was less likely to be hit rather than thinking that it's going to be a brilliant strategy.' Dip did a good job, and all credit to him, as the saying goes. I could have added that in a series against England prior to the World Cup, New Zealand's quicker bowlers had been belted a bit, especially by Botham and one or two others, and it made for a better strategy to bowl more slowly at opposition top orders. Particularly on wickets that played low and slow as was the case at Eden Park and, I think, at Carisbrook. I can't remember whether I'd forgotten to mention this during the interview, or whether it had been cut, but perhaps if those observations had appeared Crowe might not have reacted with such vehemence. The piece was not critical of Crowe but his reaction again highlighted the way many in New Zealand cricket are quick to seize on a few good performances as evidence that we've risen to new levels internationally. The ability of any international side and the level of genuine improvement can only be judged by looking at results over a far more extended period.

I hadn't seen the article myself but Crowe had. He'd torn the 'offending' page out of the magazine and attached it to a handwritten letter to me which he'd slipped under my hotel-room door. Crowe said that while I was 'entitled to my opinion' my comments were 'wrong in fact', and he wanted to know why he 'should publicly support [my] methods' when I 'freely bagged' what he'd been involved in 'in the past'? He took my remarks as being disrespectful of what others had done well. Crowe said that while he wished to make his point it was to be 'without discussion'. At times in India, and later on, I got the impression that Martin didn't like the amount of publicity I received, and this came through later on when he commented on the amount of coverage I was getting. Our media protocol certainly resulted in fewer comments from players being reported in newspapers and on radio, but I don't think this was deemed a serious absence or loss by most of the cricketing public.

I discussed Crowe's letter to me with the others on our management team and they thought it best simply to let it lie. The feeling was, 'Oh, it's just Martin belly-aching again. If he wanted to get something off his chest like that, let him.'

* * *

Our next match was the second test at Madras and we brought in Twose and Haslam in place of Young and Hart. Bryan Young had scored a half century in his first innings on tour but then had followed this with five 'misses' in succession. We felt that Twose had shown enough ability in both England and in New Zealand to warrant an opportunity. We also felt that if Twose was to play in the one-day matches then he needed to have had a chance to find some form beforehand. It doesn't pay to include batsmen in one-dayers unless they've had cricket immediately before a series starts.

As a point of interest, I am often told that test players are not always able to convert and perform effectively in one-dayers. While this may be true in a few instances, in the main I believe it is an attitudinal thing. If a player has the skills to play test cricket he certainly has the ability to play limited-overs games, providing he's prepared to trust his game and overcome some of the psychological barriers that sometimes exist.

Hart made way for Haslam partly because Lee Germon didn't think Hart was bowling well enough for him to be used with confidence. In the first test in Bangalore, Germon gave Hart only seven overs in the first innings (0 for 28) on a real turning pitch. It was true that he took the only two Indian wickets to fall in their second innings but by that stage the pressure was off. We felt Haslam's stock ball was more effective, more dangerous, at that time. He got closer in to the stumps when bowling, his arm came up and over his front leg, he got the ball to turn more than Hart did, and seemed to have a little more control. Hart did give us more batting, so there wasn't a lot in it. But it needs to be remembered that those on tour see players batting and bowling in the nets day in and day out, so it's clear who is playing well and who is struggling for form, who is on-song mentally and who isn't.

We noticed that after the first test Martin Crowe stopped contributing to team meetings, appeared to go doggo, and from there on he withdrew and often behaved more oddly than usual.

Many in the touring party had been intrigued when Martin bought a remote-controlled toy car at Singapore on the way to India. He played with it in the baggage areas in airports, and elsewhere. Once we got to Madras, and then Hyderabad, he decided to withdraw from any outings and stated that it was his wish 'not to be around people'.

Martin went to ground, moped, walked around with his head down and developed a habit of sleeping or drowsing in the dressing room for long periods. Every player – or just about every player – has 'down' periods on tours, and while sympathetic there's often not a lot that others can do about it. It is especially disappointing when a senior member of a team retires into his bunker, for the less experienced players look to the senior ones to set an example. Personally, from long experience, I can live with the fact that a few players will go into sulk mode occasionally, but there's a point when it seriously handicaps the efforts of both the captain and management.

* * *

The practice and other facilities were excellent in Madras but everyone wondered why we had been scheduled to play a match there in the south at that time of the year. The monsoon was due, so the likelihood of completing a game of cricket there then was remote. The locals and others admitted as much. Why was a game even entertained for Madras at that time? I got it from a good source that a leading Indian official was known to receive few if any votes from the region so the game was scheduled as a kind of punishment for the locals. When told that I asked, 'If that were the case, then why would the locals accept the test match?' The general consensus locally was that they couldn't afford to turn down the game because if they did it would be an excuse for the hierarchy to say, 'Well, we offered you a test last year and you refused it, so you won't get one this year.' The locals felt they had no option but to accept the game and hope for divine intervention to control the weather.

No such good offices prevailed and while we did get to play some cricket, India batting for 71 overs to be 144 for 2 wickets, that was it for the match. We bowled 35 overs on the first day and the remainder on the fourth. The most memorable feature was the amount of fertiliser that had been liberally spread on the outfield, much of it cow dung, so no one was keen to lick their fingers or the ball. It reminded me a little of the message given to golfers when greens have recently been fertilised: no licking your balls. It also reminded me of that oft-told story about Bob Charles's wife Verity, who, when asked if she did anything special before Bob left the house to play an important round of golf, said that she normally kissed his balls.

We had two excellent liaison officers deputed to look after us in Madras. One was test player Kapoor's father, and another a man known to all as Doc. They were high in their praise of the treatment and respect they received from our players. They said, 'We only noticed one person who seems to be a problem.'

As we travelled around, Gren and I asked staff at reception desks and elsewhere to tell us if they experienced trouble with any of our group. We were regularly told that they had had bother with 'Mr Parore', especially in respect to disputes over accounts.

I asked our liaison officers if they had performed a similar role with other touring teams. They said they had dealt with many other national teams. 'Which was the worst?' I asked. To my surprise they said the English were. Cricketers the world over expect the Australians to win that prize.

* * *

We moved on to Hyderabad for a three-day game against the Indian Colts and it was important for us to use the match to give our batsmen much-needed practice. Here was a chance to give Lee, or Germ as he is known, a rest and Crowe was given the job as captain for the match. He won the toss and batted first in the hope that we would get two bats in the match. On the eve of the game we had decided that it was time Germ had a rest, but during warm-ups Simon Doull was injured; and prior to that Thomson had cut himself when doing something with his knife, and Nash was indisposed, so Germ had to come into the game at the last minute. But we had already decided that he wouldn't keep wicket and that Martin Crowe would captain the side, so we didn't alter that.

The nets leading up to the game were awful and the guys were starting to get a bit titchy about nets generally, but because the test pitch in Bangalore had turned square – as pitches often did at that time of the year – we couldn't avoid practising on turning strips. So, reluctantly, we simply had to face up to the fact and adopt the attitude that the net surfaces would be good practice for what we were likely to bat on in the middle. We had vivid memories of Bangalore.

But in the nets at Hyderabad Cairns put on a performance. He got one that went through the top so he stormed out of the nets and wouldn't continue. I spoke to him about this and calmly explained why we felt there was a need to try to combat such conditions, and that if others behaved like him no one would get any practice. He absolutely spat the dummy. He didn't want to bowl in the nets either. Irrespective of circumstances, you can't have individual play-

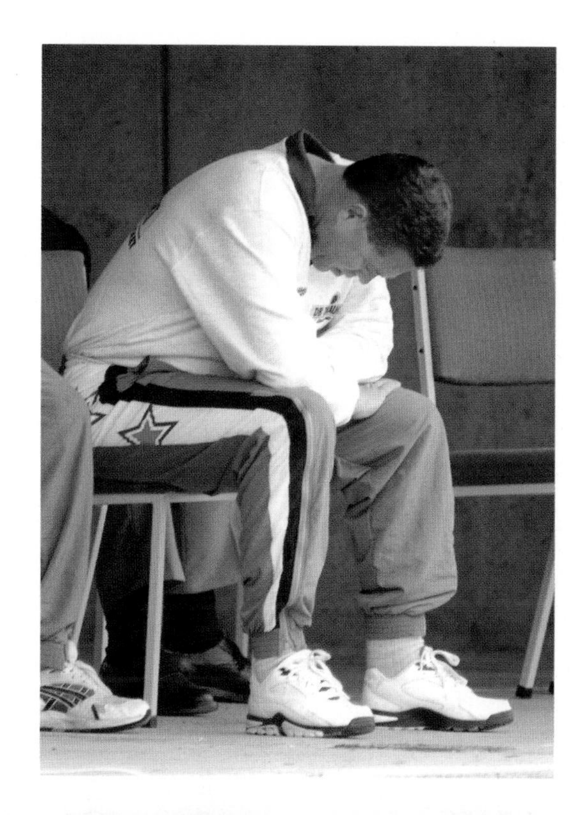

Not a good day for the New Zealand caretaker coach, John F. Reid during the first test against Sri Lanka at Napier, 12 March 1995. *Fotopress*

Below: Mark Plummer treats Martin Crowe's injured thigh muscle at Eden Park, on the eve of a match against Australia, 18 February, 1995. *NZ Herald*

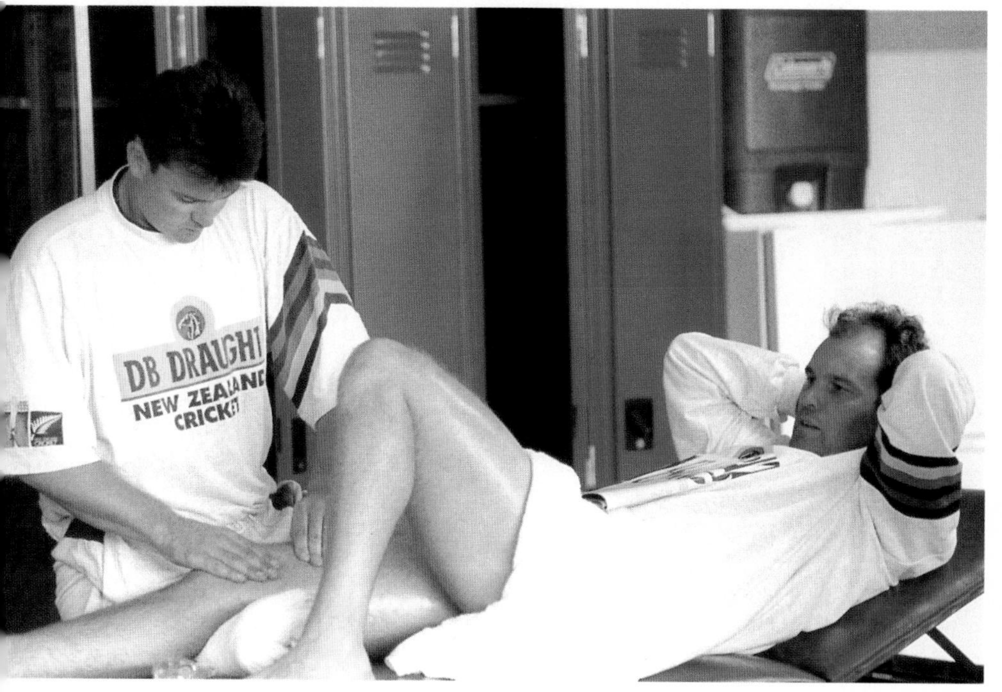

New Zealand v Zimbabwe at Basin Reserve, Wellington
Bank of New Zealand Series 1996

Back row: N.J. Astle, C.M. Spearman, C.Z. Harris, R.J. Kennedy, S.P. Fleming, D.J. Nash, R.G. Twose, M.R. Plummer (Physiotherapist)

Front row: G.M. Turner (Coach), S.A. Thomson, D.N. Patel. D.K. Morrison, L.K. Germon, G.R. Larsen, A.C. Parore, C.L. Cairns, G.D. Alabaster (Manager)

Photography by Woolf

Above: Outside the team's dressing room at Hamilton. I'd been hitting a few catches prior to a one-day international against Zimbabwe in January 1996. Team physio Mark Plummer lurks in shadows.
Photo: Richard Redgrove

Left: Lee Germon being interviewed by John Morrison at Lancaster Park before a one-day international in 1997. Soon after, Germon was sacked as New Zealand captain.
Photo: Richard Redgrove

Chris Cairns appeals to the umpire during a one-day international against Pakistan. *Otago Daily Times*

ers making such decisions for themselves, for obvious reasons.

We also decided to omit Danny Morrison from the side to play the Colts. We thought we could get him to do more work if he wasn't playing, and as it happened, because we only had one bowl in the match, this proved partly true. In order to help improve Danny's fitness we set him up with a programme devised by our physio Mark Plummer. At this stage Danny's bowling lacked fizz, or fire, and in the aborted test at Madras he'd bowled only 14 overs all up. We felt he was chronically short of quality bowling, full stop. Our plan was to get him out in the morning for a vigorous bowl in the nets, and follow this up with another session after the end of the day's play. We wanted Danny to have two good bowls each day in an effort to lift his fitness level. We had him doing some sprint shuttles and one or two other things that Plums had devised. Danny said he agreed with this approach. We all felt that it was an ongoing battle to get Danny to do more than a token amount of work.

When planning our net practices we weren't able to schedule him to bowl first because he needed extra time to warm up, additional stretching and TLC from Plums, but even then he'd come in to bowl a few minutes late on most occasions. This was slovenly and before long Plums had become fed up with the amount of TLC and extra massages that Danny required every day, on this and other tours Plums had been on. It was almost as if Plums was Danny's personal masseur. Another case of how management and selectors have to decide just how much and how many concessions should be made to accommodate certain players. This is one reason why administrators need to be very cautious about listening to complaints and whinges from some players. Unless administrators have had considerable first-hand experience of dealing with players on tour, and the realities of touring, they are not competent to properly assess the validity of moans and moaners.

Against the Colts, Twose was 'retired ill' on 119, Crowe made 110 (his last first-class century as it turned out), Fleming 65, and Cairns not out 75. Twose wasn't ill at all; he just didn't want to surrender his wicket. We declared at 454 for 4 off 123 overs.

The Colts had a mediocre batting line-up and could manage only 180. In our second bat, Greatbatch got 36, Parore 96 following his first innings 33, Fleming an excellent 100 off 110 balls, and Cairns 31 not out in our 276 for 2 off 69 overs.

So from a playing point of view things had gone well. Unfortunately Martin Crowe's conduct was decidedly odd and unhelpful. Normally when someone other than the touring captain is temporarily in charge, he consults the captain and coach to see what they want from the game. In this case, a decision also needed to be made as to whether we enforced the follow on, or went in again ourselves. The Colts hadn't made many but they did take 79.2 overs, so we felt that had given our bowlers a reasonable work-out. It was into the third day when we removed the Colts and in Germ's view, and mine, we wanted another bat.

Crowe didn't even want to discuss the issue of our batting again, said he didn't want to bat again himself, said he'd put himself at number 11. Lee told Crowe that he would go in at seven if the need arose, not 11. The team was confused by this obvious bickering and wondered what the hell was going on.

We weren't the first to find Crowe difficult to manage. We found that he was not a good role model within the team, although he sometimes provided helpful input to individuals and at team meetings. A fit Crowe was a terrific player with the ability we badly needed, but his injuries meant that his fitness was always marginal and his lack of mobility in the field, especially in one-dayers, was obvious. For several reasons it was clear that Crowe was just hanging on and no more, and we began to get worried that he was undermining management.

On 6 November Gren Alabaster was talking to Chris Doig on the telephone. In the course of the conversation Doig said that he had been in Australia and that the Australian coach Bobby Simpson had stated that Crowe was a hugely damaging force and had been undermining team management for a number of years. Doig added words to the effect that we wouldn't make progress in the New Zealand team until we got rid of Crowe. Gren said to Doig, 'That's interesting, because we've been having some problems with Martin.' Doig responded by saying, 'Well, get rid of him. You have my full support.'

Gren's response and mine was that we weren't going to make knee-jerk decisions like that during tours, and that the time for assessments and decisions was after full discussion and debriefings afterwards. After Hyderabad we had a chat with Crowe and asked what was bugging him. He simply denied there were any problems between him and management.

* * *

From Hyderabad we went to Cuttack for the third test played at Barabati Stadium, where the ground was used for a number of sports, athletics in particular. No one was quite sure how the pitch would play. Thomson felt his finger hadn't healed enough for him to play so Hart returned to the team. Three hours only was possible on the first day, then down came the rain and no more play was possible until the fourth day. India batting first made 296, Nash taking four wickets and Cairns three, before Twose and Greatbatch went out to put on 86 for the first wicket in the New Zealand innings. Twose, who made 36 in three and a half hours of solid blocking, had had to wait ten days before playing his first test innings. Hirwani with 6-59 off 31 overs went through the heart of our batting as we struggled to 175 for 8.

During the game Cairns put on a volcanic performance after I failed to send out the twelfth man when he called for another drink.

The usual procedure was for the bowlers to stash a bottle of water down at fine leg or third man so that they could take drinks when required. In Cuttack the players' enclosure was in an awkward spot, accessed from above, then down two flights of stairs, and then a walk of several metres before getting out onto the ground proper. So it was not a simple procedure for twelfth men to engage in the amount of to-ing and fro-ing that they are asked to do by players these days.

Cairns had finished his water and wanted more. The twelfth man had already been out to him several times, so, as the break was only five minutes away I said to our twelfth man, 'It's okay, he probably doesn't realise it's only a few minutes to the break.' I stood up and signalled to Cairns, tried to indicate that there was only five minutes left. I thought he'd accept that.

He didn't. He got so irritated that he started gesticulating wildly and when he came in he gave me a bollocking, wanted to know 'What was fucking going on?' I explained the situation, quietly. He said, 'If I want a fucking drink out there, I'll get one whenever it is. It's not good enough,' and so on and on. This kerfuffle ended the way it usually ended with Cairns. I'd have listened to his tirade, tried to explain what had happened and why, what we were looking for, but he seemed unable or unwilling ever to accept my explanation.

Cairns always left one with the impression that he felt he'd been wronged, perpetually. He'd storm off in a cloud of high dudgeon. No sign of remorse, no willingness, just now and then, to reflect and say, 'Okay, fair enough.'

I wouldn't normally mention incidents or episodes of the kind related here and elsewhere involving Cairns and a few others. But in light of his, and their, part in initiating my removal, and as an example of the ongoing irritation that some players – usually the same few – create, I've decided to break silence. Cairns in particular has kept sniping at me ever since, presenting himself as a sensitive individual, misunderstood and badly treated by our team management. I'm not going to protect him any longer.

Chapter 5

One After Another, One-dayers in India

Cuttack marked the end of the Clayton's test series so the job now was to prepare for the six match one-day series. We invited Martin Crowe to contribute to game plans and strategy because he'd played a lot of cricket and often came up with useful ideas. And it was another attempt to get him to 'come around'. I made some notes on the things we needed to consider when developing game plans for the series and Gren, Germ, Martin and I discussed them.

Martin's preference was to retain the batting order we'd intended to use in the third test at Cuttack: Greatbatch, Twose, Parore, Crowe, then Fleming (who hadn't batted in the test) and Cairns. He felt we needed to 'establish form and have some match play under our belts' before making 'necessary adjustments.' He didn't want us 'to force things just yet,' instead 'work our way into the correct strategy, if necessary.' Germ and I felt this was overly-cautious and contrary to the way we'd agreed earlier to approach the one-dayers. On match day we went with Greatbatch, Astle, Crowe and Fleming.

Under the heading 'Batting' I posed the question, 'Set batting order or flexibility?' Some people believe it is best to get players accustomed to batting in the one position. A case can be made for that, especially when it comes to the openers, or to the batsmen who may be required to go in and take calculated risks to up the scoring-rate in the first 15 overs. But in the main we decided that batsmen must be prepared to be moved around according to the course the game is taking, and all must be prepared to look to up the scoring-rate.

Then there was the question of whether, or how important it was, to try to maintain left- and right-hand combinations. We were conscious of the need to try to do that as much as possible. In my view it is very valuable because it upsets bowlers' lines and a captain's field placements. Captains sometimes get a bit lazy in this respect. And while left- and right-hand combinations can result in slower play, this often allows batsmen to have a bit of a breather. This can be a good thing, especially in hot conditions when the batsmen have been running a lot of twos and threes. It enables them to get their wind back and start thinking properly again. We had Greatbatch, Twose and Fleming as top-order left-handers and saw that as a possible advantage.

We also considered whether it was worth trying to line-up particular batsmen against particular bowlers. This can be worthwhile, in India especially, where the spinners are testing. So it is worth looking to see if you can get a left-hander batting against an orthodox left-arm spinner, or a right-hander against an off-spinner. In other words, give the batsmen the chance to hit with the spin rather than force them to go against it.

At that time – and it is still the case – Chris Cairns did not like facing bowlers who spun the ball away from him, so it was in his interests and the team's not to bat him in the same place in the order all the time. Cairns agreed with that. (Later, in the World Cup, Cairns was tapping me on the shoulder, not wanting to go in to bat against Shane Warne.) This line of thinking meant that Cairns would be well-suited to bat against Kapoor, and Twose, say, against the left-armers Chatterjee or Raju. Sometimes, of course, especially when a lot of overs have been used up, you just have to send out the best player left in the list. We decided to use Cairns as our main 'floater'. But once 40 overs had gone, we'd send him out, even if a leg-spinner was bowling. As for our overall approach to batting, we wanted to stick with our general policy of controlled aggression in the first 15 overs to take advantage of the fielding restrictions and hopefully set the foundation for larger totals.

There were a number of issues to be considered in respect to our bowling attack and general approach to this aspect of the game. Of course it is important to look at conditions on the day, and not go out determined always that your front-liners bowl their full 10 overs. Sometimes a bowler is not 'on-song' and you need back-up, that is why you need six recognised bowlers and one other capable of bowling a few overs too. Gavin Larsen was really the only bowler who could generally be guaranteed to get through 10 overs, for chances were that one of the other front-liners would be 'off' on the day.

Obviously, if a pitch has seam or bounce, or both, one opens with the faster bowlers. Conversely, a spinner or medium-slow bowler is best when a pitch is slow and the bounce is low. There was another consideration which related particularly to Larsen. He was noted for being hard to get away during the middle overs, between the 15- and 40-over marks, but this is often the period when there's least pressure on the bowlers. So why not use your best bowler early and late? We used him quite often early in the innings, and at the 'death'. In my view it's best to give a bowler a maximum of four overs at the death: three's okay, two is too few.

It's important to work out what line and length to bowl to certain field placements, taking into account the players concerned, varying conditions, and the number of overs bowled. But in general terms, in both India and Pakistan, the bounce is lower than in most other parts of the world. So you can bowl a line a fraction outside off stump and pull your length back a little bit – these days it's called 'bowling back of a length' – the trick being not to bowl wide or full enough outside off stump for the batsman to be able to free his arms and safely force the ball away. There's a fine line here, for if the ball is bowled close in to the batsman's body, or is a bit too full, a player can force it into the on-side with safety. Without the amount of bounce common elsewhere a batsman in India is able to stand tall on the front foot and hit the ball on the up. So the way to help counter this is for the bowler to pull the length back a little – a batsman can't afford to get on the back foot for fear of being done LBW or bowled by a scuttler. It's also more difficult to fetch the ball on-side (a captain can with confidence set a predominantly off-side field) because most times it isn't going to bounce above stump height. The dangers are real; playing the ball on, miscuing, LBW and the like. So batsmen usually still feel the need to get on the front foot but can't be certain enough of the bounce and pace to play with telling fluency.

Regarding fielding, in general terms we found that the slow-motion TV replays showed that direct hits on the stumps equated to about a yard and a half of distance at the speed most batsmen ran between wickets. So lots of practice at throwing down the stumps is very important. Which means that you want to place those most adept at this inside the inner ring. You soon find out at practice who those players are. When we got to the World Cup in 1996 we found that Chris Harris and Craig Spearman were the best in this regard.

As far as boundary riders are concerned, and especially if the boundary is longer on one side, fielders out there must have strong arms. Cairns is an example of someone with a very strong arm. So is Nathan Astle, and he is also a very good mover when boundary riding.

When it comes to the overs at the 'death' one usually has only four players inside the ring. Both short midwicket and short cover have got to be in so tight to prevent cheeky singles that they are just about standing still. Usually there's only time for them to move as far as they can reach before the ball is past, so it's handy to put players there who have good hands but who are not necessarily the best athletes. Fleming is an example and Young is another, because Bryan doesn't have the strongest arm although he is a very good mover with very good hands.

Some fielders are stronger on one hand than the other, so it pays to be mindful of this when choosing and positioning sweepers. A fielder's strongest hand ought to be away from the guy fielding on the boundary. Take when a player is fielding behind point. Then the chances are that the off-side sweeper is in front of point, so you'd have a guy who was strongest to his left fielding just behind point inside the circle. This fielder knows that if he gets done on his right then the sweeper is able to cut it off. If a ball is going down to his left it's heading towards third man and quite often goes quicker that way, and sometimes too wide for the fielder there, so this highlights the need for a fielder not to be beaten on his strong side. Of course, you have to get on with the game and get through the overs, so there are times when compromises have to be made. But a good team and a good skipper will usually get it right.

After the test series in India Gale and Hart went home and Astle and Larsen came over. This wasn't a surprise because we'd made it clear early on that it was likely we'd bring a couple of players over especially for the one-day series.

* * *

I had an extended batting session with Cairns in the nets at Jamshedpur. He had some preconceived ideas about batting that I wasn't able to alter at all. I found this was typical of his attitude to a great deal of his game generally. While on the one hand he was prone to change his methods from time to time, he also had some very fixed ideas. He'd adopted a strange batting stance, with his feet splayed so far apart that his head had to be lower as a consequence, and therefore went up and down like a jack-in-the-box every time he played the ball. This is not desirable. One of the basics of batting is that you try to have your head remain in the same plane as much as possible; the least head movement the better. I couldn't persuade him it would help if he stood up more in his stance. He told me that most of the game's best batsmen had been short men, therefore he had theorised that his best approach was to view the ball from the same height as they had seen it. He was thinking of the Bradmans and Hassetts and Gavaskars and so on. I did try to point out that there had been a few tall men who were pretty good players too – Clive Lloyd, Peter May, and so on. Barry Richards and Tom Graveney weren't short either. I tried to convince him that if you were reasonably tall, as he is, you might as well use your height. Many's the small man that would love to be a bit taller. Granted some tall and gangly types aren't as nimble on their feet, and mightn't get into position as quickly as a smaller man, but Cairns did not come into the gangly category.

As soon as the ball bounces a bit higher, and you are short, unless you are a very good cutter or puller of the ball, you just get out of the way. My point to Cairns was that given his enviable physical attributes, squatting to the extent he was, was counter-productive. He wasn't convinced. That is Cairns. I found coaching him frustrating and unrewarding, as have others; it usually seems a case of in one ear and out the other.

Part of the code of conduct applying to the tests and one-day series was that during warm-ups bowlers were not permitted to bowl at a stump on even so much as the edge of the square adjacent to the pitch to be used in the match. Some of our bowlers persisted in ignoring this, and Gren and I kept being chipped by local officials and match referees, and asked to have our bowlers stop it. One gets tired of telling guys not to do this, not because I give a bugger about the issue, but because the rules specifically disallowed it. I actually think this rule can be silly and needs re-visiting. At some venues groundstaff would sooner players warmed-up by bowling up and down a strip that had been used already, and was being retired for the rest of the season. This way the turf on the outfield off the pitch square isn't scuffed up. I believe the local groundsman should decide what he requires in this regard.

Off the field we found, too, that some players were apt to niggle staff, waiters and the like in hotels, either when dining or at the bar. Typical is the juvenile habit of fooling with language, saying, 'No, we don't want two bottles, we want three. No we don't, make that four,' and so on, all of it intended solely to confuse the waiter. Locals concerned about this mentioned it to me at Bhubaneswar, the place where we were staying about 30 km from Cuttack.

When arriving at hotels the management and other staff usually put on a little ceremony, lined up to greet us as we came out of the coach and entered the reception area. Some of the hotels are quite grand and often flower petals were sprinkled on carpets or marble floors in the foyers for us to walk over. At times a red carpet was rolled out and often two women would be at the door to apply a red powder mark in the centre of the forehead. It's a ritual to welcome guests and a sign of respect. One could guarantee some of the team would duck away and try to avoid being caught. Some staff would look to place flowers around our necks and this, too, would be dodged if possible by a few. It seemed an unnecessary snubbing of the local culture and customs.

We flew into Bhubaneswar and stayed there the first night. After seeing the road between Bhubaneswar and Cuttack we decided to shift to a smaller, less opulent hotel in Cuttack to avoid travelling daily on this bad piece of road. After the test in Cuttack we had to retrace our route to the airport, and were delayed because of a fatal accident on the section of road which we'd been scared of. The accident had upset some people so much that they'd set fire to three buses. We were diverted along side-roads, some barely more than tracks, and arrived three hours late to find a plane-load of passengers waiting for us. I doubt that a domestic airline in New Zealand would wait three hours for a busload of cricketers.

Players like to spread out on buses and use all the available room. They put their gear on the seats next to them and generally sprawl. But at times liaison people needed to travel on buses with us and a few players refused to shift to make room for them to sit down, so they had to stand in the aisle. This was the sort of culture that had developed in New Zealand cricket. Gren told some of the guys not to be so bloody rude, but it's one thing to ask people to do something, another to find they'll actually do it. Don't ask me why some guys persist with such inconsideration, but they do.

* * *

Matches in the one-day series started at 9 a.m. so there was a problem with dew on the ground. And because it was early in the season, and the monsoons had only recently departed, grass on the outfields had not been cut short and there didn't seem to be equipment available to mop up the dew. Of interest and relevance, too, is the fact that groundsmen in India have little status and appear to have to take instruction from several bosses. Instructions on the type of pitch required tends to come from high up and can get confused en route through the hierarchy.

There was also a problem with billboards which were often placed too close to the boundaries.

We were surprised to find that 12 local umpires were appointed for the six one-day internationals, plus another six drafted in as third umpires. I think this is excessive. Umpires need continuity of adjudication, just as players need regular play, if they are to give of their best. I felt that this sort of thing wasn't only a problem in India but was creeping in worldwide. Cricket authorities seem prepared to bring in an overseas international umpire for tests but not for one-dayers. I think this is a mistake and overlooks the importance of having the best umpires standing in one-day internationals.

Usually only one net was provided per team. Not sufficient. We tried to sort this out with the opposition by going down to practise at different times, but the officials had it in their minds that this net was for India and that for New Zealand, and even though India's team management had agreed to our suggestion, we still had difficulty persuading officials to let us use both nets. Without two nets it is not possible to run a proper practice.

Ground bowlers were provided in most cases, and their abilities varied greatly, as they do in New Zealand. But generally we felt local officials did their best in this regard. Balls were nearly always provided, but quite often we were given six new balls – not good for the spinners – which was why we had a supply of our own as a supplement.

Quite often in India the net behind the stumps is set well back and unless you put in a wicketkeeper then the batsman spends too much time walking back to retrieve the ball. Often, too, there is a net along one side only in front of the wicket and this means that extra fielders need to be deputed. Such anomalies can be sorted out when you are in a place to play a 3-5 day match, but when you arrive the day before a one-dayer it's not so easy. So you make do.

Water and soft drinks were plentiful and there is always someone who rushes about trying to be of service. Such servants can appear to overdo it. It is also often hard to be sure just who is in charge, so if you aren't careful you can be requesting assistance from the wrong person or persons. Everyone can seem to be falling over themselves in an effort to help and this can create as many problems as it solves. You have to be patient and take your time in your dealings with people in India. You must always remember that you speak a different English to Indian English, and that your accent may confuse or result in misinterpretation, but the one thing you can be sure of is that you won't meet a group of people who are more hospitable and willing to be of service generally.

Because of the early morning dew, and the possibility of the ball being affected, we needed to take that into account when it came to the toss. On one or two occasions the start of play was delayed in order to allow the dew to dry off. The lacquer on the new ball often lasts about six overs before the moisture takes effect on the texture of the ball. All told we decided that the presence of dew on the outfield wasn't going to be a key element in our decision if we won the toss. Dampness in a pitch is a different matter.

* * *

The first one-dayer was at Jamshedpur, about four hours by train from Calcutta, at a works ground belonging to the giant Tata Corporation, known worldwide for its steel and for buses and all manner of other things. The maintenance had been excellent and we thought it a great little ground with first-class nets and practice facilities.

Germ won the toss in Jamshedpur and asked India to bat. I'd obtained statistics which gave me the one-day international records of all the cricketing nations, and in India's case they had played 36 matches against New Zealand for 19 wins and 17 losses. The stats showed that India had won nine out of 15 times when batting second (or 60 per cent of the time), and 10 out of 21 matches when batting first (47.6 per cent of the time). So if all things seemed more-or-less equal we decided we'd ask them to bat.

If anything our feeling about India and Pakistan at that time was that both tended to meander along when asked to bat first, whereas if they knew what they had to score they went after the runs more aggressively, and were less likely to waste overs. They were apt to play the 'keep wickets in hand to go after the bowling at the death' style of game when asked to bat first and, as I have said elsewhere, more often than not I think this is a mistake.

I have noticed recently that with Tendulkar at the top of the order, India now seems to be going after the bowling right from the start.

We did well to bowl India out in the 50th over for 236, then knocked off the runs in 46.5 overs for just the loss of two wickets, Crowe not out 107 and Fleming not out 78. It was Crowe's fourth one-day hundred and, as it transpired, his last.

One-day internationals are full-on, energy-sapping and tiring both psychologically and physically, especially in hot conditions. Six in a row with no more than two days in between was a tough demand, and we were expected to get from Jamshedpur to Amritsar and play three days later.

To our surprise and dismay we were down to take a train trip from Jamshedpur to Calcutta, four hours away, travel from one side of Calcutta to the other (90 minutes from railway station to the airport) then get a flight to Delhi the same day, stay there overnight, then go by train from there to Amritsar, a journey of nearly six hours. We thought that schedule was absurd, because we knew we could fly from Delhi to Amritsar. We complained and were told that the airline which flew from Delhi wasn't the one Indian cricket was using. They said they weren't able to get an acceptable deal with that airline. We said that as both teams were travelling from Delhi they should charter a plane. We got the big NO to that suggestion so, having previously found that the only thing to do in such circumstances was to go the whole hog, we said we wouldn't accept the arrangement for the game in Amritsar. We said we weren't prepared to travel for two full days in between matches and then play on the next, so eventually the Indian board agreed to fly us from Delhi.

Although it was far from my first trip to the Punjab, for my wife Sukhi is a Sikh, I had not been to Amritsar. My in-laws came up from Chandigarh to see the game, but mostly because they knew I hadn't been to the temple and they wanted to take me there. Amritsar's

Golden Temple is the Sikh's holiest shrine, their equivalent to St Peter's in Rome.

The ground in Amritsar is not regarded as one of India's more notable cricket venues, but it had an intimacy which made it attractive. It's not a big ground and the crowd is very close. I felt it could be an enjoyable ground to play on. There were problems with the pitch: cracks had opened up and we saw this the day before the match. Late in the afternoon before the match we managed to get a little time in nets and learned that the locals were worried about whether the pitch would last, and whether the cracks would grow so wide that it would become almost unplayable.

The pitch was watered overnight and although, when we came to the ground in the morning, the cracks appeared to have gone, there was too much moisture in it. We were starting at 9 a.m. and the result was that ground staff – no doubt under instructions – had taken a big risk for the sake of cosmetics. As a consequence of the watering there was far too great an advantage to the side bowling first, and it was no surprise when India asked us to bat and bowled us out in the 45th over for 145, Prabhakar taking 5-33 off 10 overs. India knocked the runs off for the loss of four wickets but it took them nearly 44 overs and Larsen bowled his 10 for a mere 23 runs. So the game wasn't satisfactory, which was a pity, for there was keen interest in it locally and it is a fascinating place. This was Bishen Bedi's home patch and he had travelled up from Delhi to help with the pitch for there was a lot of enthusiasm for the game. It was a pity therefore that they had trouble with the pitch preparation; maybe they got their timing wrong, or simply were unlucky. With Bishen present during the net session the day before the game there was an opportunity not to be missed. I asked him to have a session with Mark Haslam; he graciously obliged, spending a good hour with him.

* * *

From Amritsar we had another two days of travel down to Goa on the coast south of Bombay. Indians see Goa as their pukka beach resort. Hotels stretch along the coast and if you are going to eat fish anywhere in India then Goa's the place.

Fun and games were to develop in Goa. Few matches are played there and they have an unenviable record of matches rained off. Here we were with 30,000 or more people in the stadium and suddenly there was talk of a delay due to overnight rain. We were keen to play but we realised that the Indians weren't. A helicopter was brought in to hover over the pitch to assist with drying, but there was a catch: the covers were still on, unsecured tarpaulin-like covers lying flat on the ground. The wind created by the chopper meant it had to get clear quickly before the covers flew up and got entangled in the rotors.

We were very keen that there be some cricket, felt an obligation to the crowd, and seemed to feel it more than the Indian team did. Even a reduced-overs game would give the crowd something. We were also concerned about how the crowd would react if the game was called off.

As we watched we didn't think attempts to dry the pitch and surrounds were very serious. It got messy. I went and saw the umpires and the ground authority and said we were willing to play. I suggested they set a hoped-for starting time, do everything they could to prepare the ground, and announce to the crowd that every effort was being made to try to get a start later in the afternoon. The absence of visible effort and a lack of communication was making the crowd restless, and us too. By now our blokes weren't all that interested in playing either, which is typical of players the world over in such situations.

Anyway, it started to rain again and the match was called off. But before that it was suggested to us that we run around the ground and wave to the fans, put on a kind of goodwill lap. That idea concerned us, and the Indian management said that could be unwise, especially if the crowd knew that the game had been called off. The advice was that before the cancellation was announced, both teams jump into a bus and get away from the ground. That, so it was said, would be the safest move. There were bound to be a lot of tired and disappointed spectators. So we got on the bus and out of there pronto.

We again had travel hassles in getting to the next venue, Pune. When we got to the airport at Goa we were told that we would fly to Bombay and then get a bus to Pune. Three and a half hours. But Ravi Shastri and other media people told us that they were flying from Bombay to Pune, so when we heard that we said we too wanted to fly. (Travelling by road in India is an experience that shouldn't be missed, for the countryside and evidence of life generally, is often interesting, but when you are pressured for time, you need to use the best services available.) Indian team players were sidling up to us and saying, 'You tell our Board that these arrangements aren't good enough,' and so on. I said, 'Why don't you tell them?' 'Oh no, we can't do that.' It was amusing to have the Indian team working through us in an effort to improve their arrangements. In the end we didn't fly; we didn't dig our heels in as we had when setting out for Amritsar because we knew the arrangements were manageable. The frustration arises when you know there are better options available.

* * *

The fourth one-dayer was frustrating for me. Chandu Borde, whom I'd played against on my first tour to India in 1969, was the groundsman and he produced what was, for India, quite a bouncy pitch. Because it was still early in the season the outfield was rough, but the pitch was a good cricket wicket. You might question whether it was ideal for a one-day game and that the toss shouldn't be quite so critical. Certainly it wasn't as important as it had been in Amritsar, but it was helpful to the side bowling first. India sensed this too, so on winning the toss asked us to bat.

The frustrating thing for me, after all the talking we'd done about how we were going to bat in one-day matches, was how our openers went about it. Greatbatch got 13 off 43 balls, Astle 11 off 34, and Crowe, when he came in, 15 off 36. We made such a slow start that we never gave ourselves a chance of getting a decent score. The top order played us into a hole; presumably because they were intimidated by the conditions. Fleming upped it by getting 26 off 39, and Twose did well to make 46 off 57. Even then we were sorely short of runs. Thankfully Cairns came in and played the best innings he was to play while I was involved, 103 off 87 balls. Till then it was his only century in limited-overs cricket (he hasn't scored one since) and we totalled 235 for 6.

The sort of innings Cairns played should have been a match-winning effort, but the ponderous early overs cost us in the end, and a quality innings was wasted. India went out and got the runs for the loss of 5 wickets in 45.5 overs. It was a disappointing result and a bad tactical effort.

In the dressing room after we'd batted and Cairns had got his hundred, I said to him, 'Well, you know you could have a good day here. If you go out there and pick up three or four wickets and only go for three an over, I'd say that you could be pretty satisfied with the day.' I acknowledged that he'd played well, but also reminded him that he hadn't finished his work. Cairns went out and bowled his 10 overs, taking 3-37, and I remember saying to him, tongue-in-cheek, 'Well, that wasn't too bad a day, was it?' He had a big smile on his face, of course, and got a giggle from some of the others. All enjoyed it.

* * *

After our unsatisfactory effort at Pune, we discussed our tactical balls-up before the next one-dayer in Nagpur. We didn't want a repeat of the top order sluggishness in Pune. The ground in Nagpur is small and is slightly crowned, which means that the outfield tends to slope down away from the pitch. Once the ball beats the field it's very hard for a fielder to turn and catch up with it before it reaches the boundary. One of those outfields where when you bend down to pick it up the ball's not there.

The ground at Nagpur had been rebuilt and the stands are very high and close. Players feel as if the crowd is virtually looking down on them instead of out at them. It's as if spectators could reach out and touch the players and it makes for a very intimate and nerve-tingling atmosphere. My guess is that the ground holds about 30,000 people.

India again asked us to bat and our top order played very well, and to the agreed plan this time! Greatbatch 38 off 40 balls, Astle 114 off 128, Crowe 63 off 62, and Fleming 60 off 40 in our total of 348 for 8, our biggest one-day score.

While we were having lunch between innings quite a commotion was going on outside. We were unaware of it. A stairwell had collapsed and several people were killed. Unbeknown to us, the officials had an emergency meeting with the police with a view to deciding whether to call off the game. The meeting decided to let the match continue because of a fear that rioting or stampeding might occur if they called it off, and the result could be further deaths. We knew nothing of this until after the game.

There was also an on-field incident when we were batting which created some controversy then and afterwards. Twose and Cairns were together when Cairns was given out caught on the boundary by Manjrekar off Kumble. From where Twose was standing he felt there was doubt as to whether it was a fair catch, and told umpire Menon that in his view Manjrekar's foot was on the boundary rope as he took the catch. Roger felt Menon ought to call for confirmation from the third umpire. In the stand I thought so too, and I signalled to Cairns to stay out there and not walk off immediately.

Some of the Indian players were indignant and claimed that Roger had called Sanjay Manjrekar a 'fucking cheat'. A reporter from *The Times of India* spoke to me and this statement appeared in the paper next day:

> During the confusion Roger asked umpire Menon whether there could be confirmation of the catch. The umpire replied that he was not allowed to call up the third umpire.
>
> Roger then asked if there was doubt involved, and, if so, it should go to the batsman. Menon replied he had to accept the word of the fielder that the catch was fair so he felt he had to give Cairns out.
>
> Roger then turned to Manjrekar in the knowledge that the decision had been affected purely on the honesty and integrity of the fielder, Sanjay Manjrekar. He said, 'if you have fucking cheated' at which stage Azhar became upset having thought Roger had said fucking cheat. The Indian players became irate.
>
> We the management believe that Roger's comments were taken out of context and he was unable to complete his statement because of the reactions of the Indian players.
>
> Further, we are dismayed and appalled that the Indian manager Ajit Wadekar saw fit to discuss the complaint which he had made with the match referee, with the media prior to the hearing.
>
> The relationship between the two teams in this series up until now has been excellent. It is a pity that what was a bit of the normal cut and thrust of hard international play should be escalated in this way.

I told the reporter that I was 'emphatic the video evidence of the catch was conclusive', meaning Manjrekar's foot had been touching the rope, and that we were 'determined to maintain high standards of discipline' in our ranks. In that regard I mentioned that we'd fined Adam Parore earlier in the tour for an incident that hadn't been seen by the umpires or the match referee, but that we didn't think Roger Twose deserved to be fined.

Roger is never short of a word but we accepted his explanation and supported him. Cairns had also been reported for remaining at the crease after he was given out the first time – we were successful in our defence of his action.

Unfortunately the Indian manager Ajit Wadekar broke the code of conduct by discussing the complaint he made to the match referee with the media prior to the hearing.

In response to India's charges we reported Manjrekar for bringing the game into disrepute: after all it was his action that created the incident in the first place. He got off scot-free.

We were prepared to back players – in this case Cairns and Twose – involved in public disputes if we felt the situation and their response was justified.

India was faced with a run-rate of fractionally under 7 an over and found it too high. They were bowled out for 249 in the 40th over. So that meant the series was tied 2-all as we went on to Bombay's attractive Brabourne Stadium for the sixth and deciding match.

* * *

Brabourne, owned by the Cricket Club of India, is now Bombay's number two stadium behind the newer Wankhede, but to me the former is the more appealing. This game was to be a benefit match for the wicketkeeper-batsman Saeed Kirmani.

We were coming to the end of the tour, a time when players start to think of getting home. They become distracted and tend to forget that the job is not yet over. I had been on so many tours when this had happened and was aware of the signs with some of our players. What occurred in the lead-up to the final one-dayer was therefore typical and predictable. It is easy for the guard to drop and standards to slip.

We flew to Bombay and that night attended a party put on by the TV company TWI. The affair took place around the pool at the Brabourne Stadium. Lee Germon and I had also been invited to join the press contingent at a dinner in the stadium's dining room. They wanted to thank us for our cooperation, and to compliment us on our media protocol which had suited them and worked well.

Germ and I left the dinner about 10.30 and went across to the poolside. It was typical of situations where you arrive sober to find most of the gathering in various states of intoxication. We quickly saw that several players had had far too much to drink and were raucous. This didn't matter much because it wasn't a public place.

But when this party finished, at around midnight, some of the team picked up taxis and, yahooing and yelling, went off to a nightclub.

Next morning, Germ asked for a meeting of the management team. He was brassed off, and thought some had been irresponsible in view of the fact that we had a very important game coming up. Lee wanted to pick out those who'd drunk the most and sweat the grog out of them during a really hard fielding session at practice. I thought that was fair enough. We split the group into two and the offenders quickly realised that they'd been singled out for extra work. There were a few rumbles and complaints. I said, 'Well, if you're going to get into the piss, you'll have to work hard to get rid of it.'

Mark Greatbatch refers to this incident in his book *Boundary Hunter*, claims that I said, 'I'm going to teach these guys a lesson.' Not true. It was Lee's idea for one group to have a fitness session in the morning and nets in the afternoon. What is true is that I didn't oppose him.

I was running the nets when I was told that Cairns had taken off from the fielding practice. Mark Plummer told me he thought Cairns had gone back to the hotel. He had. Afterwards he muttered words to the effect that he'd tweaked a hamstring, but he hadn't asked for any treatment from Plummer and had simply stormed off.

Back at the hotel, Germ, Alabaster, Plummer and I had a talk, then we asked Cairns to explain his actions. He wasn't prepared to do that, told us to do whatever we liked. We asked him if he was injured and whether he thought he'd be available for the last game. I can't recall now whether he claimed to be injured, but he did say he was unavailable. We explained that no one could simply walk away from practice like that, telling nobody and without permission. He left and we talked some more. We decided to fine him.

Discussions about such issues were chaired by Gren. The procedure then was that it was his job as manager and meeting chairperson to tell Cairns our decision. Gren went to Cairns's room and was stunned by the nature of his response. Gren said he was fearful for his own safety as Cairns started throwing things at the drawn curtains and yelling at the top of his voice, about how unfair and ridiculous we were, and so on. Cairns stormed out of the room and started screaming in the corridor, telling the world that the 'bastards' had fined him. Some players' heads popped out of their doors to see what the commotion was.

Gren had been principal of an area school in Southland, one of those with Form 1-7 pupils, and a teacher most of his adult life. He said he had never seen a performance like that in his entire career. In *Boundary Hunter* Mark Greatbatch says he couldn't see what Cairns was 'trying to achieve by his non-playing stance' and that he was surprised to see him given 'only a fine' and picked in the next New Zealand side. Batch said that Cairns needed to learn that 'you cannot put yourself in front of your teammates when it comes to representing your country' and that he ought to 'take a broader view of the responsibilities inherent in being part of a team.'

Management had another meeting and I told them what I would like to put to the players at the team meeting that evening. Normally the captain did most of the talking, covering strategy and the game plan for the match next day, and I added a few things where necessary. I asked the others on our management team what they thought of my telling the team that they were going to get their arses kicked by India. It's common for sides to put in a poor final performance, sometimes simply because they had already gone home, had lost focus. I said, 'I'll try and use reverse psychology and let them know how they'll feel if they fail through not being able to focus on the job in hand.' If I alerted them to the likelihood of a bad result it could harden their resolve to do well. That was the theory. I didn't mind if their response was to say, 'We'll show the bastard,' and they performed out of a dislike of me and my remarks. The others agreed, were happy for me to try it.

Cairns turned up at the meeting wearing a court jester's hat or something like it and sat and said nothing. Twose twigged what I was doing and afterwards said to me that it was an interesting strategy. I didn't for one minute think that I had conned them all, although I note that Greatbatch in his book was critical of my approach.

Crowe had already withdrawn due to a recurrence of an injury, and Cairns had declared himself unavailable. Not having both of them weakened the side considerably. But any strong side can perform well without a couple of leading players. Unfortunately their absence meant that we had to bring in Simon Doull who hadn't played for some time. It is a problem bringing in replacements who haven't had the benefit of lead-up games.

India once again won the toss and this added to our problems. The ground staff had produced a juicy pitch on which the ball seamed around. Srinath was very difficult in the opening overs, and then Kapoor and Kumble got assistance too and we were bowled out for only 126 in 35 overs.

So I couldn't say that my little reverse psychology strategy worked, or didn't work. The state of the pitch – a juicy seamer – certainly didn't help our cause.

There was still some juice in the pitch when India batted but psychologically our score was so small it wasn't enough to impose pressure. India knocked off the runs in 32 overs for the loss of 4 wickets and that was that.

Chapter 6

Reflections on the Indian Tour

In summary of the one-day series, India won the toss on four of five occasions. We won the toss in the first game, bowled first and won. Only once did the side batting first win the game. The pitches for at least two if not three of the matches were such that they gave the side bowling first a significant advantage. So the conditions were far from ideal for one-day games. Nevertheless we felt it had been an interesting series and that we had made some good progress all round. We had also exposed some areas that we needed to improve upon. For example, a consistent attitude and approach to cricket and everything else both on and off the park. Once again it had been proven that it is not easy to beat India at home.

At the time, I made a note of some of the positives from the tour. The first was Germon's captaincy, and the way in which he had proved himself up to international standard as a player at the same time as he was trying to improve the New Zealand team's cricket. Both he and I had to fight against those who sought to disparage and underrate Germ's abilities as a player, although the extent of this was not apparent to us for some time. Mark Plummer said that he often had to listen to a few players who kept telling him that Germ wasn't good enough to be there. Cairns in particular had been strong on this, and Germ's abilities had become a point of discussion with certain individuals over a beer. The effort to put Lee down intensified, predictably, when he took some players to task for their attitude, and tried to instil a more disciplined approach.

Back in New Zealand early in 1996, the manager of Shed Five in Napier told us how disgusted he was to hear some players running down Lee in his establishment. And he was also less than impressed by the way some of them treated one of his barmaids.

Germon had shown he could play spin better than most of the batsmen and his 'keeping was more than satisfactory. In my view he was clearly better than Zimbabwe's Flower, Sri Lanka's Kaluwitharana, and the West Indian Browne. He was also at least the equal of South Africa's Richardson. One should remember, too, that Lee was captaining the side, and was useful with the bat, so that adds up to an impressive contribution.

Another real positive from the tour was Fleming's improvement, particularly against spin, although for periods since I have noticed that he has relapsed to some extent. He is a fluent, stylish batsman at his best, and I had high hopes for him.

Aaron Gale had been selected in place of Gavin Larsen (who was unavailable for the first half of the tour) and he was one of the two to return home at the end of the test series to make way for Larsen. It's never easy for a player on tour when he knows he's covering for injury or unavailability. Aaron worked hard, never complained, appeared to steer clear of contentiousness and just got on with the job. His character and values tended to set him apart from 'the boys' a bit but we appreciated his professional attitude.

I was impressed by Mark Haslam who was very keen to learn, and had real respect for the status of being a New Zealand cricketer.

We could have done with Chris Harris's personality on tour. Harry is the joker in a team, the court jester, with that ability to lift spirits and deflate tension. There's a lot of kid in Harry – very social, but hard-working, keen, and a good tourist.

We also missed Dipak Patel, in terms of a senior player with a level head and a mature attitude.

Nevertheless, we'd developed practice and match-day routines; work habits were improving and there was a greater commitment to preparation. We'd had few injuries, and most players were keen to play and competed well for places in the team. Our team management was cohesive and so was our overall approach to cricket. We felt we were on the way to getting noticeably better both on and off the park. There were signs of a welcome, pleasing humility from most in the team; an unassuming dignity that commands respect and results in players becoming the best kind of role models for the young.

As a group in India we had gone out of our way not to be critical of the locals and their culture, and to show people respect. Overall I think we'd achieved that: generally, you don't gain much by criticising pitches and umpires when overseas. The only hiccup was insisting on a change to our travel arrangements a couple of times, but other than that we behaved ourselves like guests should, by and large.

* * *

Trying to develop or revive a team culture is a long-term project, with several stages. Before major selection changes are made you have to go through a thorough process – video analysis, wagon-wheels, the opinions of other coaches and players around the country, and so on. And then on tours you really get to know players: you see them day in and day out in the nets, in matches, and in every cricketing situation. You find out about their real capabilities and character, both on and off the field. One's information base on players becomes far greater and enables more rational and considered judgements to be made.

With teams, and especially on tours, everyone gets tetchy or disgruntled or down at one time or another. It's inevitable. Some people find touring hard, miss their home environment, don't adapt well, are temperamentally not well-suited to touring, and especially touring non-Western countries. Shane Thomson is a good example, and he admitted to counting down the days from day one. So I made an effort to help Thomson, and took him out with me in Bangalore. I'd been invited out by the manager of the Oberoi Hotel there – he was a friend of the spinner Chandresakar who'd been indisposed due to a serious accident. I was looking forward to seeing Chandra again. I thought Thomson might like to experience a bit more of a very old and sophisticated culture, and at the same time enjoy some Indian hospitality.

Thomson bowled well on tour, a little better than expected, but when batting lost confidence against spin. His finger problem became a major inhibiting factor and he appeared reluctant to play. Minor illness kept him away from practices and he was quite resistant to change. He could be very outspoken at team meetings, but this is okay. I'd sooner players spoke up and contributed rather than festering or snivelling in the background. He put more effort into physical conditioning and the appearance of his body than anything else.

Martin Crowe is another who was far from a good tourist in my experience of him, and others will readily attest to that. Someone who was surprised by Crowe's attitude was Peter Burge, the former

Australian test player, who was the match referee for the series in India. Peter often came on our bus *en route* to airports and hotels. He found India hard to deal with and said that he'd feel much more comfortable if he could travel under our wing. We were happy to accommodate him. At one point Gren said that Burge had told him that Martin Crowe sat at the back of the bus where his remarks were often critical of management, and in particular me as coach. Unfortunately Gren didn't tell me about this until very late in the tour. I wish I had known earlier. In some groups individuals don't get away with undermining others; their teammates will chip them. Sadly we hadn't reached that point. One expects more from senior players like Crowe.

One of the more useful pieces of equipment we had on tour was a type of exercycle: the front forks locked in a frame and the rear wheel spinning on rollers. The players used it a lot. Even those who were playing in a match used it, sometimes pedalling for 30-40 minutes. The machine told you how far you'd travelled and there was a bit of competition to see who could ride furthest in a given time. But a couple of players liked to jump on the machine immediately after the end of play. Mark Greatbatch was one, and Adam Parore another. Parore was quick to change and start pedalling. The trouble with that was that the team members were often needed for prize-giving ceremonies and other duties. Gren Alabaster more than once had to get him off the thing and back out to join the rest for the official ceremony. This sort of brinkmanship that he was determined to engage in is a pain. Adam is a renowned repeat offender, can't help himself. Poor old Gren, he'd say, 'Come on, you know you've got to get out there. Why are you doing this?'

Some individuals are perennially difficult, no matter who the coach or manager is. Often it's because they are not really suited to a team game. After the Indian tour I asked the Canterbury coach about this, and in particular about Cairns. He said, 'Oh, Chris, you'll always have problems with him.'

Cairns was convinced I didn't like him. In fact I came to see Chris as a victim of the negative features of the culture of our times of which cricket is a reflection. I knew his parents well when he and his sister were children and I liked them. There is no pleasure in seeing him struggle to deal with the culture of mistrust and manoeuvring which riddles New Zealand cricket.

After India my feelings about Cairns were that he was headstrong, inconsistent, defiant, with an enormous ego. Many would say that was a mask covering innate uncertainty and insecurity. Former coach Geoff Howarth once told me that he felt Cairns didn't actually rate himself able to do the job when the chips were down, especially at the top level. We found that when the pressure went on in a match, or he was getting some stick when bowling, or the opposition started a tactic which unsettled him when he was batting, he was likely to lose his rag and his play suffered. Chris was quick to speak, often thoughtless, and believed fervently that individuals have the right to do what they please. On occasion he was rude and obnoxious and would push everything to the limit. He over-reacted to any form of comment or advice, was apt to take it as adverse criticism.

He dressed in a rough and ready fashion, was poorly organised, and needed constant monitoring. He preferred to see me as the monumental problem when in reality his problem was with himself, and with the team's code of conduct.

As a batsman he was and is a big striker of the ball, well capable of winning a match on his day if only he could control his temperament. He was a poor player of the turning ball, particularly the ball leaving him. He ought to have been a more consistent run-getter but was handicapped by scattered thought-processes brought about in part by being full of changing and cranky theories.

As a bowler, he was not generally as good as with the bat, but he had and has natural physical attributes and talent which ought to produce even greater success. At the time he had yet to develop consistency with the ball. He had a habit of changing the angle from where he bowled his stock delivery from one day to the next. One day he'd jump high on delivery, the next he wouldn't.

As a fielder he has a very strong arm, sometimes inaccurate, and is a good mover in the outfield – a very fine athlete.

You have to look hard to find knowledgeable people willing to seriously argue that Cairns is captaincy material. Cairns did captain the New Zealand side in a state game in Australia in late 1997 and feedback was that he was out of his depth. I'm told the experience persuaded Cairns that captaincy is not his thing. That was then, but who knows his view tomorrow? (Indeed. As it happened Cairns again captained the team in the first game of the 1998 tour of Sri Lanka before Fleming returned from an ICC meeting in London.)

* * *

It's often said that each individual has to be treated differently in order to get the best out of them. To me a coach's principal responsibility is to show, thus help players develop the skills to regularly make the most of their own cricketing talent. In the end the players have to do it, the coach can't.

Generally I have found that the treating everyone differently according to their personality theory doesn't produce better all-round cricketers. I am more than willing to give a great deal of attention to individuals' cricketing needs, but I have found that those who want and insist on lots of individual attention, or special treatment in other areas, keep on wanting it irrespective of how it affects the whole set-up. They are an ongoing problem – you put in more than you get back – so unless you have guidelines and rules, and are prepared to stick to them, they'll abuse things all the time. This team wasn't unusual in that regard; I've experienced it to some degree in other teams too. Flexibility is necessary, of course, but somewhere a line must be drawn. In my role I wanted to be equally fair and respectful to everyone, not have favourites.

When I was New Zealand coach in the 1980s I recall Martin Crowe wanting me to sit down with him every time before he went in to bat, wanting me to go through a list of checks: 'let it come', or 'wait', or 'play straight', or 'relax', and so on. At the time I thought this was a surprising sign of immaturity in a front-line batsman, as well as evidence of our common human vulnerability. My response was to say to myself, 'All right, I'll stand on my head if it's going to help Martin Crowe get runs. And not just Martin, anyone in the team, if that's going to make the difference.' But before long you become aware that this is laughable to other guys in the dressing room who find it hard to stifle a snigger. In one way this doesn't really matter, but eventually a player has to get his own act together and not rely on someone else so often. Mollycoddling is a poor long-term strategy.

Maybe we will get to the stage in cricket where some players are earning so much – Tendulkar and Warne are examples – that they will be allowed to take their own trainers along. That would truly separate them from the rest, of course, and resentment would simmer. I doubt that it would work. But a mentor and/or a person who could work with a player from time to time would be okay.

There are usually a few players who want more, and more, and more. And some are better at persuading administrations to go along with what they want. I recall an instance when I was with Worcestershire. My friend Vanburn Holder, who also played for the West Indies, was easily our number one strike-bowler, but he was getting less money than John Inchmore who was not in Vanburn's class, and was actually lucky to hold his place in the team. But Inchmore drove a harder bargain and got his way. Sooner or later with certain players someone has to say, 'No more'.

Ours was far from the first management to have had problems with Adam Parore. Chris Doig said so himself on Kim Hill's morning national radio programme in 1996. We continued to select Adam because we felt he was worth his place as a batsman. One often hears commentators say that Adam is arguably the best player technically in the New Zealand team. That is stretching it. A problem which he had, and which we tried to solve, was his tendency to make a preliminary move across the crease which meant that he was prone to get out LBW. The timing of this movement is crucial. Back and across is okay provided you are stationary and balanced when the ball arrives. Adam got into trouble because he was still moving across the crease as the ball was arriving. This increases the likelihood of a player getting out LBW and not knowing where his off stump is. Playing at balls wider than is necessary is another probable outcome.

Adam had difficulty against leg-spinners in particular. He didn't, and doesn't, back himself to be able to stay in against leggies. As a result he resorts to sweeping, sees it as virtually his only attacking option. It's also a sign he doesn't back himself to defend the awkwardly-pitched ball. When he does push forward to the turning ball he tends to play down the initial line with his bat and doesn't cover for any turn. I hasten to add that these technical difficulties are all too common. This means that if the ball turns it either misses or catches the edge of the bat. A better technique to a ball spinning away from you is to play down the line with the pad so that you at least give yourself the width of the bat with which to make contact with the ball if it turns.

Adam's one of those characters who often puts his foot in it verbally before realising it. Off the park he works extremely hard physically, almost obsessively, but surprisingly could be quite lazy in the field, and wouldn't help others. Sometimes he meandered after the ball, ran at half pace. In fact he made it clear that he was bored fielding. We tried to get him to field under the helmet in at short-leg, a specialist position, in order to give him something to aim at, to encourage him to become the best there.

Roger Twose worked hard at his cricket and was if anything over-cautious at the crease with a habit of working the ball onto the on-side. For some reason Roger often felt he had to question or challenge management decisions on when we were to leave, what time practice would be held, and so on. Matters of no great moment. He was always wanting to know more about future tours, payments, the timing of selection of teams, and so on. There's a bit of the shop steward in Roger. Sometimes he wondered whether he should be playing at all, and was another brinkman. In the end we just wished he'd get on and play cricket and forget about the peripheral stuff.

Paddy Greatbatch was the unionist, questioned management at every opportunity. Gren became exasperated with Paddy, once told him to just shut up and do what he was told. Very jaunty after success. You can't take issue with that, of course, as players are entitled to enjoy their success in their own way. Paddy worked impressively hard on his cricket and deserves full marks for that.

We found Matthew Hart had trouble fixing his technical flaws when bowling, and I discussed them earlier. Hart worked hard at his cricket, and although he certainly listened, he found it difficult to apply what had been said or what he had agreed to do. He was no problem off the field which was to his credit.

And at the time Doig seemed happy with our progress. On 18 October he had sent us a fax noting his pleasure at the early form of the batsmen, saying, 'That's great!! Well done!' On 13 November Gren and I received a fax from Doig saying that 'we are full of admiration for the job that's being done and the vibes from the public for you all are largely positive'.

In Doig's fax of 18 October he also referred to our 'media ban' as he put it, and that certain influential radio 'journalists/presenters' found our system 'unworkable'. In fact we didn't have a media ban at all and the way we'd organised media access had suited the Indian media just fine. Some at home in New Zealand weren't happy and some were. A major part of the problem was that, initially, Radio New Zealand hadn't sent anyone to India to cover the tour. So Gren had to cope with New Zealand media people ringing up at all hours of the day and night, many unaware of time differences, to the point of chaos. We felt that the demands on us were becoming unreasonable, and applied some restrictions. Gren's attitude and mine was the principal reason why Radio New Zealand sent across the radio commentator Bryan Waddle, otherwise there wouldn't have been any prominent New Zealand media presence there other than NZPA.

We could understand Doig's concern, for there is a duty to allow the media access in order to stimulate the public's interest and meet its expectations. But open slather had proved a nightmare to all but the journalists, and we told Doig so.

Doig also raised a concern which we shared when he said that some players had been photographed wearing logos other than those of official New Zealand Cricket sponsors. Parore and Cairns had been seen in the media displaying Nike logos. Prior to the game being called off in Goa, Parore decided to go for a run, lapping the ground in front of 30,000 people wearing clothing displaying non-NZC sponsors' logos. We kept asking Parore to stop showing off non-approved logos but it is not easy to get him to alter course. You might just as well wave a lollipop at an elephant.

Gren had an ongoing task to stop players parading or playing wearing unacceptable logos. Most players got this sorted out in the end and didn't flaunt it, but not Adam. It wasn't just absent-mindedness; he well knew what he was doing, and it drove poor old Gren bonkers!

Chapter 7

At Home to Pakistan and Zimbabwe

The final one-dayer against India took place in Bombay on 29 November so there was hardly any time for rest at all before we were to play the first test at home against Pakistan in Christchurch starting on 8 December 1995. I had arranged to meet with the other selectors Pickard and Shrimpton, and with NZC's Chris Doig when we got home. Gren Alabaster came along too. I thought it was very important that Gren was there to confirm the accuracy, or otherwise, of the information I delivered. If Gren was able to add things, well and good.

We met at Auckland airport immediately after our arrival. So it was a debriefing as well as a selection meeting to pick the side to play Pakistan. Doig was keen on a debriefing meeting, and so were we. It's always worth discussing concerns, comparing notes, planning for the future, and so on. It also gives all parties a chance to hear and respond to criticism.

At the meeting Doig didn't have much to say, seemed more interested in being brought up to speed. Pickard and Shrimpton accepted that on the basis of their performances on tour it was not unfair to drop Thomson, Greatbatch and Hart. Spearman was brought in – we were impressed by his potential and we'd received favourable reports on him. Patel was deemed fit again and he was still widely regarded as our leading spinner.

Even after the fiasco of Cairns's performance in Bombay, where he'd pulled out of the team, we decided to give him yet another chance, to persevere with him. As noted earlier, Mark Greatbatch says in his book that he was amazed we'd kept Cairns in the squad. We hoped that seeing we were back in a familiar home environment he would pull up his socks etcetera. And this was something Doig did feel strongly about, Cairns having become something of Doig's special baby, his *cause célébre.*

Pakistan was coming for a short tour, one test and four one-dayers, straight after a test series against Australia. The timing for both Pakistan and New Zealand wasn't ideal, although Pakistan was at least in test match mode.

In Christchurch Lee Germon won the toss and put Pakistan in to bat. Sohail and Ramiz Raja put on 135 for the first wicket which tested our resilience, but then the side folded to lose 10 wickets for 73 runs and was all out for 208. When New Zealand replied, Spearman made 40 in his first match, Twose 59 and Cairns 76 in our total of 286. Akram took 5-53 off 24.5 overs. At half way things looked promising for us but Pakistan batted very well in its second innings, Ramiz and Ijaz putting on 140 for the second wicket and the side made 434. We folded for 195 in our chase for a daunting 357 with Spearman 33, and Twose, a marathon not out 51 off 166 balls (257 minutes at the crease) the only notable contributors. The bowler who did for us was the right-arm leg spinner Mushtaq Ahmed who took 7-56 off 34.4 overs to collect 10 wickets for the match.

Mushtaq was the major difference between the sides. Lee put Pakistan in mainly because it isn't usual for New Zealand pitches to wear greatly, and because, to win games you have to bowl a side out twice. In my view our best chance then was to have our seamers bowl when the pitch was likely to have something in it for them. Our spin attack was limited.

In the first one-dayer in Dunedin Pakistan made a modest 189, Larsen taking 1-29 off ten very good overs, and Astle 2-34 off his ten. Because of the nature of the pitch we opened with Patel and he got through seven overs, taking 1-21. Batting we fell 20 short despite Twose's 59. At one point we had slumped to 94 for 7.

Management and many in the team were startled by Cairns's performance after being dismissed by Mushtaq, who had made a bit of a monkey out of him at the crease. He was caught by Latif off Mushtaq, and he walked briskly off the park and into the dressing room where he sat quietly for a moment or two before exploding. At Carisbrook there are (or were) in effect two dressing rooms with connecting doors for each team, and Chris was in one room while the majority of us were sitting in the other watching the game and replays on TV. There was laughter about something unrelated to the cricket. Presumably Chris thought the laughter was directed at him because he started screaming and ranting. He wanted to know how we could be laughing when we were in such a poor position in the match. His volcanics were disconcerting to say the least.

When he came through a little later and sat with the rest of us, you could have cut the atmosphere with a knife. It's disturbing to be in the presence of people who rage to that extent. You think, what are they going to do next? Everyone left the dressing room and went upstairs to the players' viewing area.

There's not a lot I want to say about these games against Pakistan except that we won the second and fourth games to tie the series against the then 'current World Champions' 2-all. I don't place much store by such high rankings because there's a long time between world cups. Pakistan was a good side and we were quite pleased with the result, but it is often overlooked these days that the form of international teams fluctuates and no one nation is clearly better than others.

I'd just about come to the end of my tether with Cairns and was seriously concerned about his ability to manage his anger. I wasn't sure how to approach the issue, and neither were Lee and Gren. I wrote to Doig and detailed my concerns and said that as his employer NZC owed it to him to seek help for him. Doig arranged for Gren and I to meet an appropriate professional in Christchurch, for we both wanted to educate ourselves more and get some professional advice on how we might handle the situation with Cairns. Writing to Doig I said that, 'I realise management will always be required to accommodate and control some awkward personalities' but that we had a more serious case here. 'For Chris to face up to the stresses and strains of international cricket is like asking an alcoholic to work in a hotel. He needs to be successful to maintain stability, in a game which will never provide a stable environment.' I said that Chris needed to be helped, 'for our sake, and more importantly for his.' I said a team can't be run properly, and it's unfair to the others, if you keep giving one or two players special treatment.

Doig spoke to Cairns about my and others' concerns but didn't choose to involve me, Alabaster or Germon. He said that Cairns agreed that he'd been out of order and referred to the disciplines imposed by me and Alabaster. Doig said Cairns considered he was undervalued, particularly by me, and wanted to be given greater responsibility. He said Cairns in effect wanted to choose where he'd bat, (seven was too low) and that Doig himself saw Cairns as a vital part of NZC's future marketing objectives as well as an essential part of the success of the cricket team.

Further, Doig told me it was wrong to expect every individual to adhere to an inflexible set of rules and regulations that failed to acknowledge a person's right to be different. He talked about the flair, independence and spirit which gifted people often have in over-abundance, and which tends to make them perform but also over-react and rebel. As if Alabaster and I, with our backgrounds and experience, didn't know! Doig also reminded me what a bad thing it was to try to squeeze such individuals into a preconceived mould.

He then told me that he was convinced that the way forward was for Cairns, myself and him to meet in the near future and 'have a frank and open discussion' about Cairns's future in the team.

I thought, yes, good, by all means, even though I told Doig that I was worried that on this matter I was 'beginning to sound like a parrot'. I waited for a meeting. But in the meantime I replied to Doig. I said, among other things:

'1. The disciplines were not imposed by Gren and I. They were imposed (developed) by the players and enforced by the Tour Management Team of Alabaster, Germon, Plummer and myself.

'2. Chris is likely to continue to feel undervalued' given our experience and the opinion expressed by the professional we saw.

I said that in my view Chris's batting didn't warrant a permanent position in the top six and that his record thus far was evidence of that, but that in one-day matches we used him as a floater in the order, which meant that he sometimes went in much higher. To put him higher, 'on paper' would not suit 'the balance of the team'. Putting Chris down as number six would mean relegating a specialist batsman to number seven and damage 'the harmony of the group'.

In reference to Doig's seeing Chris as 'a vital part of NZC's future marketing objectives', I reminded him of what he'd told me, which was that a Managing Director of a major NZC sponsor had said that Chris's hairstyle did not fit with his firm's image. I then said, 'There are also obvious risks associated with hanging NZC's promotional hat on an unstable rack.'

I also asked Doig to name the 'rules and regulations' which 'have been imposed which are unreasonable?' I still haven't seen the answer to this question from any quarter.

I said that I felt, 'Chris should not be looking for a way to work with me, he should be working on a reasoned and intelligent approach towards working with a group of people and sorting out his game. His problem is not with me. By personalising his difficulties, it is too convenient and will distract him from the real issues.'

About this time NZC had received a complaint from a member of the public about a provincial player who'd allegedly returned to the dressing room, swore and then attacked a small freezer. Doig wrote and ticked the player off, told him it grossly offended members of the public and sponsors who heard the performance. This followed an earlier breach of conduct by the same player in another game. In his letter Doig told the player that I and the selectors wouldn't tolerate such breaches, and NZC would support the non-selection of players who didn't control themselves. He said that 'regrettably talent is only part of the equation' and NZC wouldn't 'condone' ill-disciplined behaviour.

Chris Doig never replied to my 10 January 1996 letter of response to his concerning Cairns. Nor did he ever arrange that meeting between him, Cairns, and me. His self-professed expertise as an administrator was not evident.

When I look back it was remarkable how few discussions I was ever able to have with Doig. He raised the issue of media access with me, and the issue concerning Cairns, but was never prepared to discuss them openly or at length. He simply seemed to make assumptions, or go by whatever he had gleaned or picked up from unnamed others, and carried on.

Gren and Lee were well aware of my exchanges with Doig in respect to these matters. They felt we and NZC ought to be doing something tangible about helping solve the problems with Cairns.

There was another matter that could have become an issue. The concerns Doig had about the contentious-to-some media protocol – which the team and management had drawn up prior to our leaving for India – hadn't been trialled in New Zealand until the Pakistan series. There was little trouble and neither the media nor the public appeared short-changed as a result. It had been a storm in a teacup.

Out of Africa, the Zimbabweans

The Pakistan side went home and a few days later Zimbabwe arrived and opened their tour with a three-day game against a New Zealand XI at Wanganui from 2-4 January. They also played a match against the Academy XI in Whangarei on 6-8 January. I attended both matches.

As New Zealand selectors, Pickard, Shrimpton and myself were interested in some new blood, and Allott, Penn, Loveridge, Kennedy and McMillan were among those of particular interest.

At the time, some provincial coaches were kicking up a fuss about players being called into the New Zealand and Academy teams for these games when the coaches thought they should have been playing for their regional sides in the Shell Cup. We felt that it was better for New Zealand cricket to give those on the verge of national selection two three-day games against a touring side than have them playing two one-dayers in the Shell Cup. Our New Zealand first-class season was limited and as selectors part of our responsibility to NZC was to give our emerging players the chance to play cricket at a higher level. The regional coaches seemed to overlook the fact that the national selectors didn't set the itinerary.

For a couple of weeks the selection panel took some flak. I got sick of it and sent a memo to all provincial coaches, saying that we hadn't appreciated the 'public and personal abuse from some of you'. Pickard, for instance, had been abused by one of his own Northern Districts selectors.

We'd picked no more than two players from any provincial side for the Academy and New Zealand elevens for the matches against Zimbabwe, so as not to deplete any one side more than others. I said that we were 'mindful that if New Zealand is to be competitive in the international arena it is vital we develop a depth of talent. Ideally we need a group of individuals whose background allows them to realistically challenge first team players for their place and recognised the benefits for them and New Zealand Cricket.'

In my memo I pointed out that one side's coach – it was Otago's Vaughan Johnson – was 'delighted for two of his players to be considered worthy of selection in the invitation sides.' Tersely I said that, 'If you have more than petty parochial utterances to make, let's hear them directly and not through public sources. If you are critical of the match timetabling and have worked out how it could have been improved, write to Tim Murdoch' of New Zealand Cricket.

The response from the coaches? Except for Bob Carter in Wellington, not a peep. He had no real problems with what had happened except to say that the announcement of the test side to play Zimbabwe in Hamilton was done whilst his side was still playing a game in Masterton. I had rung up Gavin Larsen and told him that he wasn't in the test side for Hamilton – I wanted him but my two co-selectors didn't – and Bob said he felt that no player should be advised of that while playing in a match. I tend to agree, but the time lines were tight and I felt it was better to tell Gavin then rather than have him find out by other means.

* * *

We introduced four new caps for the first test against Zimbabwe at Trust Bank Park in Hamilton: Astle, Allott, Kennedy and Loveridge. Morrison and Nash were both unavailable due to injuries, and so was Martin Crowe. We gave him a deadline to return to fitness before the World Cup which he wasn't able to meet. Of course there was no guarantee that, after our problems with him in India, and given his injuries, he would have been selected anyway. Which raises the question of selection policy generally. It became quite clear to me that the likes of Doig, John Reid, and some others tended to take the view that certain players had to be selected irrespective of their attitude. (But I did find that Reid was inconsistent there, for he told me he was quite happy to see Shane Thomson left out because he was not a fan of his. This aversion was attitudinal, more than anything.)

Some eyebrows were raised over the selection of Kennedy. It was a gamble but he had taken 4-22 against the visitors in Wanganui, and with Morrison and Nash unavailable we had to look elsewhere. He had shown real promise during the season. I hadn't seen much of him, having been away on tour, but Rick Pickard and Mike Shrimpton had. We had not been able to look at him as closely as with other bowlers – we didn't have video tape of him, and he hadn't had a lot of experience at first-class level, so he was a gamble which circumstances rather forced us to take.

Only 91 minutes of play was possible on the first day and after Fleming was run out for 49 no one was able to put together a big score, so we were bowled out next day for an inadequate 230, Streak getting 4-52 off 25 overs. Good bowling. Zimbabwe laboured to 196 with Cairns taking 4-56 and Kennedy bowling well in his debut with 3-28. In our second innings we declared at 222 for 5 with Parore on 84 not out, leaving the visitors to score 257 in 61 overs. We felt we had given Zimbabwe a chance and put them back in the game, but we also needed to do this to give ourselves a chance. I suppose you could have called it an aggressive declaration. Zimbabwe reached 208 for 6 and shut up shop. It was one of those games where I felt that one side or the other should have won. We would certainly have chased for longer than Zimbabwe did, so we assumed that they saw a draw as a good result for them. We felt that if it had not been for the rain we would likely have won.

The unfortunate thing for us was Greg Loveridge's breaking a finger when hit by a ball from Olonga. We'd had high hopes for Loveridge developing as a penetrative leg-spinner. He had spent time as a live-in member of our cricket academy at Lincoln. He was a useful cricketer, a good athlete who could run very fast. He had a strong arm in the field, was a good mover, could give it a good nudge with the bat, making him handy in the lower middle order. He could hit straight. But his injury put him out for the season and no one knows what he might have achieved.

Afterwards I felt really sorry for Greg Loveridge. The poor bugger had gone to Darwin with us before the tour to India in late 1995, and had damaged a finger in the nets before he'd got to play a match. The break was severe and complicated – a three month healing process at least instead of the three weeks or so that is sometimes the case. Later on Loveridge was sent over to Australia to join their academy and the reports that came back weren't all that encouraging for either him or NZC. One comment was that the Australians felt they had three or four leggies who were better than Greg, and the Aussies tried to change his style with damaging effects to his morale and ability. So to me sending Loveridge to Australia was counter-productive. I don't know who or what is to blame – if there is anything or anyone to blame – for him failing to fulfil his promise, but his was a talent that we could ill-afford to lose. I hope he comes again.

With the exception of Loveridge, whom we replaced with Larsen, we took the same team into the second test at Eden Park. The groundsman produced a flat, docile pitch when we'd have preferred one that gave some help to the bowlers. Batting first we made 251, Spearman 42, Fleming 94, and Cairns 57. Zimbabwe replied with 326 of which Houghton contributed 104.

In the second innings New Zealand made 441 for 5 declared leaving Zimbabwe 366 to win in just over a day. Spearman scored

112, Twose 94, and Cairns a blazing 120 off only 96 balls. Overnight Zimbabwe was 39 without loss and on the final day crept along to 246 for 4 when stumps were drawn. We just didn't have a Warne or a Mushtaq to bowl them out, and the pitch was so flat that we weren't able to be too generous with our declaration.

Our national selection panel conferred and we decided there was no good reason to delay settling on our squad for the upcoming World Cup competition, and that the one-day series against Zimbabwe was a good opportunity for the team to work on the strategies we hoped to use in India and Pakistan during the cup competition.

In the first match at Eden Park we batted first and made 278 for 5, Astle 120 and Twose 59 being the most notable contributors. Zimbabwe were bowled out for 204 in the 44th over, Thomson doing best with 3-32 off 10 overs.

Zimbabwe batted first in the second match at the Basin Reserve to score 181 for 9 off their 50 overs and we took only 39.3 overs to reach 184 for 4, Fleming 70 and Twose 41. In both games we took the approach when batting that it doesn't matter how many or how few the opposition gets, you get accustomed to playing in the same way. By persisting with a tactic, repeating a method, a sensibly aggressive approach to batting for instance, you gradually get better at it and you will win more games. Even when you are chasing a small total. Often a side will say, 'Oh, all we need to do is doddle along and collect runs sedately and aim to win with an over or two to spare having lost few wickets. There's no need for urgency.' I disagree. Lose urgency and you put yourself in danger of losing the game. A side sometimes goes to sleep and creates difficulties for itself when adopting the sedate approach, and small to moderate totals end up becoming much larger.

We wanted to learn to push ourselves more, to extend the boundaries of our capabilities. One-day cricket is all about training yourself to play on the knife-edge.

The third and final match was played at McLean Park in Napier and here we had some off-field distractions which affected our performance. All the girlfriends, wives and partners arrived like thistledown blown in on a nor'wester. In a team talk on the night before the match I said that I was concerned about the extent of the extra-curricula preoccupations. I said that it was a bit like a Butlin's Holiday Camp with elements of Hi-de-Hi. This is one of the difficulties about playing at home. On tour, particularly in developing countries, players don't have the same number and type of social opportunities and a side has a chance to become more tightly knit. But at home family and friends require time, understandably feel entitled to it, and a side can easily become disjointed and play too hard off the field. I had this feeling profoundly in Napier and our performance showed it.

Zimbabwe made 267, a good score, but the pitch was flat and the outfield fast. We did not have either Larsen or Cairns. We went out and played like millionaires, as if it was a village green holiday match, and were bowled out for 246 in 48.1 overs. Zimbabwe fielded like demons and won well, but I was brassed off about our effort. We were trying to get some consistency in our play, yet we were still finding that we had some individuals who weren't able to show the maturity and control required to put in truly professional performances day in, day out. We were making good progress but it was clear we still had a good way to go.

During the games in New Zealand against Pakistan and Zimbabwe, Doig and I had a number of breakfast sessions with sponsors at which he emphasised how New Zealand cricket was now on the right path and in the very capable hands of the right people, etcetera etcetera. The breakfasts were organised by the BNZ in major centres.

Chapter 8

World Cup 1996

We had a couple of days only between the end of the Zimbabwean tour and taking off for India again on 6 February. Our World Cup campaign was to begin with a pool match against England at Ahmedabad on 14 February. For three days – 7, 8 and 9 February – we had some net practices in Bombay. It wasn't easy to find facilities as other international teams were also there intent on preparation. Hanumant Singh, who lived in Bombay but was taking the Kenyan side, opened the right doors for us. Another to help, and who arranged for us to practise at the Gymkhana Ground, was Kailash Gattani. The Gymkhana Club's ground was where test matches were first played in Bombay. Interestingly they also played rugby there.

From Bombay we went to Calcutta for a captains' and managers' meeting on 10 February prior to the opening ceremony the next day. A necessary inconvenience! We got to Ahmedabad in time for one day's practice the day before our match against England.

There was the expected early morning dew when England won the toss and asked us to bat. Before we went out to bat I noticed during the warm-ups that the English side, compared to our guys, had no spark or spring in their stride. Our guys were miles ahead. I found that watching our players during warm-ups gave me a good guide as to how they were likely to perform.

While I sometimes got involved by hitting catches I generally preferred to stay back and observe. I let Germ run things – run the little games and grids. I feel the coach gains more that may benefit the side by standing back and watching the way the players go about their fielding routines and geeing them up when necessary. It was a different story at net practice: there I kept the time, organised the batting and bowling orders, and so on.

When we went out Astle opened and made a good 101 and others supported him with useful contributions. We felt our goodish score of 239 for 6 put us in with a reasonable chance.

England were pedestrian in most respects throughout the match and although they reached 228 for 9 we had them under control for most of the time. It was a pleasing opening game for us and took the pressure off slightly because the way the competition was organised four out of the six teams in each of the two groups would go through to the quarter-finals. Holland and the United Arab Emirates (UAE) were obviously the two weakest sides in our group, the other teams being Pakistan, South Africa and England.

In the other group both the West Indies and Australia forfeited their games in Sri Lanka out of concern over recent bomb blasts there. Both teams felt that they could afford to drop a game like that because neither of them saw either Kenya or Zimbabwe as quarter-final possibilities. The disturbances in Sri Lanka threatened the tournament. Beforehand there was debate over whether sides that refused to play in Sri Lanka should be kicked out of the World Cup tournament altogether. Some said that if this happened there could be no competition. In the end the games in Sri Lanka were forfeited without additional penalty by both Australia and the West Indies. This could have cost the West Indies dearly, though, for in the surprise result of the competition, they lost to Kenya.

After beating England we needed to beat both Holland and UAE to be sure of making the quarters. Cricket being what it is, there's always a chance that a poorer side may play above itself or strike you on a bad day, and beat you. Kenya did just that in beating the West Indies.

There was one incident during the match against England which concerned me, and which highlighted Lee Germon's determination to protect his autonomy as captain. When the England captain Atherton was out early, Hick went in and it wasn't long before he strained a muscle and asked for a runner. So convention determined that Atherton, the only batsman to have been dismissed, had to go out and run for Hick. Fine, but not so fine, for Atherton began holding discussions with both batsmen at the end of overs. It was clear to me that the England captain was in effect masterminding the run chase out in the middle. I got very irritated by this and sent out a note for Lee on which I told him of my concerns and suggested he raise the issue with the umpires. When the twelfth man ran out and tried to pass my note to Lee, he was loathe to take it, irritated that I'd sent him a note. Initially he didn't want to know about it, but in the end he did read it. When he did he realised that I wasn't querying his tactics or handling of the match, but that I was concerned about Atherton's influence. He had a word to the umpire, the Australian Randell, but Randell merely shrugged his shoulders, didn't seem to want or know how to handle the situation. I mention this incident because subsequently detractors of both Lee and myself, including Danny Morrison, claimed that Lee was little more than my puppet, that I was captaining the side from the stand. That was untrue – at no stage did I do that – and it is a slight to Lee. Lee is no one's 'puppet'. Never has been as far as I can determine from discussions with people in Canterbury and elsewhere. Anyone who thought that of Lee is a poor judge of character and misread Lee and me completely.

In his book *Mad as I Wanna Be* Morrison said that on this occasion I was 'freaking out, very uneasy that we didn't have enough runs on the board'. Rubbish. The kindest thing to say about this, and most of Morrison's assertions in his book, is that on this and many other occasions, he was mistaken.

Three days later we played Holland at Baroda. We made 307 for 8, Spearman with 68 and Fleming 66 top scorers. Holland didn't give themselves a chance and merely pushed the ball around and looked for some sort of respectability, ending up with 188 for 7, Harris 3-24 and Kennedy 2-36.

Craig Spearman's 68 came off only 69 balls before he slogged out, was caught on the boundary. It was an aspect of Spears's game that we were trying to change. He was such a casual cookie, and tended not to have the determination to go on and make a big score. Here was an opportunity to collect a really big score and I was a bit disappointed for him.

An incident at this time left me feeling dismayed by the attitude of some of the New Zealand players. By Indian standards Baroda is not a big place, perhaps 1.5 million people, but it's still big enough to have shops of some consequence. I'd gone down to a clothing shop with one of our party. I was looking for denim shirts, among other things. Staff obviously recognised us because the manager approached me and said that he would like to offer all the New Zealand players a free pair of jeans, and that if they bought anything else he'd give them a good-size discount. He said he would very much like to have the New Zealand players in the shop.

When I got back to our hotel I told the guys about the offer and asked them if they thought it was a good idea. The right noises were made, so I said that, if they liked, we could duck into the shop on the way to practice and they could pick up the jeans and anything else they might like to buy. I was to rue telling them of the shop's offer because once in there some of the comments, which were clearly audible to shop staff and the manager, were tactless and insulting. 'Aw, this is crap,' or, 'I don't like that cut,' and 'crap' and 'crap' again. I was appalled and the shop's staff and management became really upset and annoyed. Most of the guys didn't even take the jeans on offer.

We played South Africa in Faisalabad in Pakistan on 20 February and had to remain there, in the same hotel, until we met UAE at the same venue on the 27th. I could see some difficulties, not the least being a cooped up, and anti-climactic feeling. Fifteen young men holed up in a hotel in the relative outback of Pakistan can start to get on each other's nerves. But I also saw it as a chance to do some useful work, fine tuning. The hotel was right next to a cricket ground and we had access to it and nets there.

The pitch for the match against South Africa was difficult, no bounce in it at all. We didn't bat well and only got to 177 for 9. The only two players to make more than 30 were Fleming (33) and Germon (31 not out). South Africa knocked off the runs in 37.3 overs for the loss of 5 wickets.

On the 21st I held a team meeting in Germon's room at 9 a.m. I intended to hand out a programme for the time we were in Faisalabad. The purpose of the meeting was to assess where we'd come from and where we were, and to plan our practice sessions and other routines for the next two weeks. After the UAE game we were to travel to Lahore and there would be a seven-day break before we played Pakistan. We had also to plan our preparation for the quarter-finals.

We reviewed the England and Holland matches, and the previous day's game against South Africa. In the course of the discussion we spoke of South African society, their overall attitude generally and how this impacted on their approach to cricket. Generally the South Africans weren't questioning, tended to do what they were told. I had had quite a session with their coach Bob Woolmer. I knew him well, having played against him often in England. Woolmer said they were a dream side to coach because when you told them to do something they did it. I wasn't suggesting that we should be as regimented as them, but once we'd agreed to go down a certain path we should be putting more energy into it. And although the comment had been made by some of our players that they looked more professional than we did, the only reason for that was that at times we were still getting resistance to what our group had agreed to do.

Personally I don't believe it is necessary or desirable to be as regimented or unquestioning as the South Africans seemed to be. They were definitely better disciplined, which had much to recommend it, but I would sooner have more player-input, more debate. There was no suggestion from us that we should ape South African society or its values. I make this point because Danny Morrison in his book *Mad as I Wanna Be* talks, erroneously, about me latching on to the 'South Africans' militaristic approach to cricket'.

In fact, what happened was that some of our players were impressed by the South Africans' professionalism. The South Africans had a fitness trainer with them who worked with individuals, as well as the group, and this appealed to some in our side. Twose was especially vocal about this. I thought Plums was more than adequate in this respect, but maybe the sight of the South Africans out doing shuttles and sprints so determinedly hit home with some of them.

The South Africans were also reported to get up at the same time in the morning and to go down to breakfast together. Some of our guys saw this as an example of just how disciplined an outfit could be. Twose commented, 'Aw, we should be as professional as they are.'

That seemed like an opportunity to me. I talked to a few of the senior players and suggested that, particularly when there was an extra gap between matches, it would be a good idea to keep up our work ethic. Remember that on match days, 9 a.m. starts meant that everyone had to be up by 7 a.m at the latest and down to the ground by 7:30. So we floated the idea that everyone get up at 7 a.m. and go for a jog, then have breakfast, and once the dew had gone from the ground start net practices, say around 9:30.

Some of the more senior players agreed to this. Cairns was one. He was keen. It was then a matter of convincing the others. But there was an amazing amount of resistance. Shane Thomson requested a meeting of management where he said that he didn't want to go to breakfast on the morning of the match. He said that he had a routine for every time he played a big match. He said he lay in the bath for half an hour, had a cup of coffee in his room, and that did him. He wanted a special exemption. Gren Alabaster gave him a bit of a serve and said that if he got up 10 minutes earlier he could still have his bath and get down to breakfast with the rest.

Morrison also said in his book that anyone who didn't make it on time to breakfast, 'got the full fine'. What full fine? Simply untrue.

Before, and in Faisalabad, and after, I made it clear that I have never expected anyone to blindly accept anything – particularly regimentation – but without a willingness to go along with the group's decisions then there can be no cohesive team effort. I felt some in the team badly needed to look for reasons why they should do things rather than looking for reasons why not.

Some people might find it surprising to learn that at times some players do not seem to want to practise or play, and that they have to be reminded that unless they have that will it's not in their interests, or those of the team, for them to be there. If the public thinks that all players see it as a privilege and a thrill to be playing international sport, and that they are jumping out of their skins most of the time wanting to play for their country, they may be surprised to learn the degree to which it is the last thing on some players' minds at times.

It was over this issue in Faisalabad prior to the match against UAE, that Lee Germon and I had a slight disagreement. It was during a meeting, and the only time on tour when we disagreed in front of the team. He felt people should have their breakfast when it suited them on the days before the game against UAE. I didn't change the plan. We'd already been over the matter and had decided that everyone should be at breakfast at 7 a.m. on the days leading up to the match. In case there was any confusion, I sent a written message to all the players confirming that we wanted them all down for breakfast when and as previously decided. I'm not sure why Germ had had a change of heart. It didn't seem like a hell of a lot to ask, really.

News of Germ's and my slight difference over this got leaked and next thing a story appeared in the New Zealand papers saying that team management was at odds and tearing apart.

* * *

The net pitches for our practice sessions in Faisalabad were grassless strips of plain rolled mud. So we took the opportunity to draw thick chalk marks on the strips, lines to indicate what we considered to be the best line and length to bowl in Pakistan, and parts of India, too, for that matter. As I've said earlier, bowlers need to land the ball a little short of a length to prevent batsmen standing up on the front foot and hitting freely through the line. We got the bowlers to see how often they could land the ball in a one yard chalk-marked area between six and eight yards out from the batting crease. The right length was dependent on the pace of the bowler, and it was shorter than we had thought. We drew a line also between the middle of the bowling crease – half way between the stumps and the return crease, because this approximates where most bowlers let it go from – and the off stump so that the bowlers would know where they needed to pitch if the ball was to hit the stump. If the ball landed a little to the off of the ideal line and went straight on that was okay, for it wouldn't give a batsman too much width, and if the ball nipped back a bit it might hit middle. (We are talking of right-handed players here.)

The results were interesting. As you might expect, Gavin Larsen was the man. None of the other bowlers were able to land the ball in the area very often, which shows just how difficult it is for bowlers to control their line and length. Since then I have often thought that it would be very useful if our cricket academy, and coaches elsewhere, adopted this method of finding out just how good a bowler is at consistently bowling a tight line and length. Coaches and selectors need to look for and encourage bowlers with pace and an ability to swing or cut the ball, but generally the tighter a bowler's control of line and length the more useful he or she is.

Prior to the match against UAE we decided that we wanted to make doubly sure that all our pre-match routines were in place, so we made a particular effort to get it right. Some people may be interested in the routines we instituted. Give or take a few minutes it went like this at Faisalabad: 7:45 - 8:00 a.m., team warm-up (a few minutes jogging, then some stretching); 8:00 - 8:05, 1 grid (diagonal running, the idea mainly to wake people up, get them accustomed to space, ducking and diving); 8:05 - 8:10, fielding skills in pairs (line up with stump, ball and glove); 8:10 - 8:20, fielding group session (target work from mid-wicket to cover); 8:20 onwards, individual skills (short and long catching stations available).

The toss is usually made at 8:30, so if we were to bat some of the guys might have a few more throw-downs after that. Alternatively they might go in, change their shirts, then go out for some more throw-downs immediately before the match starts. If we were to bowl, the guys might spend a bit more time rolling their arms over.

Batting first we made 276 for 8 off 47 overs, Twose getting 92 off 112 balls and Spearman 78 off 77. UAE battled to 167 for 9, Thomson 3-20 off 10 overs.

Some players find touring difficult. Cairns is one. He is an extremely restless character. Because of that, from time to time we went out of our way to give him some responsibilities, make him feel included, important. In Faisalabad, for instance, we asked him to look after Kennedy, take the young bowler under his wing. I do not know if this helped either of them.

We had a rest day and then travelled to Lahore in a coach, a trip of about 3 hours. There were good facilities available at a ground close to our hotel and locals arranged a game for us on 3 March, one of the 5 days we had to wait before our last group match. We welcomed this as a change from net practice, to keep things alive, sharp and fresh. We played a team drawn from members of the club side that illustrious former players such as Javed Burki, Majid Khan and Imran Khan had played for. Most of the old boys played so they didn't provide much opposition, but we were grateful for the outing.

Socially Lahore has more to offer than Faisalabad and we managed to link up with the British High Commission and drink some Australian beer and scoff some English tucker that the diplomats enjoyed. I don't know if there was a stash of tinned baked beans of the kind favoured by a noted Australian leg-spinner.

It's worth noting that for lengthy periods the guys are able to do what they like. It is important that players get such time to recharge the batteries and so on. Sleep in, read a book, catch up on filling in their records, thinking about their game, or *not* thinking about it.

At our team meeting on the night before the match against Pakistan we closely examined the pattern of play that Pakistan seemed to follow. Both Lee Germon and I talked about the Pakistanis' style and Lee had done an analysis of both their bowling and batting strategy against England. He'd researched other games and found the Pakistanis had followed a similar pattern. Lee pointed out that when bowling they usually opened with Akram and Younis. Aaqib was brought on as early as the 8th over in place of Younis who returned when Akram came off. Akram usually bowled overs 1, 3, 5, 7 and 9; Younis 2, 4 and 6, then 11 and 13. Aaqib 8,10, 12, 14 and 16. Mushtaq came on for 5 overs from the 15th over on, then he bowled another 5 from the 38th to the 46th. The remaining 7 were shared between Younis, of reverse swing renown, overs 41, 43 and 45, Akram (overs 47 and 49), and Aaqib (48 and 50). In between overs 15 and 40 they tended to bowl out Sohail and use Malik for 5-6 overs. Lee drove home the need to get after Sohail and Malik, a minimum of 4.5 an over he felt, and he wanted us to aim for 220 runs after 40 overs because it was always hard to score 6 or more per over against Pakistan's attack in the last 10. He also, looking to have a bit both ways, said it would be good if some of our top order survived through until the final overs to counteract the threat of their quicks.

Then we raised the vexed issue of whether or not to sweep the right-arm leg-spinner Mushtaq. Lee and I decided that it had to be a personal decision for the batsmen, especially for Parore and Twose who had great difficulties playing the leg-spinner. (Mushtaq kept bowling googlies at Twose.) Parore found that his best way to score was to sweep, and we did not object to that, because on tour is not the place to try to develop a greater range of skills with the full blade of the bat. We emphasised that each player had to think carefully and decide how they were going to score off each type of bowler. A coach can suggest ways of attacking various bowlers, advising what the best percentage shots are, but in the end individual players have to go with the strokes they have most confidence in.

Regarding their batting, we had noticed that Pakistan were starting to attack more in the first 15 overs in ways similar to ourselves and the Sri Lankans. Their openers Sohail and Anwar were big shot merchants, and as left-handers liked width which enabled them to thrash the ball behind point. But after 15 overs and through to about 35, we felt they tended to go to sleep a bit, were happy to collect runs sedately and keep wickets in hand for a 15-over dash at the death. In the past they'd appeared to confine their dash to the last 10 overs. So Lee emphasised the need for the bowlers to settle on the right line and length and bowl to their fields at each stage. He proposed we use our slower bowlers in the middle stages in short spells of 2-4 overs, and that they bowl straight to straight fields. In other words, don't allow batsmen to use the pace of the ball to run it away behind the wicket and collect easy runs. He said that once the ball had lost its shine bowlers should go round the wicket to left-handers and make all the batsmen work hard for runs.

For my part I reminded the players that when batting our policy was to stretch ourselves in the middle overs and not waste them. Put pressure on the field without throwing one's wicket away. Urgency in the middle stages. My advice was for batsmen not to think in terms of runs per over, but to do the best they could with every ball. If that policy is adopted – if you concentrate on the process – the outcome looks after itself. What can often happen in the middle overs is that players tend to set their minds on collecting at 4.5 to 5.5 an over and start to panic if, say, four balls have gone and only two runs have been scored. Some batsmen then say, 'Jesus, I'd better hit a boundary'. Conversely, if 5-6 runs have been scored off the first 4-5 balls there's a tendency to say that's enough. Along comes a very loose ball and the batsman doesn't put it away. This is an example of how one-day cricket is often much more difficult than test cricket because the one-day game demands your utmost concentration and effort ball by ball. When the mind wanders performance suffers.

If you can't play Mushtaq with the full blade and decide you are going to sweep him, then you'd better practise it. He is the sort of spinner who is slow to arrive; he's slow-ish off the pitch, so it's hard to push him around for singles. The best way to play him, if you are technically accomplished, is to use the full blade and hit him down the ground and collect runs that way. But to do this you do have to get your body weight coming forward into the ball, because of his lack of pace from the pitch. Mushtaq usually has either mid-off or mid-on placed well back. But if you don't have the confidence to come down to him, and can't read him, you have to find an alternative.

When bowling I encouraged our team to play with urgency and try to get through the middle overs as quickly as possible. That gives a side the chance to slow down the over-rate in the final overs if the opposition is scoring quickly. You have to use all strategies possible to stop the opposition running hot in the final overs. Adjust the field. This helps bowlers collect their thoughts. They have to be thinking all the time just as batsmen do, and if batters really get after them earlier in an innings they may have to bowl the line and length normally reserved for the slog at the end. That means block-holers, perhaps, aimed in at middle and leg and to a re-set field. But if the tail-enders are in at the death, it's often better for a bowler to mix things up a bit on the theory that the poorer batsmen just don't have the skills or confidence to handle a variety of balls. Tail-enders prefer a predictable line and length, and if they know the bowlers are intent on block-holing they often handle things better. Quicker bowlers are often better to bowl just short of a length as most tail-enders struggle to lay bat on ball when this happens.

What had been happening – and this was one area that Germ and I discussed several times – was that we were having to rush through our final overs to fit them in to the time remaining. I know it was hard for Germ because it's not easy to keep wicket and captain the side in one-dayers. My message was, keep up the urgency, get through the overs quickly but without undue rush. Three and a half hours to bowl 50 overs ought to be ample time. How? Simple really: walk quickly between overs, make sure bowlers are aware in advance that they are going to bowl, mid-on and mid-off going to collect the bowlers' sweaters to take to the umpire so they don't have to walk the extra distance themselves, telling bowlers that when they follow through they should turn around and go back (they ought to be getting back alongside the stumps anyway) and not stand around on the pitch with their hands on their hips, and so on.

Although the match against Pakistan was not vital – a loss wouldn't stop us getting to the quarter-finals – it was another opportunity to work at imposing our attacking strategy. We were also looking forward to playing at the Gaddafi Stadium which was to be the venue for the final on 17 March. Gavin Larsen was still unfit – he'd damaged a calf muscle – so we badly missed him. The more so because Morrison, who went for 17 off 2 overs, broke down and had to come off. That reduced our options and Pakistan reached 281 for 5. Too many, and it showed that without Larsen, and Morrison at his best, our bowling was vulnerable.

When we batted we were bowled out in 47.3 overs for 235, Germon at number 3, Fleming, Twose, Cairns and Parore all getting handy but not big scores. It was, to use the sorry expression New Zealand cricket has often uttered, 'a respectable loss'. The upshot was that we qualified third in our group behind South Africa and Pakistan, and were to wait until 11 March before playing Australia in the quarter-final at Madras.

World Cup Quarter-final against Australia

In Madras lights were used for the first time. With day-night games the lights are turned on the night before so that sides can practise and get accustomed to any peculiarities of the lighting. Catching practice is important, among other things, and we were certainly keen to try out the lights in Madras. On some grounds lights are lower than others, in which case boundary fielders may have to return the ball on the bounce so that it doesn't come blasting in straight out of the lights.

We were having some high catching practice when Cairns dropped a couple, whereupon he ran over and said that he'd injured a finger. There was no sign of an injury, but it was an indication of the beginnings of a pattern. I recalled discussions with Geoff Howarth, and one or two others earlier. It was certainly becoming evident that Cairns did have doubts about his ability to come up with the goods when it really mattered. I might add it's a common affliction; all who have played at the highest level have experienced it, but it's something you have to overcome if you are regularly going to perform well when it really counts. All cricketers are afraid of failure to some degree and will dodge putting themselves under pressure if they can. Some deal with it better than others.

Regarding playing under lights, in his book Morrison says 'a lot of guys' told me that 'it was hard to see the ball batting second under lights'. I can't recall anyone saying that to me. How many of New Zealand's 26 one-day games did we play under lights while I was coach? Danny doesn't say. Actually, two only, and on one of those occasions we batted first. What is Danny on about?

In the game against Pakistan we'd put Germon in at number 3. For our strategy to work, because we acknowledged we were prepared to run the risk of losing three – and possibly as many as four – wickets in the first 15 overs, we needed to give ourselves as much depth of batting as possible. If we did that we believed that we could still recover from the position of losing early wickets and post a competitive total. By using Lee at 3 we also didn't unnecessarily expose another of our top players early on. And while I am a great believer in sending one's best players in as soon as possible, we felt sending Lee in, given his abilities, was both a protective and attacking strategy. Our batting was such that we had players down as far as number 10 who could bat. Lee had shown that he wasn't a mug facing spin, but more than that he was also capable against the new ball. We felt that we weren't going to lose much by batting him at 3 because otherwise he was probably going in at 8. At 3 we felt he could do well enough to give us quick runs at the top of the order and in effect lengthen our batting order. So I am very much in favour of floating a capable but not necessarily front-line batsman further up the order. In the quarter-final against Australia we were to have Thomson at 9, Patel at 10 and Nash at 11, so our batting was about as long as you can get.

Lee and I discussed the reasons for putting him at 3 at some length. He found it mildly amusing to have to grant that if he got out early then it would not be too great a loss to the team. Nothing if not a realist.

For the game against Australia, for the first time I put together as comprehensive a game plan as I could devise. I drew together everything we'd done previously. I had a preamble which I presented to Alabaster and Germon but not to the players, for naturally there were parts of the plan that were best for the eyes and ears of those two only. I felt that our plan needed to take account of the fact that *at that time* our opposition was better in most respects. The exception was our fielding; we had excelled there.

The issue of motivation is interesting and open to debate. These days international teams play so often that I believe it can be counter-productive to give a side a big verbal 'ra-ra, go get 'em' talk. Cricket isn't a big physical confrontation game like rugby or league. But now, even in those games, my impression is that coaches there are questioning the validity of that sort of talk. It's possible to arouse players to such a level that they go out onto the field and do silly things; conversely they can have become so excited beforehand that they're on a downward spiral by the time they get out on the park. Coaches have a term for this which is the 'inverted U'.

I believe a coach should build towards helping players develop the will from within, but on this major occasion I made a similarly big effort to convey everything I could helpfully and constructively offer. I think it's more effective if a coach is discriminating and saves his most thorough and insistent efforts for when it matters most. Players are more likely to prick up their ears, and find it more telling when you do get wound up about an event.

We believed that we couldn't expect the Australians to go out and lose the game, so we had to introduce additional strategies to those that we had already applied during the World Cup. I felt that our best chance of winning hinged on our producing an exceptional batting performance, for there were still grave doubts as to whether our best one-day bowler Larsen was going to be fit to play. It was highly likely that our bowlers were going to take some punishment – the previous game against Pakistan had proved that. With Danny Morrison unfit our resources were stretched, although conditions in India didn't really suit him and he was past his best.

Our team for the game against Australia was Spearman, Astle, Germon, Fleming, Harris, Twose, Cairns, Parore, Thomson, Patel, Nash. Our strengths were: three left-handers in the top order; the flexibility of having seven players who could bowl; a very good fielding side. But we had also to face the fact that so far, Astle excepted, our batsmen tended to be 60-run men on a good day. New Zealand's record showed that in recent years we'd produced few batsmen who had developed the ability to go on and win a game for their side. Batsmen who can win one-day games for you on their own are those who can go on and score a hundred or thereabouts at a good rate. Quick thirties and forties will often turn a game round, help you win it, but they are not usually enough in themselves.

When it came to bowling we really only had one bowler with the ability to take the edges and nick batsmen out early, Dion Nash. With Larsen gone – in the end he decided that he wasn't confident of lasting the match – we had no one we could be assured of bowling 10 overs.

I went through our plan. The target for batting was 300. Actually I meant 300-plus, and said that we should not alter our batting approach unless we were chasing fewer than 220 runs. Even then, I am reluctant to adopt a slow accumulation approach to run-getting in one-dayers. If a side can knock off a modest total in say 40 overs well and good.

We felt we couldn't afford to take a conservative approach to batting against Shane Warne; if we were to make 300 or more we couldn't allow him to bowl his 10 overs for as few as 25-30 runs. That would mean we would have to gather runs off the other Australian bowlers at a rate that was probably beyond us. Nevertheless we had extreme depth to our batting – Thomson, Patel and Nash at the bottom – so 300 or more wasn't unrealistic.

In order to make a big total we had to go for it from the outset and not alter our approach if we lost a few wickets in the first 15 overs. We decided that if a wicket fell in the first eight overs, and provided Warne hadn't come on, Germon would go in at number 3. If Warne was on we were going to put Germ down at number 8. What we were looking to do was have three left-handed batsmen in succession there to counter Warne who was the key to their bowling and to our success. Harris's position in the order was vital as far as Warne was concerned. We'd got in a couple of local leg-spinners to bowl to us in the nets and Chris had practised belting them over the top in preparation for an onslaught against Warne.

In many ways Harris is – or was – our best all-rounder. He is also our biggest striker of the ball; when in form he hits it further even than Cairns. Of course it is easier for a left-hander to hit a leg-spinner to and over the boundary because he can go with the spin.

We assumed that Fleming would be able to keep the score moving against all the bowlers, and our hope was that if necessary Twose could collect runs against Warne, but if he wasn't needed in that role we could push others above him in the batting order.

There was a whisper that Mark Waugh could be asked to open the bowling for Australia, but with three right-handers at the top of our order we felt we had that possibility covered. My overriding feeling was that Australia probably thought that it wasn't necessary to spring surprises on us. Australia tends to under-rate New Zealand as recent one-dayers have shown.

Also, again, I reminded the guys that the records showed that in most one-dayers played on good pitches, sides ran out of overs before they ran out of wickets. I impressed on them that we really had to play out of our skins and that we had to be committed to our plan, had to have the confidence to follow it. I tried to drum into them the importance of new batsmen being aware of the need to maintain the required tempo from the outset.

In regard to the bowling, I didn't say to the team that Germ and I felt that Nash was the only one likely to take the edge of the bat, but re-emphasised the need to create pressure by bowling a tight line and length to particular fields. Change of pace, the odd yorker at the right time, is a far better strategy than trying to bowl 'magic' balls of the sort that pitch on leg and knock over off stump. Even change of pace has to be on the right line and length.

We knew that we were vulnerable and were giving away too many runs with the new ball, so rather than having our two quicks Nash and Cairns bowling at the same time, we decided that we would use Patel in the first few overs. The plan was to use Nash for 4-6 overs in the first 15, and that he needed to be followed by the medium pace of Astle or Twose, and that Patel would be best replaced by Harris or Thomson. I also reminded them of the need to keep up the over-rate and that they should look forward to doing their job and not seek to duck it. With seven bowlers, a player who is a bit over-awed by the occasion, or is not feeling very confident, can start to hope that he is not going to be asked to bowl. That sort of thinking simply has to be suppressed.

Again I gave targets as far as the over-rate was concerned so that the team would only have to get through say 12 overs in the last hour and not 15 or so which creates real pressure on the fielding side.

We had to look at the advantages and disadvantages of batting first or second. In day-night games, natural light is generally good for the first two and a half hours, and although it is often said that the twilight period can be awkward, in India the light fails quickly and there isn't a long twilight. However, it is a factor to consider. Everyone's fresh if you bat first, for you haven't had to sweat it out in the field in hot conditions. Early morning freshness in the pitch doesn't come into calculations with day-nighters. We were also mindful of how well we'd played batting first in a match against India at Nagpur the previous year. But the clincher was that according to statistics we'd obtained, in previous matches against Australia we had won 40 per cent of the time when batting first and only 8 per cent of the time when batting second. Or to put it another way, we'd won 15 of 37 games batting first, and only two of 23 batting second. So naturally we wanted to bat first.

Of course if you bat first and fail to get a decent score, the opposition has more options on how to approach getting the total – and less pressure in doing so. Although at that time the weakest part of our one-day game was the difficulty our bowlers had defending a total, the evidence of other factors in regard to Australia outweighed that fact. We were also in a position where we felt it was an all or nothing situation, total commitment at the risk of bombing out. By and large I am a believer in bowling first in one-dayers but on this occasion we felt there were stronger grounds for batting first.

What we didn't take into account in our list of disadvantages, and which became a factor, was that a lot of dew came down. One doesn't expect that early in the evening in India, but it arrived and the ball became damp and our bowlers had trouble gripping the ball late in the match.

The game itself was riveting. We lost two early wickets, Astle and Spearman, at 15 and 16. Germon went in at three, then Fleming left with the score at 43. In came Harris and they batted magnificently to put on 168 for the fourth wicket at an excellent rate of scoring. The loss of our third wicket for only 43 tested our resolve to play shots and be committed to the team plan. It would have been easy to chicken out and try to conserve and consolidate.

When Germon left after a wonderful 89 off 96 balls the score was 212. We were in a great position given the time and the batting resources we had left – Harris was still at the wicket, and Twose, Cairns, Parore and Thomson, plus Patel and Nash were left to come, if needed. I thought that we were headed for 320 and a bit, and so did the Australians. If we'd made 320, Australia was history, and their coach Bobby Simpson knew it. But we folded and Lee and I knew that while 286 was a damned good score, it wasn't necessarily enough. The few runs at the end of an innings can sometimes act almost as double runs, and a score of 320 would have forced Australia to go all out from the beginning, risking all. Australia would have had to adopt a strategy, a style of play entirely different from any they'd followed before.

In the earlier stages Germon and Harris had clobbered Warne, but when he came back towards the end we had at least three batsmen padded up because we wanted to juggle the order and if possible send out a left-hander to face him. Cairns was due to go in at the time Warne returned and he said to me, 'Now that Warne's back on I should bat lower down.' But it was so late in the innings that it didn't matter for we had wickets in hand and we had to commit ourselves with a hitter the likes of Cairns. It was very disappointing that one or other of Twose, Cairns or Parore couldn't have made say 30 on this big occasion for it was clear to us that we were on the point of batting Australia out of the game. Cairns hit one straight up in the air off Mark Waugh; Twose got into knots and tied himself up trying to sweep. The crowd seemed right behind us, animated, noisy, encouraging. They loved seeing us hitting the Australians to all parts of the ground and tension was high throughout the match.

As far as our bowling, and the use of bowlers, was concerned, I gave Lee my views and then left it up to him to adjust things as he saw fit at the time. This was always our way. On this occasion I think he erred a bit in that we had planned to replace Nash with a medium-pacer, and for some reason he changed that and brought on Cairns in the first 15 overs. He went for over 20 off two overs, and all told bowled 6.5 overs for 51. Cairns had been bowling inconsistently and we didn't want the Australian batsmen to be able to take advantage of his additional pace in the early stages of their innings while the field restrictions were still on. I'm not sure why Lee deviated from our plan at this point. The Australians didn't really smash it around in the early stages of their innings; their strategy still tended to be to keep wickets in hand for the death. They relied heavily on Mark Waugh and he beat us, making 110 off 112 balls. But the Australians had been frightened, as Bob Simpson said to me afterwards, which was the reason why they floated Warne and put him in at number four where he thumped 24 off 14 balls. The Australians felt they were getting behind in the run-rate and Warne had a bit of luck being dropped – a half-chance really – out on the sweep to Nash. He also plopped the ball into space. But his innings just turned things their way and they got home in 47.5 overs. For us it was a near miss against a side which, at that time, had been performing better than us.

I must admit that during that game I was fairly uptight, unusual for me. It was a big occasion for us; we'd put a lot of time and energy and thought into planning and preparing for it, and I had a lot of problems getting into a position to sit so that I could see the whole field. The organisers were trying to reserve the prize seats for some dignitaries due to arrive later in the match, and I was shunted from one place to the other three times and got into arguments with the local police over where I could or could not sit! I basically lived every ball, and because Lee Germon was out there for most of our innings when batting, I had to decide and control who batted next, and had to be on hand to ensure people were ready. I hasten to add that I hardly missed seeing a ball bowled on tour, or in the nets; I regard myself as a good and inquisitive watcher of cricket, and I don't like to miss any of what is going on. That day and night I had to make some decisions on behalf of the captain to an extent which didn't usually occur.

I recall Roger Twose saying to me that I must have got a real kick out of being out front calling the tactical shots, a kick out of the power involved in that. Interesting: I didn't feel like that at all. I saw it as a requirement.

In one-dayers, especially when you bowl second and lose, there is the inevitable flatness. It's dispiriting, emptying. If you don't feel that way then you can't say you have given it your best shot. But as long as you have, you can hold up your head. We had come within a whisker of doing the very best we could have done, so had grounds for satisfaction.

* * *

Because we had made the quarter-finals there wasn't time for us to return to New Zealand before flying off to start our tour of the West Indies. Given our disappointment at Madras, and the length of time we'd spent away from home in the previous few months, we knew the West Indies tour was going to be an extremely difficult test. This situation created even more stresses and strains and put everyone's relationships under far more than the usual, or desirable, pressures. Future tours just have to be planned with gaps in between so that players can return home and see families and friends.

Thinking back, I felt the timetabling of the matches was unsatisfactory. A gap of almost a week between our games on more than one occasion was just too long. Too much hanging around – six days in Faisalabad, five or six in Lahore. Far from ideal.

As for the format, two groups of six teams made it fairly obvious which sides would make it through to the quarter-finals. Thereafter it was a knock-out system to find the semi-finalists and finalists, and I don't think this is the best way to determine the best sides. South Africa was an example of a team that had played so well in the pool matches, then lost one game and didn't even make the semi-finals.

We played some good cricket and some average stuff. I felt encouraged, felt we were making progress, and that most players felt the same.

For the record, in the other quarter-finals, England 235 for 8 in 50 overs lost to Sri Lanka 236 for 5 off 40.4 overs. India 287 for 8 beat Pakistan 248 for 9; West Indies 264 for 8 beat South Africa 245.

In the semis Sri Lanka 251 for 8 was awarded the game when the crowd became unmanageable after India collapsed to be 120 for 8 off

34.1 overs. In the other semi Australia got 207 for 8 and the West Indies flopped to 202 all out off 49.3 overs.

The final was won by Sri Lanka. Australia 241 for 7 and Sri Lanka 245 for 3 off 46.2 overs, de Silva not out 107.

Moored in Fisherman's Cove

At the end of our World Cup campaign we got stuck in Madras. While we waited for a suitable flight to take us to London, and then the West Indies, it was suggested we might like to spend some time at a resort, Fisherman's Cove, about an hour and a half's drive away on the coast south of Madras. We thought this was a pretty good idea, for it is a nice place, one I'd visited before. What we didn't realise was that we were going to be stuck there for almost a week, and that communications from Fisherman's Cove were poor, virtually nil as far as phones or faxes were concerned. Our liaison person was a Pakistani. He was likeable and did his best but wasn't making much headway, so we got in contact with Indian liaison people in Madras with whom we had become very friendly. They came down to see us and then went back to Madras to see if they could get us on an earlier flight from India. It seemed that the Indian cricket authorities had been unaware of the difficulties the delay caused us.

Two or three days in Fisherman's Cove would have been fine, but kicking one's heels for five days or more was frustrating. Nevertheless most of the guys had a good time there by the sea. I had time for thinking and some writing. In particular I responded to Dayle Hadlee who'd been reported as saying that New Zealand was going to use the Australian Cricket Academy in Adelaide. I said that although I didn't have any big objections to that, I hoped it had been thought through carefully and that if we were going to send players there, there would have to be very good reasons. I asked, What were they doing that we weren't, or couldn't, do ourselves? Also, at what stage were our players going to be slotted into their programme? (The Australians had a programme that lasted several months.) The idea was for us to send players for 2-4 weeks. I emphasised the need for caution, to be sure that we got what was best for us. It seemed to me that Doig was hell-bent on plugging into the Australian system, was sure that what they were doing was right and that it was in our interests to be a part of it. To me this was an example of Doig's bull-at-a-gate, knee-jerk way of going about things.

My contract stated that I was to be involved in these decisions.

I agree with information-sharing and exchanging visits from overseas coaches, but brainstorm things and consult first. Granted I was overseas, but it's not hard to make contact. I thought, as national coach, I should have been asked my opinion on moves to establish more links with Australian cricket and its academy. It is my impression that Doig takes the view that Australia and Australians have a more refined, sophisticated, and deeper knowledge of cricket than we do. They don't. Australians have a great enthusiasm for cricket, but their best cricketing brains are not better than ours when it comes to technique, tactics and so on, nor are they intellectually more astute. It is ironic that with all the gabble about the need to be 'positive', many of our cricketing hierarchy preface their remarks with an acknowledgement of Australia's cricketing superiority. We have long been far too deferential towards Australian cricket. What we ought to have been doing is saying, Yes, Australia is usually going to be, on paper, a bit better than us, but their players have weaknesses which can be exposed and we shall do it. But are the best cricket brains running New Zealand cricket?

I'm all for observing what people are doing in other countries, learning from it and applying it to our own environment, but the New Zealand cricketing psyche is quite different. Aping the Australian style is usually going to be a mistake. We need to mould, graft, modify. I think it's generally accepted that everyone needs to look to other nations to see what tactical and technical ideas can be picked up, but one never buys in holus-bolus to another country's systems and ways.

I keep hearing what Doig told me more than once: 'I don't know much about cricket, but I'm a good administrator.' He has made no secret of the fact that he has a big ego. To me it was a pity that all that energy couldn't have been used differently.

I told Dayle Hadlee that I'd had a talk to Bob Simpson who'd said he wasn't a great fan of their academy, and felt that it had many shortcomings. In effect I wanted to warn Dayle of the dangers of NZC taking it for granted that sending our players to Adelaide would be beneficial. Sending our promising leggie Greg Loveridge to Adelaide had ruined his confidence. I'm not sure that Dayle had all that much say in this for my feeling was that it was already a *fait accompli*.

During our World Cup campaign Doig had been sending through

written material relating to future player contracts. I had had no input into this material at all, and I felt that his timing was quite wrong. Ultimately it wasn't going to be my job to present contracts, but in the absence of Graham Dowling, and before Rod Fulton got pushed out, Rod and I had put in a lot of work on proposals for future contracts and I had committed it all to paper before we'd left New Zealand. I wondered why Doig didn't consult with me and Gren and Lee.

Players were having meetings and discussing the acceptability of terms and conditions while we were involved in the World Cup. To my surprise the players had deputed Adam Parore to approach sports lawyer David Howman and ask him to negotiate with NZC on their behalf. Parore collected money from players to pay for faxes back and forth to Howman in New Zealand. Adam was not flavour of the month for most of the players – few wanted to room with him – but in this case most players obviously felt he was the horse for the course. In a group Adam is more vocal than most, is quick, and can be relied upon to make the most of any opportunity.

When talking on the phone with Gren Alabaster, Doig said he wasn't at all happy with the way the players had responded. Doig's naivety can astonish. By not consulting me and others in team management he appeared to be acting unilaterally. But the players were not to know that. The reaction of some suggested that they assumed we were happy and *au fait* with the content of the material, the timing, and the way Doig had chosen to open negotiations. We weren't. Faxing his work through wasn't the right way. We felt this subject ought to have been advanced only after he'd sat down and talked it through with us.

While at Fisherman's Cove Gren Alabaster was faced with an awkward problem. We'd found that early on at Fisherman's Cove the team's daily expense allowances hadn't been getting through, so Gren said that any expenses for food and miscellaneous items could be put on his account and that individuals could pay him when the allowances came through. Once the allowances did arrive, a couple of days before we left, he told players to pay their own expenses. He thought that this had been happening, but when about to leave, he received a large bill for approximately 18,000 rupees (roughly NZ$750). It appeared that one or two players had either failed to clear charges they'd made to his account, or had decided to see if they could get away with putting additional expenses on Gren's account. Gren had quite a heated exchange with three players who he felt had been charging items to his account – Parore, Nash and Cairns. Gren and the players concerned got off the bus and went back into the hotel, and the players did acknowledge that some of the expenses charged were theirs. Nash was quite cooperative and apologised for it. Gren and Parore made two visits to hotel reception. In the end he felt he had cleared most but certainly not all of the expenses. It was unpleasant and Gren was pretty angry about it. The players weren't happy about being publicly exposed like this either.

Around this time Adam had told Gren that once the main part of the West Indies tour was over, he would have to come home and not go on to Bermuda with the rest of us. He said that the company he was working for, Coca Cola, wanted him back in New Zealand. Gren contacted Chris Doig and asked him to check with Coca Cola. Doig came back and said that Coca Cola denied that they were putting any pressure on Adam whatsoever, and that they were quite happy to see him complete the tour.

The dispute over charges on his expense account was the straw that broke the camel's back for Gren. It was at Fisherman's Cove that Gren, who had spent so much time trying to bring Parore in particular to order, admitted defeat. He said, to those of us in the management team and no one else, 'I give up. I think he should go home. I think we should replace him, not take him to the West Indies.' We thought about that and, although we understood the extent of Gren's exasperation, decided that we would persevere with him, again, and see what others thought after the West Indies. My rationale was that we didn't have players to burn. Unfortunately I think our tolerance was actually to work against us in the end.

Above: With Harold Bird, the English umpire best-known as 'Dickie'.

In Arab attire with commentator Henry Blofeld, right, and TVNZ producer Doc Williams in Sharjah.

Photography by Woolf

New Zealand v Pakistan at Basin Reserve, Wellington
Bank of New Zealand Series 1996

Back row: G.M. Turner (Coach), R.G. Twose, G.R. Loveridge, D.N. Patel, S.P. Fleming, C.L. Cairns, D.J. Nash, M.R. Plummer (Physiotherapist), G.D. Alabaster (Manager).

Front row: G.R. Larsen, A.C. Parore, C.M. Spearman, L.K. Germon, N.J. Astle, B.A. Young, D.K. Morrison

Top-level discussion between the cell-phoned modern manager Gren Alabaster, Harpreet Gill and Kieron Goodwin (both from the BNZ) at Eden Park, 1996.
Photo: Richard Redgrove

Below: Shell Cup captains Shane Thomson (Northern Districts) and Lee Germon (Canterbury) awaiting an interview with Grant Nisbett of TVNZ.
Photo: Richard Redgrove

World Cup Team and West Indies Touring Team, 1996

Back row: R.J. Kennedy, R.G. Twose, S.A. Thomson, C.Z. Harris, C.L. Cairns, S.P. Fleming, D.J. Nash. C.M. Spearman, M.R. Plummer (Physiotherapist)

Front row: N.J. Astle, A.C. Parore, G.R. Larsen, G.D. Alabaster (Manager), L.K. Germon (Captain), G.M. Turner (Coach), D.N. Patel, D.K. Morrison

Chapter 9

Fun and Games in the West Indies

Before we'd left Madras I'd had a long chat to Bob Simpson. I thought it would be good to pick his brains because the Australians had been the last side to tour the West Indies and I wanted his views and suggestions. He felt that the best bowling line of attack against the West Indians was simply to bowl line and length consistently and persistently. 'Don't try to bounce the top order out, however let the tail have it: they don't fancy it!' That was the gist of his message there. Of course we weren't able to succumb to the temptation to bounce their top order much because we didn't have bowlers able to do that.

Simpson said he was quite surprised to find how much the ball swung in the West Indies and he put this down to the fact that they were using Dukes, an English brand that is renowned for being a bowler's ball. He said that Lara really smashed anything wide but that he hit in the air through the covers, and that he preferred to hit square of the wicket rather than straight. He also said they had a group of players reluctant to graft at the crease, hence denial of scoring opportunities was very important. I was glad to hear that because it has always been my belief that when bowling to the better players, the fewer scoring opportunities you provide the more chance you have of capturing their wicket. Most top players hate to be tied down; they are accustomed to dictating play, that's why they are good. So a strategy of denial becomes an attacking strategy.

Bob said that the pitches gave uneven bounce, and that they deteriorated and became more and more uneven as games wore on. He felt that it was usually best to bat first in the longer form of the game, except in Trinidad where it could be damp to begin with. We had found that when I was playing way back in 1972, so little appeared to have changed there. He also said that we should be careful not to judge pitches on their appearance the day before a match.

This was because the ground staff put a lot of water on them, which they got away with because of the high rate of evaporation.

Simpson said that he felt the Australian off-spinner Tim May had bowled too straight and he thought it better to bowl a line slightly outside off stump. He also felt that the West Indies relied heavily on Ambrose and Walsh and that they had few good back-up bowlers. Benjamin appeared to be out of favour. The opening bowlers tended to bowl very short and Steve Waugh was highly successful because he let the short ones go, wouldn't hook, and was prepared only to cut wider deliveries. He said that the old days of the West Indies having four quicks to mount an unrelenting fast attack had gone. Simpson spoke of the need to assert a psychological dominance, which is something we all agree with, but you need to get on top first if you are to enforce and maintain that. It had been shown before that if you can get on top of the West Indians they do not respond very well. I might add that the same applies to the Australians and that, although it takes a while to rupture their self-belief, once you do knock in their cans, their self-doubt is glaringly obvious.

Simpson also had other information and advice, most of which we found to be accurate. He suggested we pick up our own cricket balls, say three dozen Dukes in London, and take them with us, and that all travel and accommodation arrangements be secured a.s.a.p. He said that the practice facilities were poor and that they'd experienced luggage difficulties when using smaller planes to travel between islands. Insist, he said, on gear arriving 48 hours before matches – easier said than done! – and on receiving expense allowances in U.S. dollars. Overall he found the islands' infrastructure and organisation on a par with India.

Bob said that their opening bowler Glen McGrath had been very successful because of his height and ability to get the ball to carry through between waist and shoulder height. McGrath was particularly effective bowling against the tail, and because he knew the West Indies quicks would bounce him, he didn't show any mercy and got rid of their tail smartly. With our resources we had to adopt a different strategy.

* * *

When we got to the West Indies we had to pick ourselves up, prepare for a testing time. Our first practice in Kingston, Jamaica, was on 18

March. We couldn't get on to Sabina Park so we practised in the middle on the Melbourne Cricket Club's ground. This meant that team members were able to come down at various times of the day. The English-born West Indian Dean Headley had come across from England to play for the Invitation XI which we were to meet on 23 March. Dean is the son of Ron Headley with whom I opened the batting for Worcestershire for many seasons. Dean started playing for Worcester when very young, struggled to make it there, went down to play for Kent and became a seam bowler for England. As he'd come out of the English winter he was keen for a good bowl so we were happy to use him, for it is much harder to obtain local bowlers in the West Indies than in India. We then had one practice in the nets at Sabina Park before the game, so it was clear that what Simpson had said about practice facilities was spot on.

Subsequently, Simpson was sacked as coach of the Australian team. A rumour circulated that Mark Taylor wanted more power but whether there is any truth in that I have no idea. I can say that Simpson spoke highly of Taylor and said that he was able to have good debates with him on matters relating to cricket. Interestingly Chris Doig mentioned to me that he didn't much like Simpson's style. My impression was that Simpson and I had somewhat similar views on the need to have solid structures, good routines and disciplines. I note that when looking across the Tasman, NZC didn't choose to approach Simpson to take over from me.

Our first game was a one-dayer against the University of the West Indies Vice-Chancellor's XI, quite a good side captained by Vivian Richards. The opposition had brought out Nasser Hussain, Dean Headley and Devon Malcolm from England; there was Maurice Odumbe, Kenya's World Cup captain, and the West Indian test players Chanderpaul, Holder and Adams. We batted first and gave them a bath. The invitation side opened with the young up-and-comer Patrick Thompson, reputedly the quickest bowler in the West Indies. He certainly charged in and got it through, taking 2-52 off 8 overs. He actually 'crusted' Astle – meaning he hit him on the head, but not seriously enough to do perceivable damage. We sent Lee Germon in at three and he stood his ground and whacked Thompson, making 29 in 25 balls.

Spearman made 42, Fleming 89, and Cairns a blazing 107 off only 73 balls. The opposition folded to be all out for 141 in 35 overs, Larsen

2-13 off 7 and Harris 1-13 off 6. Morrison got 2-31 off 7. This was the only lead-up match we had before five one-dayers in a row against the West Indies, but the lack of practice matches didn't really bother us because we didn't feel we were short of one-day cricket.

Chris Doig sent Gren and me a fax and referred to 'the splendid win in the opening game about which Don Cameron' had 'reported so glowingly in today's *Herald*. Lee's bravery and courage were given particular attention... Good stuff. Equally, all the people I spoke to in India were effusive in their praise of the team and your progress with them which made my job in negotiating tours considerably easier. Many thanks.'

We had a few extra days in Jamaica and had some fun. The makers of Coruba rum hosted us royally for a day on a small just-offshore island. Swimming, eating, drinking. Very pleasant. On another day we went across to Ocho Rios on the north coast of Jamaica and everyone liked that.

Three days later we fronted up to the West Indies at Sabina Park. We decided to continue with our policy of going for it in the first 15 overs and taking a long batting list into the game, having Patel at eight, Larsen nine and Nash ten. Astle made 41 off 46 balls but the rest of the top order flopped. We lost our fifth wicket at 70 and our sixth at 113 before Parore and Patel put on 111 together and we were bowled out in the 50th over for 243. Patel finished up with 71 off 63 balls and Parore 61.

When the West Indies batted they went well early then lost eight wickets for 73 runs to be 197-8, then 221-9. The West Indies looked dead in the water, gone. Unfortunately for us Harper and Walsh got them home with five balls left, about as close as you can get when coming second. Once again Larsen was the most economical bowler in the game with 2-29 off 10, highlighting just how serious was his unavailability through injury in the World Cup, and Harris did well with 3-45 off his 10.

The second match was at Queen's Park Oval in Port-of-Spain, Trinidad. Our only change was to bring in Thomson for Morrison. Batting first the West Indies made 238 for 7. Astle, Patel, Larsen and Harris were our best bowlers. Spearman got 37 off 47 balls but we were in danger at 71 for 4, then Fleming, who made his maiden one-day hundred (106 off 108 balls), Cairns and Harris provided the runs we needed to sneak home with one ball to spare. It was New Zealand's first one-day international win in the West Indies.

Already it was clear that the sides were evenly-matched and the series was set to be extremely close. The first two games could have gone either way. The games were proving to be thrilling and demanding, both mentally and physically.

Next day we fronted up again (two games in consecutive days!) at Queen's Park Oval. We played Twose instead of Nash who'd bowled 6 overs for 46 at Sabina Park and 6 for 29 and one wicket at Queen's Park. With Twose in the side our batting looked pretty strong when you consider that Larsen was relegated to last man in. Few sides could boast a more accomplished number 11. We had found that in the West Indies, as far as our attack was concerned, the faster we bowled in the opening overs the more quickly the ball disappeared over the boundary. For the third, fourth and fifth one-dayers we decided to open the bowling with Patel and Larsen, having concluded that dibbly-dobbly bowling (not a term I use in any disrespectful way) irked the West Indians who found it harder to score off than faster stuff.

Twose (48) and Astle (43) put on 94 for the second wicket, but Ambrose, Walsh and Simmons made it difficult and we battled to 219 for 8. Not enough. Even though Larsen took 3-26 off 8.4 overs, Lara got away and plundered 146 not out off 134 balls as the West Indies cruised to 225 for 3 off 45.4 overs. It had become increasingly obvious that if Lara got a big score the West Indies usually won, for he got his runs pretty quickly. Another example of how in one-dayers, more often than not a top batting effort, rather than bowling, wins games.

The fourth match was at Bourda, Georgetown, Guyana. We'd called for an additional player and got Justin Vaughan over from Auckland. After watching him have a long bowl in the nets we included him in the team at the expense of Parore. In retrospect, given the slower wickets in the sub-continent, we could have done with Vaughan in the World Cup.

At practice in Guyana on the day before the match, Cairns put on another performance. The ground at Bourda is small and there were no practice strips round the edge of the park, so we used the one and only in the middle on the main square and put nets around it. When practice started we didn't have as many good balls as we wished. Cairns was unhappy about this and started yelling at me, complaining about the lack of quality balls, much to the surprise of the quite large group of onlookers standing out on the ground. I just told him to get on with the job.

There was a moat around the outside of the ground. For it to 'come into play' as they say in golf, you had to hit the ball over the little stands around the ground. When Cairns came to bat he proceeded to belt one of the first balls he received out of the ground and into the moat. If a ball went into the moat it was effectively lost. After all we were on the South American continent, so what with the jokes about piranhas, no one was likely to willingly enter waterways. Bounding forward and roaring, he slogged the last ball he faced out of the ground, over the stand and into the moat once more.

It had got to the stage with Cairns that this sort of performance was typical of the man. We could have justified fining him every other day, or so it seemed.

Ideally we could have done with a few more quality balls, but what happens is that over time balls get lost despite one's best efforts to keep them. Every cricketer knows that. Thrashing balls out of the ground is one way of ensuring they get lost. Sometimes a team arrives at a ground and the person who has been looking after the balls announces that he didn't manage to pick them all up last time, or that more than usual have been lost, or that a box of newer ones had been left behind at the hotel, and so on.

When the Australians had played at Bourda they'd made quite a large total – about 270 – and we expected to be able to do the same. On a small ground and a flat pitch a side feels it has to make a big score to be competitive, and our batting strategy was geared to setting out to make 300. We hoped to reach 100 in the first 15 overs. Astle went for 20 off 16 balls at 55, our second went at 77, and our third at 90 in the 15th over. The 14th over had actually been a maiden. Spearman made 41 off 39 balls, Germon struggled a bit (19 off 33 balls) and then got run out. We weren't worried because we were set up for a really good total, but then we went haywire and with the exception of Cairns with 29 off 36, the others played badly and we collapsed to be out for 158 in 35.5 overs. Crestfallen is the word. We felt we'd completely blown it. I laughed to myself, for it seemed a bit absurd. My argument has always been that it doesn't matter when you are bowled out as long as you have the score to win, but we never dreamed that 158 would be enough. The crowd, for their one big game of the year, was dispirited to say the least. It was looking like a fiasco, another blow for Guyana whose currency had been greatly devalued and whose water supply was so dodgy that the hotel we were in had difficulty guaranteeing an adequate supply. They'd struggled, too, to complete games in their domestic cricket competition because rain had devastated many of them. So even though Guyana has, over the years, produced some terrific players – Alvin Kallicharan, Roy Fredericks, Clive Lloyd and so on – and currently had Harper and Chanderpaul in the West Indies team, clearly Guyana was going through hard times.

The stands at Bourda are small and low to the ground. The ground holds about 12,000 people and that's all, and the spectators are very close to the players. We were being booed and hissed at where we sat on the balcony near our dressing room, because it appeared that we hadn't provided much opposition and the game wasn't going to have been worth watching.

At 104 for 5 the West Indies looked home and hosed, but then they blew it and were bowled out in the final over for a miserable 154. Once again we'd opened with Patel and Larsen, and in the context of the game, Dipak's 10 overs, 1-35 wasn't especially economical, but Larsen was parsimony personified with 2-18 off his ten. Chris Harris took 1-23 off 10 overs. Vaughan also bowled well with 2-26 off seven, and so did Cairns and Astle. It really was a resolute, gutsy effort, and another cliff-hanger. Our 158 was the lowest total that New Zealand had defended in a 50-over one-day international.

Vaughan was actually a bit brassed off that he wasn't asked to bowl the last over, for he'd been bowling very well. Germon gave it to Cairns. Vaughan's reaction showed that he wanted to be put in the gun, wanted to face a pressure situation, and backed himself to do the job. That was heartening.

I tend to try to sit quietly on such occasions. I don't try to orchestrate responses to victories or losses. I prefer to let the team members decide that. When a side wins a close encounter – a gripping encounter like that – invariably they come in emotionally drained but elated. This was the situation, precisely, on this occasion. I sat back and really enjoyed seeing the satisfaction – admittedly laced with bewilderment – on the faces of the guys.

The crowd and the West Indies team were stunned. And the booing of us was profoundly absent.

So, two-all with the decider to come at Amos Vale, Kingstown, on the island of St Vincent. Well, so near... it was Lara, wasn't it, for if he gets a hundred, or any batsman does at the rate he usually scores (104 off 103 balls in this instance), the side often wins the game.

Our score of 241 for 8 was quite good. Thomson had a shoulder injury and Parore returned to the side. Germon (55), Fleming (75) and Harris (42 off 49 balls) were our best contributors but we struggled to up the run-rate throughout. Even though Germon and Fleming put on 120 for the third wicket, both had difficulty with their timing and were pretty exasperated.

The West Indies got home fairly comfortably thanks to Lara and Simmons (who made 103) and reached 242 for 3 in the 49th over. Towards the end of the West Indies innings I felt that they were on the point of panicking a bit – even though they still had plenty of wickets in hand it seemed to me that they were putting pressure on themselves in terms of the number of runs required per over. I don't think that our guys really appreciated that, and we relieved the pressure just enough to let the opposition back in.

Larsen bowled 8 overs for 31 and Vaughan 10 for 37 but none of the others could quite shut down the batsmen enough on the day. It was hard not to wince about the series. We were just so close to winning it.

* * *

Crowd behaviour can be very entertaining in the West Indies. At Sabina Park in Jamaica, where we played our first one-day international, the firm which brews the Red Stripe brand of beer had hired part of the spectator area. It's quite a big, grass-covered mound. Large speakers are mounted there and they pour out reggae music. If you pay $US 50-60 you can go in there and drink us much rum or beer as you like. New Zealand and the West Indies are the only two countries I know of so far that play music loudly at the grounds. At Sabina Park you got it blaring even between every ball.

The crowd is quite a sight – colourful, noisy, antic, writhy. Loose-limbs really movin', maan. It takes some getting used to, especially when they start doing the grind. Rubbing, gyrating, squirming and rubbing against others' bodies and from all angles... basically sex with clothes on. A sight to divert and behold. It is hard to avert the eyes.

The gyraters go on all day. They start before the match and go on after the match for two hours or more. One of the Red Stripe 'girls' came across and we had a chat with her. I asked, 'Don't you have a problem with drunkenness and so on? Isn't that a risk?'

'No no,' she said, ' there's no problems there.' They do get drunk all right, but they don't seem to misbehave to anywhere near the same extent as Australians and New Zealanders are prone to. The only real problem they'd had, she said, was the year before when the Australians were touring. She said some of their supporters got involved and became very drunk and obnoxious. They started throwing things and misbehaving. 'But of course,' she said, 'the white man can't drink.' So, not only can't the white man jump, he can't drink either.

Down in Antigua we experienced something similar. A guy there hires a section of the stand and puts a small stage out in front of his area. The stage is elevated, several metres above the level of the ground, on the first storey and right alongside where the players sit. The entrepreneur is a noted local character who puts on different costumes each day of a test match. One day he's there in drag and moves to the beat of the music; next day he appears as a cricketer and starts playing shots to the music. He looked as if he knew something about cricket for he had a fairly convincing range of attacking and defensive strokes, could be elegant and aggressive. I liked his poise and rhythm. Another day he appeared in a graduation gown complete with mortar board. But when we were there he had a problem with another guy who fancied himself in a similar role and kept getting up on stage and trying to upset him. So he went on strike for a couple of days.

The same gyrations and movements which were practised at Sabina Park were in evidence in Antigua. Booming reggae, lots of the grind. The rival – or interloper – who'd taken over from the regular performer was dressed in a red dress, rather like a cancan dancer. She was dancing away as Robert Kennedy walked down to fine leg and straight towards her on the stage. When he got to the boundary at fine leg she lifted up her dress and yelled out to Robert, no more than 10 metres away, 'Maan, you want to eat pussy?' Kennedy turned away, didn't know what to do or say. Thereafter, whenever Robert came down to that area of the ground, he got half way to his position, turned round and walked backwards for the remainder of the distance. His shyness and embarrassment were plain for all to see.

At the same ground in Antigua I watched a dwarf come in. I was sitting beside a West Indian guy just outside the dressing room. Watching the dwarf I said to the guy beside me, 'This could be interesting.' It looked as if the dwarf wanted to dance on the stage. My companion said, 'Oh, yeah, that dwarf there, he's a famous dwarf. He's well-known around the island here as one of the top reggae singers.'

In the group of revellers was a European woman who had been in Antigua for some time. She seemed to be dancing with every Curtly, Everton or Clive, and when the dwarf came along he wanted to dance with her too. It was highly entertaining. She got down on her knees so that he could perform the grind with her without him being disadvantaged.

Tetchy Times in Grenada

After the one-dayers we had a three-day, then a four-day match to get into test mode. The first game was a three-dayer at St Vincent against the West Indies Board XI and we saw a chance to give Germon, Larsen and Patel a deserved rest.

At St Vincent the surgeon John Heslop, a Life Member of NZC and an old friend from Dunedin, Gren Alabaster and myself were invited on to the yacht of American Paul Getty Jnr. He is a very keen cricketer, was chairman of the Surrey County Cricket Club and has his own cricket ground near Beaconsfield in England. Getty was sailing the Grenadines and timed his arrival to coincide with our one-day international. His private 'yacht' had two or three funnels and anchored just off our hotel. We were picked up by two of Getty's staff in a snazzy little fizz-boat and taken out to the yacht. Opulence? Rather. The loos were astonishing. One of our group returned and said, 'You must go and look.' Grand and shiny fittings galore!

One of the Grenadines is an island called 'Mystique' on which many famous people have houses. I was told old lips Mick Jagger himself was one. The whole team had a day out on a large keeler and stopped in on Mystique.

The hotel was well-located at St Vincent, right by the water, so anyone who wanted a swim could choose between the sea or the swimming pool. If you didn't want to eat in the hotel you could try the bar and restaurant a short distance away along the beachfront. There were locals willing to take us sightseeing round the island and I certainly did that.

An influx of wives and partners arrived in St Vincent and while this was pleasant for some, it posed problems that we could have done without. The pot gets stirred. Players reveal their anxieties, tell their partners about what they like or don't like about the way their tour is going. Partners get dragged into wanting to have an influence, quickly reach a conclusion as to whether their man is or isn't getting a good deal. A few went to Lee Germon's partner, Toni, and put pressure on her. It can become very tricky and disruptive.

My experience has been that the disadvantages of having wives and partners on tours outweigh the advantages. The truth is that the playing of professional sport, especially cricket, is a very selfish business. Wives and others can have an expectation that they are there for a holiday and they want their partners to be available. This of course can interfere with the practice and playing of cricket, and additional pressure goes on. Misunderstanding and disharmony is common.

Some partners understand this and are better at accommodation, are able to go off on their own where necessary. But the younger, or less experienced ones, find it hard. Most cricketers are too young to have established a tolerant, mature relationship, and that's what it takes. I was lucky with my wife when I was playing: Sukhi didn't understand cricket and wasn't really interested in it. When she was with me – not that she came on many cricket trips at all – she'd go off to museums and galleries, or visit friends; the last thing she wanted to do was get caught up watching cricket. In the West Indies, of course, it's very much an eating, sunbathing, socialising scene, and perhaps this creates more of a demand on partners.

I am all for arranging a holiday for players and wives and others at the end of tours. That gives everyone something to look forward to and time to unwind. It would also give players and management a chance to clear their heads, reflect, and not have to rush straight home to a barrage of post-morteming, and possibly witchhunting from administrators and media.

The night of the wives' and girlfriends' arrival was marked by a significant party at the home of an ex-pat New Zealander, Kelly Glass, who'd set up a successful business on the islands. Glass was into putting up telegraph poles and the like for tele- and other communications. He had his own small aircraft which he used to fly between the islands to keep his eye on the business. He had a lovely house on a big section; he invited the New Zealand team, wives, partners, and all his friends. One of the team stumbled on another in the foliage with his partner, both of them with their trousers round their ankles, and was highly amused to report that his teammate clutched his leg and tried to make him believe that he'd dropped his strides because he'd hurt his leg and wanted to examine it.

In the days prior to the arrival of partners some players had engaged in extra physical fine-tuning. Roger Twose ran back from practices and even swam across the about 300 metres of water between our hotel and an island. We were a bit concerned about that, because neither we nor he knew about the local tidal currents.

Shane Thomson's injured shoulder had prevented him playing in the final one-dayer, and Mark Plummer said the injury wouldn't allow him to play again on tour. The normal procedure in this situation is for the player to go home, and we had already organised for him to return. However Shane had arranged for his girlfriend to fly over from New Zealand, so we agreed to let him remain with the party until after the game in Grenada which was to finish in just over a week's time.

For the game against the Board XI, we decided to appoint Vaughan as captain. We knew this would disappoint some players, for there are always two or three guys in any team who think they should be captain. That is okay, as long as they don't undermine the one who is chosen. To our mind none of the pretenders to Germon's throne were candidates in the immediate future. I suppose the three who appeared to consider themselves the most suitable candidates were Parore, Cairns and Twose. Remember that Parore had told me the year before that he thought he was the logical person to succeed Martin Crowe should Crowe be captain again. And Cairns had often indicated that he thought he should be manager, coach and captain. Roger appeared to think that with his background in English county cricket he ought to be a serious contender.

Although we felt that Fleming might be ready to take over from Germon in, say, three years time, our management team decided to use the only player then captaining a provincial side in New Zealand – Justin Vaughan. He showed no sign of reluctance. To us Vaughan had more maturity than those vying for the position, but there was no doubt our decision caused a few waves. I don't think this was especially significant, for as Dipak Patel said to me earlier this year, there was a certain group in the team who were never going to accept what we were trying to achieve irrespective of what happened or how things were done. Nor were they ever going to fully cooperate with or support Germon. In the end I think Lee was surprised and disappointed to find that one or two of his Canterbury teammates were also less supportive of him than they ought to have been. Flickering ambition, or sensing an opportunity? Who knows.

Morrison says in his book that I gave Vaughan 'a hard time' when he chose to bat not bowl on winning the toss. Untrue. Beforehand, both Lee and I said our preference would be to bowl but as captain he could do what he wanted. In fact I didn't have a strong preference one way or the other.

We wanted to give Chris Harris a chance to gain more batting form by placing him at number 6. Cairns was not a happy boy. After the team was announced Cairns was thunderous and called for a meeting of our management group. He said that we were preventing him from reaching his full potential, that he should be number 6, that he wasn't just an all-rounder, he was a batsman and a bowler, etcetera. The toys were thrown out of the cot. I think Cairns's act here may have resulted from his being miffed at not having been given the captaincy. Our response was that we needed to think of the whole team, and that meant giving Harris the best opportunity to get into good batting form. We were gruff with him in this instance, asked him who he thought he was, and told him to have more thought for the team's interests. To us he'd been getting worse by the day.

As it happens, while I was coach Cairns played in 19 one-day internationals and batted at number 7 four times, 6 seven times, and 5 eight times. In six tests (nine innings) he batted at 6 six times, twice at 7, and once at 5. After my axing in tests between May 1996 and April 1998, in 14 tests (25 innings) he was at 6 nine times, 7 ten times, 8 five times, and once at 3.

While sitting watching the game against the Board XI I became disturbed by Cairns's conduct on the field. There was no obvious place for us to sit, so we tended to be amongst spectators. Some of them were irritated by Cairns's behaviour. He was being no-balled, and disputing it in a way that some felt was obnoxious. To me he abused the situation where Vaughan was captain: he abused the umpires. Vaughan didn't seem willing to reign Cairns in, presumably because he didn't want to be seen as too pushy given the reaction of some players to his appointment. I had a word with the umpires, basically apologised, and said that if there was any more nonsense they should let me know about it.

In the match we declared at 319 for 9 off 76.5 overs, the middle order of Fleming, Astle, Parore and Harris all batting solidly. The Board XI was bowled out for 158 with Cairns doing well with 5-29 off 14 overs, including an efficient mopping up job of three of the last four batsmen. In our second innings we declared at 204 for 7, Harris 55 not out. Batting last the Board XI could muster only 209, Kennedy, Morrison and Cairns all taking three wickets to give us a win by 156 runs.

We were a bit disappointed, and so was he, when Twose scored only 9 and 6 opening the innings, and from this time on his heart didn't seem to be in his cricket to the same extent. This was a pity because it was at a time when it was important that our leading batsmen got some decent batting practice for the forthcoming test matches, as I was to point out to him when we got to Grenada. Undoubtedly the arrival of his partner had a lot to do with it. Subsequently Roger admitted that he had become distracted. He also made it clear more than once that he didn't like touring, and that he'd have preferred to be back home setting up a business and being with his 'lady' as he called her.

Travel arrangements became quite chaotic at this time. Only small aircraft fly in and out of St Vincent and Grenada. We had difficulty getting our kit from one place to the other as it had to go on another aircraft – sometimes gear arrives late. The presence of players' partners also complicated the travel arrangements. Locally the airlines run what they call a bumping system; this means that seats are often double-booked and even though you have rung and confirmed your seat, you can arrive at the airport and be told that staff have decided to give your seat to another passenger. This system is quite widespread around the world these days, but it seemed worse in the West Indies. Gren Alabaster decided to try to please everyone and, although the team had agreed prior to the tour that travel arrangements for wives and partners would not be management's responsibility, he attempted to make arrangements for them all. He didn't get many thanks for it. Some of the women got bumped and didn't arrive in Grenada with their partners, and when they got to the hotel there was no guarantee of beds. Gren copped the blame.

We also found that one or two of the women had approached Lee Germon's fiancee Toni and wanted her to tell Lee that their blokes weren't being bowled enough, or weren't batting where they preferred to be in the order. We were quite concerned about the evidence of more than the normal simmerings of discontent.

When this sort of thing is going on it's easy to become distracted and start neglecting one's main purpose, the cricket. Danny Morrison hadn't played any of the last four one-dayers so it was important he get in some longish spells at the bowling crease against both the Board and President's elevens. He bowled 13 overs in each innings in the match against the Board XI, taking 4-70 overall, which was handy. But he was far from being overworked.

There was only a day in between our match against the Board XI and the first day of the President's XI game in Grenada. On the day before the match I said to the side, very calmly and politely, that the difficulties with travel arrangements, and the presence of wives and partners, seemed to be contributing to a lapse or two, and that we had to be very careful that our standards didn't slip. Gren remarked that I had been very restrained and polite.

The airport at Grenada was fairly modern. When the American military decided to intervene and eject the Cubans some years ago they built a very good airport there. The hotel where we stayed, by the beach, was also very modern and nice. There were a couple of small restaurants on the beachfront and it was close by these that the Pakistan cricketers had been alleged to have purchased some dope and smoked it the year before. Grenada is a noted little fishing port and the buildings are interesting and quaint. The roofs of shops, warehouses and houses are red-tiled, a colourful sight in contrast to the blue of the ocean. I gather the tiles arrived as ballast in ships and were off-loaded there. As for the cricket ground: very rural, the one small stand in a state of disrepair, the outfield only just adequate, and practice facilities virtually non-existent. But for all that a very nice spot for cricketers to visit, play or reside.

On the morning of the match against the President's XI the bowlers warmed up by bowling on the edge of the square on which the game was to be played. One of the umpires came up to me and officially complained. He said, 'I've asked your bowlers to get off the square and they won't do it. Will you deal with it, please. I'm not happy. As far as I'm concerned they're on the square and they're not allowed to be there.'

So I went out and spoke to them as a group. I said, 'I've had a complaint from the umpire. He's not happy. He says you're bowling on the square.' They indicated that they felt they weren't. I said, 'Well, it's marginal. You're half on and half off. But there's no point in arguing about it. The umpire doesn't want you on there, so just move across.'

They took no notice of me and carried on. So, I got grumpy and said, 'Get off the bloody square. We're not going to win this one. Just do it.'

To my surprise Gavin Larsen was as unhappy as the others. I thought, Gavin's reaction will pump up Cairns, encourage him. Sure enough, Cairns yelled at me, 'You never fucking well support us in things like this.' I'd said my piece and ignored him. Soon afterwards Mark Plummer was throwing balls to me and I was nicking catches to our slippers, when Cairns stormed over and said to Plums, 'Here, give me that fucking ball.' It was obvious he wanted to throw the ball at me. I said, 'Don't be bloody stupid, piss off.'

Subsequently Larsen said that he was pissed off with the umpire and thought the ump was being needlessly picky. I agree. Gavin said that his reaction was principally because he is 'big into fairness' and he felt the umpire was being unreasonable. The thing he was scared of was that he might 'turn an ankle on rough ground.'

A little later, Germ and I went out and looked at the pitch. We wanted two bats in the match, and because it was a four-day game, we thought this was assured. We felt there was a bit of moisture in the pitch so Germ decided to bowl. It's always necessary to remember that if there is a bit of moisture in a pitch and you bat first, you can lose the top order fairly quickly. And even though later in a match you can sometimes find the ball will squat, it still usually takes longer to get batsmen out. We wanted two full bats and thought it made no sense to risk the conditions. It was important that our bowlers got a decent bowl as well. So I'm sitting in the dressing room about 20-25 minutes before the start when Morrison comes in and says, indignantly, 'Aw, why are we bowling first?' I replied along these lines, 'You know the procedure. If you're a bowler you must be prepared to do your job first and you have to gear yourself up psychologically to do that. The same applies to batsmen. Fifty per cent of the time you don't have a choice anyway.' I looked at Danny and thought, How often have you got to tell these guys these things. Don't they claim to be experienced, mature, international cricketers? Then I said, 'We've talked about this before.'

'Aw, yeah,' he said, 'I know about that, but Christ, I've just bowled at St Vincent, I don't want to have to bowl again straight away.'

I said, 'You bowled 26 overs in three days up there. You've had a full day's rest. You've got to get ready for the test match. You think you've been overworked?'

I also pointed out to Danny that if we bowled first in the game then chances were he'd get an extra day's rest before the test match. Mind you, as the Grenada match was going to finish on the 15th, and the test wasn't to start until the 19th, so what?

Then, all of a sudden, Cairns appeared in the dressing room and started yelling, 'What the fuckin' hell's going on. We're bowling first. Do they see something that I can't fuckin' see.' I ignored that. He looked at me and wanted an answer. I very quickly said, 'Look, I've already been through this with Danny, I don't want to go through it again. Let's just get on with the game shall we.'

Cairns went out and bowled lollipops by his standards, no more than Gavin Larsen's pace. After about four overs Germ took him off for there wasn't any point in bowling him at that time. He'd basically gone on strike. When you get this sort of petulance and nonsense it creates a highly unpleasant, disruptive atmosphere in the dressing room.

Samuels played very well and his hundred earned him his first test cap. Reifer, batting at 5, also made a century and the opposition compiled 454. We were out there for 113 overs. When Cairns had spent some hours grazing safely in the outfield Germ brought him back on and he took the wickets of numbers 6, 7, 8 and 9 to end up with 4-66 off 15 overs. It would have been nice if he'd done a professional's job and put in the effort at the start.

Our batting performance was woeful and we were rolled for 113 in 34.1 overs. Beforehand I'd had a word with Roger Twose. We were planning to open with him in the tests. I said, 'Now listen, Twosey, we want to try to get you into opening form. You've wasted two innings in St Vincent due to extra-curricula preoccupations, so just try to get your head focused on the cricket and make good use of this game to find some form.' To his credit, he agreed with me. In the first innings he batted for 163 minutes and made 19, then for 44 minutes for 26 in the second when we followed on. Hardly a success, but at least he was trying.

In our second innings Cairns went out and slogged 94 off 71 balls. As he came in from batting I was sitting with Gren Alabaster just above the players' tunnel. It was almost behind the bowler's arm, so it was a good spot from which to watch the game. Twose had turned up and was in my ear. He'd heard that on the scheduled fourth day of the match – for it had become obvious that it wasn't going to be needed – I had planned an open wicket practice. I didn't realise it at the time, but Roger had made an arrangement to go scuba-diving with his girlfriend. He was trying to tell me that he should have the day off, and that we shouldn't practise. At the same time as I was listening to Roger, Cairns got out and walked from the ground. Suddenly there was an almighty crash. Gren and I were sitting in the front row. I said to Gren, 'Jesus, what was that!' Gren said that while Roger and I were talking, Cairns had looked up, abused me, swung his bat over his head and smashed it against metal tubing attached to part of the stand in front of us. In a way it was farcical: Twose ear-bashing me in the stand while Cairns was ranting and bashing below.

Germ, Alabaster, Plums and I agreed that we'd reached an all-time low with some of the guys. We could, for instance, have fined Cairns most days. We'd left New Zealand at the beginning of February and it was now mid-April. The question we were asking was, how do we hold it all together? I said to the others that as far as I was concerned, Cairns had stretched things beyond the limit. He'd created serious waves in the party. I said we couldn't risk going to Barbados for the first test and have Cairns pull the plug half way through the game. As far as I was concerned we needed to bring things to a head. So we discussed it. I said that with Cairns we'd had him in and talked things through several times. Maybe it was time to have one of those sessions that Nash had mentioned to me when I went to see him and Cairns and others in England almost a year before. To reiterate, Nash's idea had been that we hold team meetings similar to those run by Middlesex where everyone openly got things off their chests about other individuals and anything to do with cricket. I said, 'Maybe this is the time. We have got to show the rest of the team that we can't put up with this sort of nonsense any longer.' I thought and hoped, too, that it would clear the air quickly, and we could get on and put in a good performance in the tests.

That night after our loss to the President's XI, Germ said he had heard some fairly mutinous talk from a group of players (among them Cairns, Morrison, Nash and Thomson) sitting out on the balcony above his room. He thinks they meant him to hear it. Some of the players' partners were there, and Lee's partner Toni was being attacked, too. It was rich that Thomson was in on it; we'd kept him on the tour out of goodwill, when he was of no further use as a player. Some players who were present at the start of this bitch session left in disgust, saying they weren't going to have any part of it, that the talk was 'shit'. One player says he thinks Astle and Harris were two who left.

I called a special team meeting in Grenada on the evening of 15 April. Gren Alabaster had prepared a written statement which he wanted to present to the team. Everyone sensed that something out of the ordinary was imminent. Alabaster spoke, Germon spoke, some players spoke. I said that as far as we were concerned there was a small group trying to undermine management and railroad the team, and send us back to where we were 12 months ago. I made it clear that as far as I was concerned that was not going to happen.

I had barely got started when Twose and Nash piped up and wanted to have their say. (Nash had gone doggo a couple of weeks earlier and wouldn't communicate with anyone. He later apologised to Gren for having been so sulky.) I got stuck into Twose and said that to my surprise and dismay, three of the most unprofessional players in the team happened to be the English pros, which meant him, Nash and Cairns. (Some months earlier the umpire Peter Willey, himself a former England player, had told me that standards had slipped badly in English county cricket. I note that English umpires in 1998 were suggesting that it was time red cards were introduced in England, so that they could send players off.) Twose didn't like this. He was close to tears. Nash, possibly because he'd had experience of such meetings, had a bit of a smile on his face and chuckled.

Cairns tried to defend himself. I said to him, 'You didn't try at the start of this match.' He wouldn't admit that he was in any way at fault. Cairns's repeated childish and arrogant attempts to put me down had riled me. I didn't see how I and others could have been more patient or tolerant towards him. He was told that henceforth he was to cease undermining management, accept management decisions, and perform to the best of his ability at all times.

Morrison told Gren that he was going round patting players on the back and making up for the fact that I didn't do that. Gren replied, 'No, that just happens to be my style.'

Gren recalls a few players, 'putting the hard word on Flem to say something, because he was obviously saying things in the background. He said, "What do you expect me to do, shoot myself in the foot?" When Fleming was pushed he said "the trouble was communication". We then had a discussion along the lines that communication happens to be a two-way thing and it can't all be from the top down, it has to be from the bottom up as well. We then resolved to go away and try to communicate better.'

In discussions with Doig, Gren said that, 'When I was talking to him I said that this was the most communicated to, and with, New Zealand cricket team that's ever been sent away. I pointed out all the processes that they'd gone through before they went away. I said we saw the players every day, talked to them individually and as a group in the bus, in dressing rooms. We had news/information bulletins which we put up on my door, then delivered to their rooms. What more, I said, could one require by way of communication?'

Personally I can't think of much more. You ask players things but mostly they don't come up with much. In retrospect, Gren thinks that we'd have been better off with another player in addition to Lee in the management group. That would have, he said, 'perhaps, been politic.' Then the players, he feels, wouldn't have had any comeback, wouldn't have been able to say they weren't being communicated with, etcetera. Gren added, 'But our style – the size and way our management group operated – was far more liberal than any have been in the past.'

Chapter 10

Goodbye Adam, Goodbye Chris

Adam Parore had kept telling us that he had to return to New Zealand after the West Indies section of the tour, and that he wouldn't be going on to Bermuda with the rest of us. His job with Coca Cola had to come first, he said, and he'd told the company he'd be back immediately after we'd finished in the West Indies. We'd already told him that Chris Doig had checked this out with Coca Cola, but it didn't seem to register.

It is worth reiterating that the Bermuda tour wasn't an add-on, something sprung on the players at short notice. It had been arranged before we went to the World Cup and the players knew that. It was in their contracts. Parore had signed.

Of course no one – or few – were all that keen to go to Bermuda but we didn't have a choice. In other circumstances and at other times it may have been a more attractive prospect, but most of us were already looking forward to getting home. However NZC and the Bermuda Cricket Association had agreed that we would go there and play and it was part of our job.

In the meantime we had to focus solely on the tests against the West Indies. We were aware that most of the players hadn't had enough time in the middle leading up to the first test, so we'd arranged for the locals not to water the pitch that we'd just played on, and allow us to have an open wicket practice on what would have been the fourth day of our match against the President's XI. There wouldn't be a chance for a practice in the middle before the test in Barbados. Contrary to what some players thought, it wasn't intended as a punishment session.

To give a little bit of edge to the practice we decided that if a batsman nicked it and was caught, he was out. This keeps bowlers interested as it stops batsmen having a go at them without fear of the consequences.

It was astonishing at this practice to find that Twose, Nash and Cairns went on strike. They wandered around in the outfield, trotted or walked after the ball. Cairns goose-stepped and fooled around. Twose, when batting, nicked one and was out after about two overs. With open wicket practices you need all the players you have to field or the object of the practice is defeated. He was slow to come out of the dressing room after removing his pads and when he did he came over to me and said, 'Well, what's the point in me being here. There's nothing left in this for me.'

I said, 'Yeah, it would have been all right if you'd batted for a couple of hours while others fielded for you.'

What we did was give any batsman who'd failed a chance to bat at the end, but we didn't let them or the bowlers know that beforehand or it would have taken the edge off the practice.

* * *

From Grenada we flew to Barbados for the first test at Kensington Oval, Bridgetown. Barbados is easily the wealthiest of the islands. Lots of capital has gone in there and the place is very much set up for tourists. We stayed at the Rockley whose complex includes a golf course. There was another hotel within walking distance on the waterfront where we could eat if we wanted to, and charge the cost to our accounts at the Rockley. Some of us played golf, and quite a few spent an evening out on the *Jolly Roger*, which is like being on a shipboard disco cruising along the coast. It's easy for some, given the difficulties and friction that occur at times, to overlook the amount of pleasurable recreation and relaxation that is part and parcel of touring, particularly in a place like Barbados.

I'd had a close look at the scores and runs per over in the test series between Australia and the West Indies the previous year. In Barbados the West Indies had been bowled out twice for under 200. And even in Antigua, which is normally a flat deck, the scoring hadn't been high. I was keen to see the run-rates and found that during their four-match series the West Indies had scored at a rate of 3.08 per over and the Australians 2.84.

In pre-match discussions with the team I drew their attention to the fact that in a five-day test there would be a minimum required number of overs of about 440 (5 days at 90 per day less, say, 10 for changes of innings). That meant about 220 overs per team, so in order to get on equal terms it was probable that a team would have to make 600 runs or more. We spoke of the need for batsmen to let balls go, work out their best shot options, to be patient and set time targets, session by session. Although my cricket philosophy is that one shouldn't abuse the time available – as many overs as possible should be bowled, you should look to win the game from the outset, and so on – the reality is that a lot of one-day cricket makes batsmen look to score first, defend second, utilising their natural aggression. So what one tries to do is temper that aggression so that it's there for a long time. Players who come off a one-day series have sufficient shots in their repertoire to score at a good rate in tests provided they can occupy the crease.

Bowlers needed to persevere and be prepared to bowl at least 18 overs each per day, some more and some less depending on conditions and form. Everyone had to be determined to hang in for a long period of time. We also had to stop the petulant behaviour that had been a feature of the previous two matches where players, when having LBW appeals turned down or when being no-balled, were frequently questioning the umpires. It was almost as if the absence of match referees and the lack of TV cameras had contributed to the lapses in on-field conduct.

At practice prior to the test we found that the pitches in the nets were lively. After looking at the strip set aside for the match we thought it might be quite lively too. For about the first time only on the entire tour I stepped away from the nets for about seven or eight minutes. (The usual procedure was that we had two nets running and a batsman had seven to eight minutes in each net.) My old friend Don Chivers from Worcester had turned up at the ground and he beckoned me over. It so happened that while I was chatting to Chivers, Cairns broke down, left the nets and went inside. He didn't come to me. Mark Plummer went after him to see what was wrong. Cairns said he had tweaked a muscle but that he didn't require any treatment. It was the culmination of a period whereby he'd basically stopped communicating with the majority in the side, and certainly no one in management. Cairns had chosen not to inform the captain, manager or coach about his condition. It was clear that Cairns wasn't prepared to talk to any of us; he was even reluctant to communicate with Plummer. Mark told us that Cairns said he'd sustained an injury and that he had ruled himself out of any further part in the tour. I asked Plums if Cairns had indicated that he wouldn't be fit enough to play as a batsman either and he said, 'Yes, Cairns said he wouldn't be able to play in any capacity in either of the two tests'. Plums didn't really believe Cairns was injured. He felt it was just another performance from this player. To us Cairns basically just took off, on the eve of the first of two tests against the West Indies. Most of the players were pissed off with him pulling the plug at this time. Some of his peers had actually forecast his withdrawal. Hardly anyone bothered to see him off; he simply disappeared. It was sad and ridiculous.

As management we'd talked and talked to Cairns over an extended period and couldn't see any point in trying to talk to him yet again. He was better off out of it, for his sake and ours. (Interestingly Cairns wanted to come home from Australia when New Zealand had been knocked out of the one-day series there in 1997. The main, or only difference, between what happened in the West Indies and in Australia was that we were happy to see him go, whereas in Australia the present management insisted he remain, advising him that if he came back he'd never play for New Zealand again.)

When he got to England he tried to claim he hadn't been wanted as a batsman, and actually rang up Mark Plummer and wanted Mark to say that he'd been keen to stay on and play as a batsman if required. But Mark wouldn't play ball, despite pressure from Cairns, and was adamant that Cairns had said he wasn't going to be fit in any capacity for the rest of the tour. When Cairns got to England he told his county Notts that he was available to play for them immediately.

The person in charge of the pitch preparation in Bridgetown was Richard Edwards, also known as Prof, who was one of the few whites who'd played for the West Indies. He did well in New Zealand as an opening bowler on their 1969 tour. He had told ground staff to leave quite a lot of grass on the pitch: too much, in fact, for one end was matty. He wanted it to be a good cricket wicket, but I think he went too far. It actually turned quite a lot, and Adams, not a noted bowler, got it to sit up and grip in the coarse grass. He took 5-17 off 9 overs. The seamers also got quite a lot of help, for while the pitch wasn't quick, the ball bounced, and the game took a similar course to that of the test against Australia the year before. Only this time we performed like the West Indies did against the Australians.

The pitch was very different to the one I'd played on in 1972. Back then it was rolled mud and had quite a sheen on it, so the ball got through quickly. Bruce Taylor took 7-74 and the West Indies were out for 133, to which we replied with 422, Congdon 126 and Hastings 105.

This time we were bowled out for 195 in 62 overs, Parore 59, Astle 54, and Vaughan 44.

West Indies replied with 472 of which opener Campbell got 208 and Chanderpaul 82. The seamers stuck at it. Larsen bowled 40 overs, 3-76; Vaughan 2-81 off 34, and Harris 2-75 off 34. Morrison was in his 30th over when he got Thompson, their number eleven, to finish with 2-130.

Nash was injured and Cairns had vamoosed, so we'll never know if their presence would have helped.

Astle starred in our second innings when he made 125 off 150 balls in our total of 305. So we didn't capitulate even though a 10 wicket loss was emphatic, comprehensive. Parore strained a groin muscle when fielding and went in at number 7 in the second innings. After the match he went home. Before that, Mark Plummer checked the injury and said that it seemed serious enough to prevent him playing again on tour. So he didn't get to play in Bermuda after all.

Arrival of the White Knight

Chris Doig arrived while we were in Barbados. As far as we knew he had always planned to come, in part to discuss future tours by the West Indies. Given what was to follow I think that he was there in part to gather material to help him develop his case to get rid of me. I was clearly the problem, in his eyes; at that stage Lee probably less so, and Gren absolutely marvellous in every respect.

Unbeknown to me, Chris Doig was interviewed by Kim Hill on her Nine to Noon show on National Radio back in New Zealand. Speaking from Barbados, Doig was asked about Adam Parore's return to New Zealand and his reference to a 'summer of discontent'. Doig replied that Parore was 'grossly overstating the case' and that there was 'nothing new' when it came to Adam. Doig said there are problems 'in all teams... under all regimes', and that 'we've had ongoing difficulties with Adam in practically every team that he's played with.'

Further, Doig told Hill that he'd 'met with all the players last night' and found 'all of them focused, contented and ready to do battle in the second test'. Doig was at pains to point out that some strife was 'inevitable when players have been together for a long time'. He said Gren Alabaster had told him that he'd been home for only about 20 days in the last seven months so a 'certain amount of grumbling and disaffection' was inevitable.

Doig described Parore as 'difficult to fit into the team' and that 'some of his comments' should be taken 'with a grain of salt'. Parore, he said, 'is a player who will buck discipline if possible' and had been that way 'with New Zealand Cricket for a long time. It's unreasonable of him to say it's wholly because of Glenn Turner'.

There followed a long and tortuous explanation about Cairns's flight to England. The players and management were in little doubt as to why Cairns had packed his tent and his subsequent utterances were sometimes vague, sometimes evasive, sometimes contradictory. To team management, Cairns's departure was like the lifting of a heavy burden from our shoulders.

Doig said that 'New Zealand has a history of having difficulties with players', that he was 'a very good supporter of Chris Cairns', that he understood 'what makes him tick', and that Cairns wasn't 'being absolutely straightforward in saying' that he'd told Mark Plummer 'he was available to play in the second test'. Cairns, said Doig, had 'chosen a collision course with management' that was 'wholly inappropriate'. 'He's part of a team structure and the style that the team was going to use both on and off the field was discussed and accepted by the players prior to the tour, and therefore neither he nor Parore has a right to contravene it.'

Doig reiterated that there was 'a very good spirit in the side' and that they were going into the second test 'as a united group'.

When Hill asked if 'Parore and Cairns were too damaging to play for New Zealand in the future?' he replied, 'No,' and said they were 'strongwilled people who in this instance have not got their way with management and are frustrated by that and have reacted with a certain degree of petulance'.

Doig wrapped it all up by saying that we could 'hold [our] heads very high in terms of what [we'd] accomplished on this tour'. He said that the West Indies manager Clive Lloyd remarked that New Zealand had given them 'the best one-day series they've had', and that Clyde Walcott, Steve Comacho, and Peter Short had told him we were 'one of the most popular sides' to have 'visited the West Indies'.

Little did I know at the time that, as the English say, Mr Doig would prove to have more faces than Big Ben.

* * *

The second test was at St John's in Antigua, the ground where Lara had made his world record test score. So it was a ground noted for runs, although when the Australians had played there the season before scoring had been quite low: West Indies 260 and 80 for 2; Australia 216 and 300. Because there was a hint of moisture in the pitch, and because we thought that if we were to have any chance of winning we needed to bowl first, Germ asked the West Indies to bat. Our strength still lay with our seam bowlers rather than our spinners, so if there was something in the pitch it was more likely going to help the seamers early rather than later. Germ and I discussed the pros and cons of playing Kennedy or Mark Haslam who'd arrived to replace Thomson, and I left it to him to make the call: he went for Kennedy. We had Patel and Harris in the side so presumably he felt that was adequate slow bowling resources.

Batting first, the West Indies made a massive 548 for 7, Samuels 125 and Adams a big 208 not out. Our guys stuck at it, bowled 166 overs. All except Kennedy bowled 25 or more overs; Patel 38 in all, taking 2-131 and Harris 2-83 off 35.

Our reply was impressive. Spearman made 54 and Astle became the tenth New Zealander to score a test century in consecutive innings when he made a gutsy 103 in 217 minutes off 165 balls. Fleming 39, Vaughan 26, Harris 40, Germon 49, and Patel 78 at number 9, contributed to the total of 437.

When the West Indies went in for the second time our bowlers did a great job. At the end of the fourth day they were 146-7, Lara 74 and Campbell 34. That night I called a team meeting. Beforehand Germ and I exchanged ideas. Both sides in the match knew that time was of the essence. The pitch was now very slow-paced and difficult to score quickly on, but not hard to stay in on if you decided simply to bat time. Nevertheless we were determined to try to force a win. So we needed urgency on the last day. Morrison was invited to soften up Ambrose, and privately Germ and I discussed field placements. We emphasised the need to get through the overs quickly for we knew that if the West Indies were in trouble, when bowling they simply slowed down their over-rate. This is a very effective tactic because short twilights and rapidly failing light is a major worry for the batting side in the West Indies.

The next day they scratched their way to 184. The pity was that they took up 15 overs which made our task harder. Morrison, after a desolate 0-124 in the first innings, gave his best performance of the tour, 5-61 off 20 overs. The prevailing wind had sprung up and was blowing in from about extra cover to the right-handers. Danny took advantage of this and got the older ball to reverse swing, and it was this movement rather than pace which got him wickets. The ball moved away from the left-handers and he got Samuels then Lara, too, after troubling him for a while. He could have had Lara a few times before Fleming caught him at slip. Morrison also bowled another left-hander, Chanderpaul. Vaughan strangled the batsmen to the point where his 3-30 came from 16.3 overs. Larsen also kept it tight, 1-27 off 11, and Kennedy 10 overs for 30.

We never had a debrief after this test because it was the last game, but I was dismayed when we bowled only about 12 overs in the first hour on that morning. I could not believe how sluggish our guys were. The lethargy was obvious. I got irritated with them. For instance, Morrison, after bowling an over, would wander down towards fine leg, not get there and turn round just as the next bowler was running in.

However, we'd been left with a winning chance; not a big chance – 296 runs off 75 overs (just under four an over) – but a definite chance all the same.

When we went out we were determined to give it a real go. But at 39 for 3 we were in trouble. Ambrose and Walsh were a handful. Their height makes them troublesome, even on a slow pitch, when they put in a big effort. They were trying. For our part we weren't going to give them a victory, so we had to consolidate for a while. When it became obvious neither side was going to win, the game was called off early with Fleming not out 56 after a very responsible, gritty four hours at the crease. The pitch had got slower and slower, making it nigh-impossible to up the scoring-rate.

We felt that we'd competed well and that given more time would have been in with a chance of a win. Given the recent ructions we were also pleased that we'd shown some steel. After the frustrations and upsets in Barbados, and the departure of Cairns in particular, there was a sense of relief and a more relaxed atmosphere about the team.

Last Days in the Caribbean, then Bermuda – Reviewing the Tour

Although everyone wanted to go home, and hardly anyone wished to go on to Bermuda, I was admiring of the way our guys performed there. Bermuda was nice: nice weather, nice accommodation on a golf course resort, nice beaches. Ten minutes on a ferry to the downtown area.

We had a full programme so there wasn't a lot of time for R and R. It's the sort of stopover that might be better scheduled as a prelude to a major tour. Bermuda's a smallish island of the sort that leads to what's called 'rock madness', so the wealthy break out to-ing and fro-ing to New York.

We just let things wind down. No team meetings, no talks on tactics, but we still wanted to play well and acquit ourselves appropriately.

We played on small grounds with very ordinary pitches against teams which were mostly made up of ex-pat West Indians. They were for real, really got stuck into the games, and in one instance the opposition was ugly, and engaged in an unusually excessive amount of sledging. Some of our guys were a bit taken aback by the extent of the enmity and were given to say, wryly, 'And to think that we had gone out of our way to come here when we'd far sooner have been back home with family and friends!'

We scored 383 in 50 overs against BCB President's XI on the Somerset Ground, Spearman 110, Mark Bailey (whom we'd called over when Parore went home) 100, and Harris 67; then bowled them out for 143 in 42.2 overs. Against St George's Cricket Club at Wellington, Harris made 160 of our 269 for 9 in 49 overs, to which they replied with 153 in 34.1 overs. Bermuda scored 177 batting first at Lord's Cricket Ground in St David's and we got them in 44.2 overs for the loss of 6 wickets, Astle 64 and Harris not out 47.

* * *

During the West Indies tour we had continued to work on developing a style of play and tactics which would improve New Zealand's performance in the long- as well as the short-term. That's not easy, of course, because individuals have their ideas, and wish them to be followed. One soon finds that players' ideas change, swing back and forth, depending on how they feel at the time. It's not just because they are fickle, it's the emotional and physical wear and tear of the game. Their current form influences their thinking, naturally, as does whether they feel their position in the team is under threat. What can happen then is that they put self ahead of the team's requirements, and team plans and consistency are the first casualties. Individuality of shot selection, of course, is fine, but it has to be with the intent of furthering the team's tactical plan and style of cricket. A coach will sometimes get it wrong, as players do, but in the main the coach should know more than the player. The coach should have a more experienced background and knowledge base to draw from, and what is more, his decisions are more likely to represent the good of the whole.

In the West Indies one official said to me, 'You don't have any fast bowlers, but we appreciate the way you use your medium-pacers, the way they use their brains.' In the limited-overs matches it wasn't just a question of us getting the most from our slower and slow-medium bowlers, it was that we had bowlers – Larsen, Vaughan and Harris, and Patel too, generally – who we could normally rely on to bowl well enough to get through their full quota of 10 overs each. This was an advance on what had pertained at the World Cup. Unfortunately, in the World Cup, with Larsen out, we didn't have one bowler on whom we could rely to bowl 10 overs, although Harris came on in that regard later.

We also felt that we were starting to get used to a one-day system where, with Germon at three, we were able to have left- and right-hand batting combinations and a depth of batting right down to number ten and, sometimes, eleven.

Our decision to use bowlers like Larsen in the first 15 overs was also seen as a brave, new and effective tactic. I felt that by bowling him early we got even more value from our best one-day bowler.

The two tests were seen as something of an add-on by West Indian authorities. The one-dayers were given priority. Two tests really doesn't sort out which of the teams is clearly better – unless you have mis-matches such as the 1998 New Zealand-Zimbabwe tests in New Zealand – but what they did prove to us again was, that *at that time* we were better to use our slow-medium bowlers and create pressure that way.

Most of the New Zealand bowlers who are deemed quicks at home are not quick at all by the standards applied by other international sides. Wicket-takers are not guys who mistakenly think they are quick, they are guys that run up and put the ball in the right place time and time again, and get the percentages working for them so that if the ball moves off that ideal line and length, then they are likely to be in business. When it doesn't they are still bowling dot balls and exerting pressure that way.

We didn't have a Glen McGrath or an Ambrose or a Walsh. We had one bowler, Danny Morrison, who at one point in his career was capable of tickling a few batsmen up with pace but couldn't any longer; we had Nash, injured for quite a lot of the time, who was no more than a brisk medium-pacer when fit, and who relied more on movement than pace, but at that time was still lacking some consistency in line and length. We had a young lad, Robert Kennedy, promising but who sprayed it a bit as he was still learning his trade.

Now and then mention was made of the fact that we could have done with Simon Doull, and why wasn't he there? He may have been if he hadn't been injured back in New Zealand prior to the World Cup. Shrimpton and I asked Rick Pickard to find out about Doull's condition and prospects. Pickard came back and said that he'd been advised that Doull had a serious leg injury which would keep him out for quite some time, if not for good. As Rick was in the Northern Districts region we assumed that he would have been given the right story and we accepted it.

Our spinning resources were limited. Wouldn't New Zealand have loved to have the likes of a Warne or Mushtaq, those who come into their own especially in the longer form of cricket and get people out.

The batsmen were making progress. Astle for one showed that, even in the West Indies against their bouncier bowlers, he could play well. His two hundreds were impressive. His hundred in Barbados was on a bouncy pitch. I liked his fearlessness against Ambrose and Walsh, his general willingness to tackle anyone. There's a lot to be said for someone who backs himself and can score quickly. It was disappointing to see his batting go back in Australia in 1997.

Germon was most useful going in high in the order. Basically Lee was a middle- to lower-order batsman who was in the same parish as the quickies. In other words he was able to catch up with the quicker bowlers, which meant he was good enough at times to go in at 3 and have a reasonable chance of success. With his natural aggression this enabled us to lengthen our batting order. Lee was not one to duck a challenge. And, as he showed in India, he was more capable than most against spin.

Fleming was starting to play spin fairly well in India, better than he often showed in Australia and New Zealand in 1997-98. Flem is naturally a fluent player, likes to play shots, and with the right assistance could become a very good player indeed.

Craig Spearman did not get very big scores for us but he was decidedly useful, especially in the limited-overs games in the West Indies. He got his runs quickly at the top of the order, got us rolling. In 10 innings in tests for New Zealand, at the end of the 1996 season, Spears had scored 352 runs at 35.20. Spearman was similar to Astle in that he had a fearlessness, a confidence that wrests the initiative. In our low-scoring one-dayer in Bourda, Guyana, which we won, he top-scored with 41 off 39 balls. The fact that he was whacking their attack, and wouldn't allow Ambrose to bowl his overs cheaply, got us away to a good start. Spearman was learning, was on the way. Spears was easy to manage and coach. Since the West Indies I think he's had a rough deal.

Harris became very useful all round, both with bat and ball, in one-dayers and in tests. He had trouble with the quicker bowlers. His foot movement meant he struggled to catch up with them – at times his feet didn't move in the right sequence. So Harry was more of a middle-order player. However, as a left-hander, it is worth moving him around in the order. He was capable of coming in and attacking from the outset or, as we've seen in more recent times, pushing it around and lifting the side to a respectable total. There's no doubt that Harry can cane spinners. He was very handy as a bowler in the tests and took some wickets. He is an excellent fielder. Good to have in a team. His absence from test cricket in recent times seems to me illogical.

As for other batsmen ready for introduction into the national side, I would have brought in Craig McMillan in 1996. A very promising player, a clean hitter and capable of development into a top performer at both test and one-day level.

These players were well able to play the sort of game and style we

Left: My pre-match pitch report at Hamilton in 1997. I have my shoe off showing how it slides on the sheen on the pitch. *Photo: Richard Redgrove*

Above: John Morrison and I in the commentary box at Lancaster Park. *Photo: Richard Redgrove*

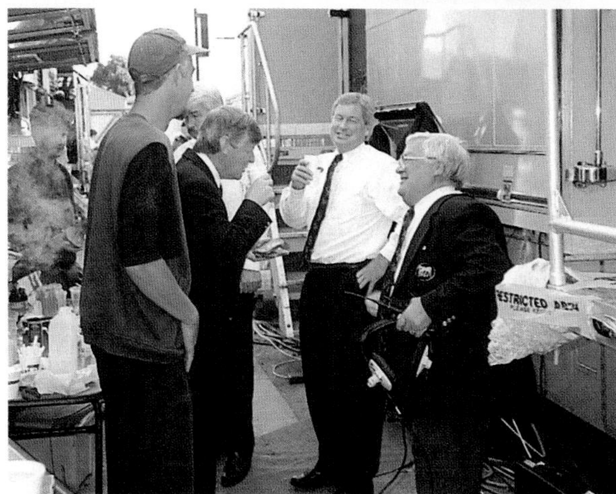

Left: Some of the crew and commentators breakfasting between two TVNZ outside broadcast vans in Christchurch. From right: Jimmy Biggam, Ian Smith, me, John Morrison (obscured) and Robert van der Laan. *Photo: Richard Redgrove*

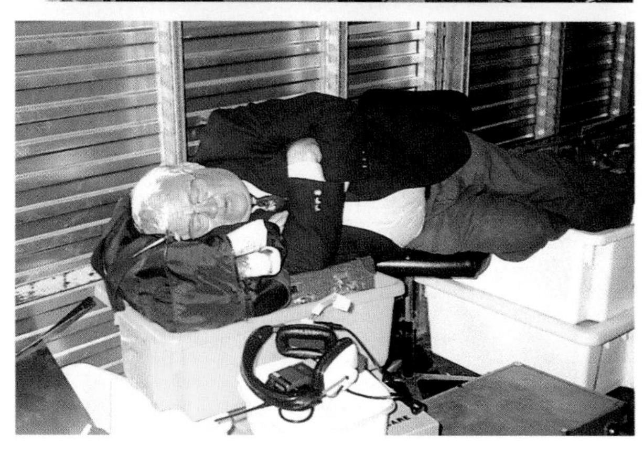

The Unit Manager, Jimmy Biggam, hard at work recovering from his labours. *Photo: Richard Redgrove*

Cartoon by Garrick Tremain
courtesy of Garth Gallaway

On top of his game. New Zealand Cricket's CEO Christopher Doig at the Basin Reserve. *Photo: Richard Redgrove*

Above: At Mt Hutt, doing a promotion for Ski New Zealand. From left: Shaan, Natasha, me, Annelise Coberger, and Sukhi.

Down memory lane. Revisiting my old club's ground at New Road, Worcester: Natasha, Shaan, me, and Sukhi in 1994.

Right: Sukhi and I in period costume during Otago's 150th anniversary celebrations, 1998.

were refining and the signs were very encouraging. Conviction, confidence and faith was evident.

All of us charged with the management and development of the side felt that we had made progress towards developing better cricketers and restoring widespread respect for New Zealand cricket. But what we had also provided, because of the length of time we had been on tour, was an opportunity for some players who were hell-bent on getting their own way to concertedly work at destroying what we had been trying to achieve.

The tour over, and before we left to return home to New Zealand, Alabaster, Germon, and myself sat down together and I suggested we each write down a list of the players we'd not take on tour again, if it were our choice. There was no prior discussion, apart from deciding that we'd use three categories: those we'd rather not have; those we'd maybe have; those we'd be happy to have. We dropped our lists on the table. Somewhat to my surprise we'd all written down the same names on the rather not list. We had four names on that list, and three on the list of maybe nots.

It will come as no surprise that Cairns, Parore, Thomson and Morrison appeared on our no thank you list. Morrison was there because we felt he was no longer worth a place in the side. It was only when I read parts of his autobiography in 1998 that I realised the extent to which he was anti our team management, not to mention the number of his misconceptions.

The truth was that in terms of ability New Zealand did not have, at that time, any players who were rated as exceptionally good by international standards. I disagree entirely with anyone who asserted that the New Zealand cricket team could not hope to compete internationally, or in spectator appeal, without the presence of its more notable recalcitrants.

We had also had time to sort out which players weren't going to make it as players at international level. There was a group of emerging players coming through, some of whom were ripe for inclusion. We knew where we were going in most respects and felt we'd got to the point where we were poised to present to the New Zealand public a team that they could admire.

The phase on which we were ready to embark over the next year was to get together a group of players whom we knew would work well as a unit. We may have had to take a punt with one or two, but not many. Having said that we still felt we were in a development stage. There are no quick fixes in cricket. But we were sure that removing a few players would improve team structure, behaviour and performance in every respect. This could only have been to the benefit of any new players that were introduced. New Zealand cricket would have become more enjoyable and rational for both players and supporters. This does beg the question, 'What provides enjoyment?' Of this I am sure, unless the players respect each other, even allowing for difference and differences, then a side will not function well.

But I don't think it's good for things to become too cushy, not if you are trying to stretch players and get them to extend themselves and improve their performance both in their own and the team's interests. International competition isn't comfortable. Teams that become too pleased with themselves, too relaxed, get lazy and complacent. It sounds calvinistic I know, but a side has to maintain good discipline and a rigorous work ethic if it's to achieve a lot regularly.

No team runs smoothly all the time, nor will it, so there have to be limits. A few New Zealand players repeatedly went far beyond acceptable limits. We made no apology for seeking greater integrity all round: we were determined to get rid of the sledging and to insist that other people be treated with more and due respect. Many, if not most adults I speak to with an interest in cricket, hope the members of the national team come across as good role models for their kids. They feel there is an absence in some quarters of such role models and they did not – and to some extent still do not – feel that cricket has yet met that expectation.

Lee Germon's wife, Toni, is a teacher. She's listened to players say they don't want to be role models, they just want to play cricket and be paid for it. That annoys her. She's told them of kids who see them as role models and act like the players. 'I've told them they are role models whether they like it or not.'

By the end of the West Indies tour I thought that the majority of the New Zealand players had improved in every respect related to the practice of being an international cricketer. A few had got worse and would not, or were unable, to take the step up.

* * *

On our last cricketing day in Bermuda Doig, now back in New Zealand, sent Gren Alabaster a fax. His purpose was to inform Gren, and ask him to let me and the team know, that the NZC Board had decided, on his 'recommendation to engage the services of Robin McConnell, an expert in elite team leadership, & coach-player interaction' to interview everyone shortly after we got home. McConnell's report was 'to form the basis of a report to the Board on the season's achievements, the strengths and weaknesses of the current system & make recommendations as to what might be a better and more complete management & coaching structure for future New Zealand teams.' McConnell, said Doig, had been 'highly recommended by Laurie Mains' the All Black coach and by the NZ Hockey coach Keith Gorringe. Doig said the NZC Board was meeting in Christchurch on 24 May and he hoped to have McConnell's report by then.

That fax turned a few heads, came as a surprise to us. The feeling was, 'Oh, so we're going to be put on trial. That's interesting.' I didn't like this, didn't like the fact that Doig hadn't discussed it with us, particularly since he'd been in our company less than two weeks earlier, but it's not my nature to automatically think *conspiracy.* I was and had been so preoccupied trying to make things work that I hadn't thought of the politics going on. I don't think any of us, at this point, foresaw what was to come.

Chapter 11

The Stealthy Inquisition: Fact, Fiction and Evasion

It was to become clear to me before very long that Doig and his confidants thought Gren was marvellous and popular, an admirable figure, and that they had thought, or hoped, that the players shared their view. Doig and others preferred to assume that Gren was the one largely responsible for any success the team had: it was convenient to attribute our success to someone other than those they wanted to replace. Subsequently I learned that Lee Germon was deemed a major problem, and that I was seen as completely irredeemable. No one has been able to explain to me how Lee, so highly thought of during his years as an unusually successful Canterbury captain, could have become chronically unacceptable so quickly. As I've said elsewhere, to me Gren did a very good job, was even-handed, extremely patient and fair. But what Doig hadn't realised, ironically, was that some of the players were more averse to Gren as manager than to me as coach.

When gathering material for his report, McConnell talked to me and Gren but NZC did not follow up by giving us and Lee Germon the chance to jointly discuss the report with them and the Board.

We were angry that Doig, as CEO, and his Operations Manager, John Reid, weren't prepared to give us that opportunity. We all might have learned something. We felt that it was extraordinarily arrogant and presumptuous of Doig, and then Board Chairman Sir John Anderson when he declined our request, to disregard our months of experience with the team as a whole. I found it a slap in the face. One just does not treat people and employees that way. (Soon after my demise I learned that a former employee of NZC, who left after the arrival of Chris Doig, had taken a personal grievance legal action against NZC, and that another was seriously considering it.)

There was to be a meeting of NZC's Board on 24 May. Presumably, I thought, the Board would spend a good deal of its time discussing and considering the performance of the national side and its management, both home and away, over the best part of the preceding seven months. I assumed that the Board members would be keen to pick the tour management team's brains.

Personally I felt a mixture of relief, bemusement and satisfaction to be home, but before long it became starkly clear that Doig and Reid in particular, thought that the players had had a rough time.

At the time I was unaware of the extent of the weevil workings behind the scenes. Not long after I'd got home the *New Zealand Herald*'s Don Cameron told me that no sooner had Doig arrived in the West Indies than he had asked him, 'Who are we going to get to replace Turner?' For a start Cameron thought Doig was joking, but it soon became apparent that Doig was keen to discuss this, was for real.

While we were in Antigua a New Zealand journalist, Martin Davidson, had approached me and said that in New Zealand Martin Crowe had been reported as saying that I lacked compassion and sensitivity, etcetera. This was after Cairns had done a bunk. Crowe also rang up Murray Deaker's sports talkback programme, off his own bat, and told listeners much the same thing. At the time I didn't realise what was happening, but in retrospect I should have recognized the same old troops were mustering again.

The players' payment structure remained contentious. After discussions with the players in mid-1995 it had been agreed that contracts would be offered to them within a couple of weeks of their return from the West Indies. Doig knew this and had acknowledged it when speaking to me on the phone when we were in Trinidad at the end of March. He said that we were to give him a list of names and that they should be put into three categories, A, B, and C. The category would be used to determine the size of retainers and other aspects of players' contracts.

The players expected contracts would be offered to them by the end of May 1996. When I arrived home on 15 May I was ready to make my recommendations to the other selectors, Pickard and Shrimpton, as to who should be included in a national squad to undergo winter training. And, of course, to make our recommendations as to which category the players should fall into for contract purposes.

Doig decided to put all this on hold and gave me no reasons. I found this odd, and saw it as a breach of faith with the players. But, aside from a discussion with Robin McConnell, who was preparing a report for Doig and the Board, I had to write a tour report myself which had to be ready for NZC's Board meeting on 24 May. (McConnell informed me that he told NZC that he found me to be 'friendly, communicative, direct and open' and the phrase appeared in his report to the Board.)

Apart from what I wrote in my report, I hoped to be able to arrange a separate meeting with the Board in order to discuss the previous few months, go over concerns, and look at changes and plans for the future. Generally bring them up to speed, for it was mostly a new Board. I was never able to do this.

A couple of days before the Board meeting Doig rang and told me that I had come out of McConnell's report okay but that Gren Alabaster hadn't. Both Gren and I were to be given separately a few minutes each to table our reports to the Board. Doig asked me to shift my time-slot on the agenda so that I came up after Gren. This was so that I could answer any concerns they might have had about him. Doig was keen to see Gren continue because he thought he'd done a great job. He wanted me to rebut the comments on Gren's performance as laid out in McConnell's report. Neither Gren nor I had been shown McConnell's report. McConnell said he insisted that Doig at least allow him to discuss parts of the report with me before he, McConnell, talked to the Board about it. Doig wasn't prepared to let us see it, but later, during a meeting with Doig and Reid, I was able to look through McConnell's report.

However, I certainly thought Gren had done a very good job, and was more than happy to say so to the Board. Therefore I went along with Doig's request that I swap time-slots with Gren even though it looked like manipulation to me.

The Board Meeting

I had been looking forward to presenting my report on the period from October 1995 to May 1996 and discussing it with the NZC board.

As it turned out, I don't think it was an important part of the agenda for the Board, as very little comment or discussion was forthcoming. No one asked me to explain or elaborate on any aspects of my report, but I assume readers will be interested in some of the comments I made concerning the players.

I said that as captain Lee Germon did an excellent job under very difficult circumstances. He was better than just handy with the bat and proved to be very versatile in where he batted in the order and the type of innings required.

As wicket-keeper he was always adequate and sometimes much better than that. Occasionally the captaincy appeared to affect his concentration, and as he preferred to stand closer than many 'keepers he got beaten for pace at times.

It's interesting to compare his batting results with other 'keepers who have played for New Zealand. By the end of the 1995-96 season Lee had played eight tests (13 test innings, 268 runs at 26.80), enough to give a fair indication of what could have been expected of him if we'd continued together. Other New Zealand 'keepers: Tony Blain, 20 innings at 26.82; Arty Dick, 30 at 14.73; Warren Lees, 37 at 23.57; Frank Mooney, 22 at 17.15; Adam Parore, 46 at 26.80; Eric Petrie, 25 at 12.90; Ian Smith, 88 at 25.56; Ken Wadsworth, 51 at 21.49; John Ward, 12 at 12.50.

In one-day internationals Germon had had 19 innings at 25.06; Blain, 38 at 16.37; Lees, 24 at 11.31; Ervin McSweeney, 14 at 8.11; Parore, 50 at 34.78; Smith, 77 at 17.29; Wadsworth, 11 at 30.20.

Lee was a good listener and where we agreed on a policy he mostly actioned it, but as captain it was always his call. He prepared well for team meetings and delivering team talks. Lee's a clear thinker, puts words together well, is concise and constructive. He doesn't suffer fools easily and doesn't always put things delicately. Germon was totally committed to the interests of the team and to improving the performance and reputation of New Zealand cricket.

I respected Nathan Astle's abilities and approach. I said that he'd developed from just a one-day player into a test player, and that with more exposure to top class spin, and a tighter approach to playing the new ball, he had the potential to make double hundreds.

As a bowler I said Astle was useful as a cover in limited-over games, that he had the potential to be better than that, and that he needed to work on gaining more movement from the seam.

In the field Nathan was very versatile, had above average hands at second slip, was a good mover who anticipated well inside the circle, and had a strong arm but needed to work on accuracy.

He tended to give his wicket away too often but by the end of the West Indies tour was not as reckless as he had been.

His attitude towards team requirements was good. He worked

well with others, was always prepared to cooperate and support decisions, though he didn't fully understand that in some situations batting recklessly doesn't help the team.

Astle practised well, considered others at practice, didn't expect special concessions and got on with the job. He had no injury problem, had good mobility and stamina, and wasn't physio-dependent. I found Nathan didn't ask many questions but did listen and made an effort to improve his play. Perhaps his easy-going personality didn't always help him take a tough enough approach.

Nathan was a good timekeeper, didn't go in for brinkmanship like a few others and had a healthy zest for living. I found him pleasant, well-mannered, and sometimes shy with strangers, but he related well with his peers.

Stephen Fleming was a gifted striker of the ball still well short of reaching his full potential. This was not surprising given his age and experience, and was partly because he played quite loosely and struggled to apply himself for long enough periods to make big scores more often.

Fleming had the best pair of hands in the team (first slip); he had an accurate arm from the deep but not much of a throw. Inside the circle his target arm was average in accuracy but his excellent hands lifted his value in tight in the final overs. Stephen had a desperate wish to succeed but his laid-back personality sometimes worked against that.

I thought Fleming had suffered some fallout from the previous team culture and influences, but seemed to have shrugged that off and responded positively to team requirements and philosophy. I felt that he could be easily led – and misled – by those with doubtful agendas, and at the time he tended to be a follower more than a leader. Like Astle and Spearman, at times he didn't always make the connection between his approach to batting and the team requirements.

Fleming practised well and considered others' requirements. Just occasionally he allowed the pitch conditions to upset him. He had no injury problems of consequence, appeared to have sufficient stamina, and was not physio-dependent. He came to me more often than previously for advice and tried very hard to action it.

Fleming was a good timekeeper, and had the ability to solve problems. Although tending to be reserved, Flem liked and enjoyed socialising.

Chris Harris was the court jester, very popular with his peers. He was always on time, turned up neat, clean and tidy. Harry's batting was still developing and was inconsistent. He hit a bigger ball than anyone in the side.

As a bowler he developed more consistency and proved to be very economical in both limited-overs and test cricket. His unorthodox delivery and persistence also resulted in him taking wickets.

As a fielder Harry had excellent agility and anticipation inside the circle, and his target arm was so good he hit the stumps often. Good hands. An average throw from a distance. I gave Harry full marks for effort; he tried very hard. His attitude towards team requirements was never in question and I found him cooperative and supportive. He was a fanatic for practice and couldn't get enough, and as an all-rounder his practice sessions were full-on.

Fitness? He had no injury problems which was surprising since he releases an enormous amount of energy. Not physio-dependent at all.

To me Harry thrived on advice and tried very hard to action it, although due to his shyness in this regard I found I had to approach him in most instances.

Gavin Larsen was our most economical bowler in most forms of the game. On unresponsive pitches in India and the West Indies he is proof of the value of bowling accurately with persistence at a slow-medium pace. I felt bound to say that 'over the past eight months he has easily been our most valuable bowler.'

Gavin had good hands and was capable of pulling off a brilliant catch. He threw well from the deep and although he's not what's termed a 'gifted athlete' he gives it his best shot always. I found he applied himself like a professional, was fully supportive towards team requirements, had an excellent attitude towards practice, and that he worked hard on his fitness. Unfortunately for Gavin, injuries were a problem for him for the first time in his career and he played the last few weeks of the West Indies tour with an abdominal strain.

All in all Gavin was what is called a reasonably self-contained unit and I left him to his own resources because he was working so well. That said, I feel that he may have appreciated a bit more feedback from me.

They don't come much better in teams than Larsen. He was popular with his peers, helpful to management, and all round a good role model for younger players.

Dipak Patel I had known since he joined Worcestershire and played with me for a few seasons before I retired from county cricket in 1982. A more mature cricketer than most.

Justin Vaughan. Cooperative, thoughtful, determined, committed. I wish we'd taken him to the World Cup.

Adam Parore has often promised more than he has delivered as a cricketer for New Zealand. We found him a tough competitor who produced some useful innings but usually failed to go on and make big enough scores. He worked hard at his batting at practice, and applied himself well when batting in games, but when it came to team requirements we found he had his own agenda, didn't work well with others, and would not cooperate nor support team decisions.

In the field he had very hard hands which resulted in dropped catches and fumbles. He admitted he got bored and perhaps as a result didn't always chase the ball hard. Had a strong, accurate arm and was capable of flashes of brilliance.

Parore was and is a fitness fanatic, spent a lot of time running and working out in the gym: the highest aerobic fitness level in the team.

He asked for advice on his batting and actioned it, but sought advice on nothing else and certainly took no notice of any other advice that might be given.

I told the Board that Adam is the original brinkman who takes everything to the line and beyond.

Craig Spearman had talent and was still learning about shot selection and how to bat for long periods. He had a run of four bad decisions (two in the tests) in six innings in the West Indies and took it well, considering he was in the early stages of his international career. I thought he needed to sell his wicket more dearly but had a healthy arrogance towards the opposition.

In the field I said Spears looked as if he might make a good third slip, he had a reasonable arm from the deep with good accuracy, was a committed fielder who hit the stumps often from inside the circle.

He practised well, considered others and didn't get upset with conditions nor did he expect favours. Was happy to cooperate with team philosophy and supported decisions. He was not physio-dependent, didn't get injured and his stamina and mobility seemed more than adequate.

Spears sought advice when he felt it necessary, not otherwise; he wasn't into communicating for the sake of it, and responded best to a more delicate approach. Curiously he was sometimes very direct and harsh with his tongue, sometimes gave better than he took, but it wasn't a major problem.

Craig was never late, was reserved but not anti-social. He preferred quieter scenes. I had him down as 'a trouble-free tourist'.

Although Roger Twose and I didn't always see eye-to-eye I found him intriguing and diverting, a man with more than his share of contradictions. Overall, both entertaining and exasperating.

Twose loves to talk cricket and seeks advice which he'll follow for a day and then move to another theory. He goes around in circles which doesn't make it easy for anyone to help him much. It was surprising how often Roger needed to tell others about what he should be doing instead of playing cricket – like setting himself up in business or raising a family for instance – and he was forever challenging boundaries so that he could organise himself differently, irrespective of how it affected others. Twosey is big into the 'I know what's best for me' syndrome, which is okay except when it's not in the best interests of the team.

He tried very hard in the field, had good hands, anticipated well and was prepared to dive around, particularly in the circle.

Dion Nash was capable of bowling a good outswinger at medium pace. He had a lot of trouble with injuries. Unfortunately, the reality of touring is that there's little time for rehab and recovery. As a result Nash wasn't able to make as big a contribution as he and we would have liked, and he tended to look to blame others for his difficulties. For some time on tour we had noted that Cairns's influence on Nash was largely detrimental. After Cairns left the team, Nash had apologised to Alabaster for his sulking, an apology to his credit. His batting had fallen away in the West Indies, too, and he developed a fear of the ball and a habit of slogging across the line. Nash is a natural athlete who moves well in the deep. He had safe hands and an accurate throwing arm. We felt that Nash needed to take time out, give his body time to repair, get fit and ease himself back into cricket. Which is what he did.

Shane Thomson was a very good all round fieldsman both inside and outside the circle. His throw was strong and accurate, he was capable of throwing the stumps down often, and in the outfield he moved well and had good hands.

Thomson's batting was limited. His bowling was adequate most of the time but for some reason he wasn't willing to try hard to improve himself. He certainly worked hard in the nets, and while he put in a lot of effort pumping iron in the gym, his cricket was handicapped by an ongoing knee injury and, later, by a shoulder injury.

Tom, as he was known, looked for reasons not to play and wouldn't always cooperate or support team decisions. We felt he worked against management.

When I tabled my tour report to the Board I indicated that I would like to see the same management team kept together, and Doig himself told the Board that I was willing to continue as coach. I also gave a verbal Yes to the question of my availability.

In the course of my brief appearance in front of the Board, McConnell's report was not raised.

Distanced from the Board

At this time I was somewhat mystified by what was going on, was unaware of what was afoot. It wasn't until later that I was to conclude that Doig was prepared to make a case for the retention of Gren but not for me.

I was taken aback when I learned that the jobs of coach, manager, and physiotherapist were to be readvertised, and that consideration was being given to altering the size and make-up of the selection panel, possibly increasing it to four. I've always thought the decision to readvertise the jobs was at Doig's instigation, but he denied that. He always stated that the Board wanted it.

There was a whisper, too, that the coach might not be the convenor of selectors, and that he might not be a selector at all. To me having four selectors was unnecessary and I was surprised it was even considered. In my view it makes sense to have the coach on the panel and for him to be convenor – a coach gets to see and know more about the players' cricketing and associated abilities than anyone else.

A day or two after the Board's 24-25 May meeting Doig told me that it had been decided that the coach's new contract would be for a two-year period, and that he assumed that wouldn't 'suit' me.

It wasn't until a year later that I learned that, prior to this, at a birthday party in Christchurch, a close friend of Doig's said that Doig had told him that NZC had an Australian in mind for the coach's job, and that by altering the terms of the appointment – a two-year rather than a one-year contract, and not guaranteeing that the coach would be a selector – I would be disinclined to reapply.

When it was made public that the jobs were to be readvertised the announcement hinted at the possibility of someone being appointed who was unfamiliar with New Zealand cricket and its players. There were words used to the effect that the coach may not be a selector, depending on his knowledge of the players.

My contract with NZC had a clause which said, 'The board of New Zealand Cricket, Chief Executive and the Chief Executive's nominee will work in conjunction with the Cricket Manager to appoint a tour management team with the mix of skills necessary for particular home and overseas tours.' I was the current coach and convenor of selectors, yet no one in NZC consulted me about proposals for change. On reading a newspaper report which said that the Board had decided to readvertise the jobs and reconsider the selectors I got in touch with Doig on 28 May. I hadn't been asked for my views on the need or reasons for changes, and I found this both rude and perplexing. I hadn't even had time by then to put together a selectors' report. I asked Doig how the Board could come to such decisions, and how much discussion had taken place, and he replied, 'Not much.'

My contract with NZC was due to run out at the end of May. NZC had waited until a few days before its expiry to tell me my job was to be readvertised. As a window-dressing exercise they rolled my contract over for two more months whilst they tried to reorganise themselves. It became farcical, everything else had been put on hold: what was I supposed to do?

It looked to me as if the horse had bolted, in terms of anyone wanting to look at any input from me, but because I knew that the Board meeting was being reconvened a week or so later, on 6 June as it transpired, I wrote down a few thoughts on selection panels.

My thoughts on why the coach ought to be a selector went this way: because he is touring and living with a team a coach has far more knowledge of the players than any of the other selectors; if he is employed by NZC for 12 months of the year, his travels put him in touch with coaches and selectors throughout the country; because the coach has been a party to selecting the players this is more likely to add strength and mutual confidence to the relationship between a player and the coach; players who may be tempted to go off the rails, should think twice when being observed by a selector.

Convenors of three-person selection panels don't have any more power than the other two – there's no casting vote situation as there is with four-person panels. I felt that if a convenor is going to be given the most power on a panel then the coach ought to be convenor simply because he's almost certain to have more knowledge than the others. But if the convenor is away on tour say, and it's inconvenient for him to deal with administrative matters, and act as spokesperson, then it may be more practical to use as convenor a selector who isn't the coach. I remarked that 'It won't matter how many selectors you have, you will never satisfy everyone' and pointed out that our panel had consulted extensively, used local talent scouts, and put in a great deal of viewing time personally. I suggested that consideration be given to nominating a person in each major area as a formally recognised selection scout.

By now I had started sending copies of my communications with Doig to the Board chairman Sir John Anderson, just in case information wasn't being passed on and therefore he wasn't aware of what was developing. I had yet to lose faith in the Board. I saw its members as Doig's boss, as the final decision-makers, so as long as I kept them informed through Anderson then things would be looked at constructively, and Alabaster, Germon and I would get a fair hearing.

Doig had tabled a paper for the Board, which I saw, in which he commented on aspects of our team management. The opening sentence stated that 'there is sound evidence that the current Team Management structure is deficient in a number of areas.' I found this presumptuous and open to dispute. On 2 June I wrote to Doig and said, 'I disagree that evidence is sound unless due process has been conducted. The process must include the opportunity for the incumbent team management to a) read the findings of Robin McConnell,' and 'b) have the opportunity to respond to them'. I also said that we should be given the same opportunity 'to discuss the issues with team members'.

I told Doig that 'To dismantle a structure without due process increases the risk of poor decision making', and that 'In this instance a consultant was given a mere 10 days to come up with some recommendations on a number of complex issues' which involved us. I said McConnell had 'made a useful beginning to what should develop into a very worthwhile exercise.' I concluded by saying that in light of all that 'I would like to suggest a meeting be held between John [Sir John Anderson], yourself and the management group to discuss details of the consultation process, timelines and any other matters pertaining to these issues.'

Doig replied in a letter dated 5 June which I received two days later. He said that he was 'satisfied that the Board will receive a balanced and complete overview to enable it to make an informed decision.' He said that he thought I would 'agree' that it had been his 'policy to consult', and that it was his 'intention to continue to consult.' By now I was really sick of being treated as if I'd come down in the last shower.

The next bit took the biscuit. Doig asked me if I 'would be good enough to give [him] a formal indication as to whether you would be likely to accept a further contract if one was offered to you by the Board and, if so, the term of the appointment you might wish to seek.'

I found this incredibly ingenuous. The Board had met on 6 June, the day after Doig had posted this letter, and the day before I'd received it. At the Board's meeting on 6 June members decided to readvertise the coach's, manager's, and physiotherapist's jobs and to offer two-year contracts. Doig announced this in a 'Media Release' on 7 June. Although Doig had privately said that he didn't expect the two-year bit would 'suit me', the release said that 'the current incumbents' would be encouraged 'to reapply'.

I talked with Gren Alabaster and Lee Germon, then faxed Anderson saying that we'd 'agreed that I ask for an urgent meeting... between yourself (or your nominee), Chris Doig, John Reid and optionally, Mark Plummer.' I said that we were 'bewildered by the attitude of NZC' and especially by 'the actions of the CEO' since we'd returned from the West Indies tour. I told him that 'I was sorry to make the approach through you, but at this time I have lost confidence and trust in the CEO.'

Anderson replied. He said that I and the others had been appointed by the previous administration and that the new Board and CEO were going to 'redefine' things. He said that the Board had made it clear that they 'fully supported' us and that we'd all been 'contacted individually', told this and invited to reapply for our jobs. He said that 'the past is now irrelevant to the process', and so on. As a consequence he saw 'little relevance' in meeting with me, 'Lee Germon and Gren Alabaster as from a Board point of view there are no issues to discuss with the group.' He did say, though, that he and Doig and John Reid would be prepared to meet me after he and Doig got back from Australia on 19 June. (Perhaps it was only a coincidence that Doig and Anderson got on a plane to Australia a couple of days after the advertisement inviting applications for the coach's and other jobs appeared in the papers. I later learned that Anderson and Doig had been to see Steve Rixon around that time.) I decided not to avail myself of this sop, and gave up there. I told him that I couldn't see any more being achieved by holding a meeting 'without the collective thoughts' of Alabaster, Germon and myself.

I was surprised and disappointed by Anderson. And not for one moment do I buy the one about the past being irrelevant. That is never the case. As William Faulkner observed, so I'm told, the past is never dead. Then there's the oft-quoted bit from Santayana who said words to the effect that those who refuse to heed the lessons of history are doomed to repeat them. The truth of this was highlighted on more than one occasion in the ensuing months.

Subsequently Anderson let slip that the current coach Steve Rixon had been approached by NZC in March 1996. Clearly the die had been cast as far as I was concerned. In time I was to note that NZC was apt to say one thing about me through the media and others elsewhere.

Publicly Supportive, Privately Condemnatory

I am aware, naturally, that all of us involved in the game say that we have the future good of New Zealand cricket at heart. So, a kind way of looking at the situation is to say that we were embroiled in a dispute over ways and means, and that ours were seen by Doig and his aides as the wrong way. But no one in NZC had the guts to say that outright and no one there, in administration or on the Board, was willing to debate the issues and areas of concern with our management team. When we returned from the West Indies Alabaster, Germon and I took it for granted that there would be a debriefing as a group, that such debriefings were the norm. They have been since our departure. Doig has more than once been reported in the media as having had debriefings with Steve Rixon and co. It was actually done with us, once only, albeit briefly, when we returned from India in 1995.

By now I was feeling that Doig was distinctly unsympathetic towards my stance and attitude regarding matters concerning the coaching and management of an international cricket team, and that, due to his refusal to thoroughly discuss issues with me and others of our management team, there was a strong likelihood that my views were being misinterpreted and possibly misrepresented. I think it's fair to assume that Doig would have voiced his views and concerns in reports to the Board. I'm still mystified as to why the Board members did not decide to have a full and frank discussion about matters of mutual interest and concern with Alabaster, Germon and me.

I feel it came as a shock, and I dare say a disappointment, when Robin McConnell's report revealed that the players, if anything, were less happy with Gren than with me. I'm sure Gren doesn't mind sharing the Bogey Man title with me and Lee Germon. Meanwhile, whatever Doig might, or might not, have been saying about me to the Board and elsewhere, he was assuring me that he was supportive of me.

In the *Sunday News* on 16 June 1996, Campbell Mitchell asked Doig who the New Zealand coach was going to be for the tour to Pakistan. Doig replied, 'I have no idea, but... Glenn Turner as the incumbent would be a very strong contender.' Really? How could that have been given that I was informed that in March that year, at a social gathering prior to our tour of the West Indies, Doig had told a prominent person there that he couldn't stand me, found me arrogant, and that I thought I knew much more about cricket than I did, and that at the time he was stuck with me.

I also learned, after Rixon had been appointed, that earlier Doig had met sports broadcaster Murray Deaker and told him that he was keen to get rid of me. He wanted Deaker's opinion of the public reaction if he did. Deaker told Doig that he'd be mad to dump me.

Deaker has said that both Doig and I are passionate about cricket. Okay, but that doesn't mean that he has a similar depth of knowledge regarding what is required of an international professional cricketer. Deaker remarked that Doig had played senior cricket, but thousands have done that. I played golf off a single figure handicap, but don't feel that equips me to direct the New Zealand Professional Golf Association.

Months after I had been sacked, Lee Germon told me of a meeting he had had with Doig and Reid. Germon said they had told him some of what was in McConnell's report and had advised him that he was in dire need of remedial treatment. He was seen to be 'too much like Turner'.

I felt that NZC's treatment of me was undermining my reputation as a cricket professional and was also starting to undermine my credibility as a human being.

The impression I gained from both Reid and Doig was that they were convinced that I wouldn't accept that some people have personalities and individual idiosyncrasies that have to be lived with. This is not the way I feel. Many, if not most, of my friends inside and outside cricket are highly individual characters, which is what I like about them. But I do draw the line at megalomania, in officials, and at players who are persistently uncooperative, unreasonable and disruptive.

I particularly take issue with Doig's view that I will not recognise and accept difference. How about his aversion to accepting mine?

I concluded that he clearly didn't see any relevance in acknowledging, when it comes to the acceptance and enjoyment of difference, that I'd played in a great many teams internationally, toured country after country, taken a real interest in other cultures, had married Sukhi, an Indian, and am still married to her 25 years later – not out! My children are mixed race, Indo-European if you like, so it incensed me to have this man accusing me of arrogance and intolerance of difference. I could, too, hardly contain my frustration at members of the Board; could barely contain my disappointment when not one of them came to me seeking clarification or information on any criticism made of me and our management team.

I have often tried to fathom what it was that Doig really couldn't abide in me; why he wouldn't discuss issues and argue the toss. Early on Doig admitted that he had a big ego. I don't think he liked seeing me, Alabaster and Germon putting in place methods, standards, systems that he would not have been able to operate under himself. So he said, in my opinion, 'I'll get rid of him.' There's no room for more than one Top Gun in Doig's world. This is far from just my assessment; others who have worked with Doig have expressed similar views, have had similar experiences.

I often wondered, then, as I have since, how players could really trust an administration that was prepared to treat its team management the way it treated us.

My conclusion was that the management of NZC was grossly deficient in human terms, doubly ironic really when one had to listen to their frequent statements about the crucial importance of 'people skills' and 'man-management'.

Misunderstanding or Misrepresentation: Exercises in Futility

In mid-1996 I found myself between a rock and a hard place. The public and NZC's sponsors generally seemed to think that Alabaster, Germon and I had done a good job. But it was clear that Doig and management of NZC, and certain players, were hoping like hell that I'd pack up my tent and go away, back to my stoic Southern Man fastness. That would have made it easy for them. I wasn't prepared to act at their convenience. I'd put in too many of the hard yards for all that work to be thrown to the four winds. At this point I did not know who was going to be on the selection panel for the coach's job.

NZC made play of the fact that I'd been appointed for just the one year. Doig said both the former Board and I had 'welcomed' this. No. I'd simply accepted the offer of a year because the then Chairman of the Board Peter McDermott had told me that the contract was – as he was quoted saying in some newspapers – 'initially for one year... but that the appointment is open-ended'. I'd been told short-term contracts were common these days and that they were normally rolled over. Graham Dowling, Rod Fulton, and McDermott all used the phrase 'initial 12 month period' when talking of my appointment. Deputy Chairman Cran Bull also confirmed that this was their thinking.

They said that if they had felt there were problems with my performance they would have discussed them with me during the term of my contract and given me an opportunity to remedy them as they had done with Geoff Howarth. Both McDermott and Bull said that when I was appointed they saw the task I was to undertake as a difficult one and believed that the Board of NZC thought I would be coach for longer than a year. They personally hoped I would be involved for at least three years.

After Doig's advent, neither McDermott nor Bull were approached by anyone from NZC to discuss any aspect of my employment.

* * *

There was clearly a concern, which came through from my discussions with John Reid, that Doig and NZC felt I was determined to get rid of a whole heap of players in whom we had invested a lot of time and money. I couldn't understand why Doig, with no experience of first-class or international cricket, would think he was qualified to take issue with me over the merits of players. Both seemed to think that I was too harsh on players and quick to discard them. In fact, our team management and selectors went to great lengths to retain players and gave them repeated opportunities to prove their worth.

Some of my critics, including Doig, allege that I was of no help to the senior bowlers, and that I don't understand them, or bowling. John Reid told me of this bizarre claim, which was made by some senior bowlers (predictably Cairns and Morrison in particular) after the West Indies tour. In fact my knowledge of where and how to bowl to different batsmen in order to expose their weaknesses, of the strategies and line and length required in various conditions, is greater than most. The length of my career as a batsman made me well aware of how and where bowlers need to direct their attack to get players out, or to restrict their scoring. Richard Hadlee acknowledged my help when I was cricket manager of the New Zealand team in the 1980s.

I am of course well acquainted with the basic techniques – I know my MCC book on bowling. Over the years I did quite a bit of bowling in nets, in club cricket, and even, early in my career for Worcestershire, in one-day cricket. In fact I have a career-best first-class bowling performance of 3-17 for Worcestershire against Pakistan. Hanif Mohammed was in my bag. That will teach him to under-estimate me!

John Reid said he thought this claim by a few bowlers was a load of cobblers. Reid said he saw me as hard-working and well-organised, that I had good tactical and technical knowledge, and that I knew more about bowling than I was being given credit for. But his main concern was that I wasn't able to motivate players before they went out to play. I tried to explain my way of operating which was to give thorough team-talks which focused on the individual and collective weaknesses in the opposition. I said I thought this is more convincing because it shows players that the opposition is vulnerable, hence beatable. It seems to me that a more convincing way of motivating players is to give them something tangible to focus on, and build their confidence with, by highlighting their opponents' weaknesses. Nevertheless I do give individual players a special chat occasionally, when something exceptional is needed.

Reid thinks about cricket, but his touring experience was limited. His preferred approach – heavy into coddling – in my view doesn't produce hardened and accomplished international cricketers.

Sources tell me that he also said that I had lost the support of senior players. Some, but not all. There were very few problems, if any, with admirable senior players like Larsen and Patel. So I'm assuming that Reid was referring to the likes of Parore and Morrison, for instance. Cairns, too, saw himself as a senior player. What Reid overlooked, in my opinion, was that these so-called senior players were, had been, and still are one of New Zealand cricket's more serious problems.

Reid had not been in his job long when I saw that he wanted to be involved in selections. (Since 1996 he has been a non-voting member of the selection panel, why I don't know.) Of course I was interested in Reid's views, but not obliged to go along with them. Initially I didn't have a problem with him expressing his opinion, but I was surprised when I learned that he thought he knew better than Alabaster and I did, for instance, who was worth retaining. He wasn't willing to concede that our months of touring with players gave us a better grip on individuals' abilities than he had.

I accept that there is a perception among some players that I don't have much sympathy for their situation and I would certainly have had another look at how to assure them that this was not so. When depicting me as cold or hard-hearted the likes of Crowe, Doig and others either overlook or are unaware of my own struggles as a player. Early in my career I was a delicate, sensitive lad who had to endure more than my share of media attacks. And attacks from administrators as well. I had to work hard (and without much support) to overcome the pressures, problem solve, and toughen up to become professional and successful.

I know exactly what players go through emotionally and in all ways associated with having to perform day in and day out in international cricket. Anyone who has read my reports on players, or seen me work with them individually on their cricket, would see that I actually like most of them a good deal, find them interesting and diverse personalities. But I make no apologies for keeping my distance and for trying to avoid favouritism.

As for self-belief, it is terribly important. It is one thing I emphasise again and again. But how to develop it? Now there's a debate. I don't believe bullshit baffles brains.

There were ten or a dozen players who were, in my opinion, no longer first choices for New Zealand teams, for one reason or another. This list included both current and past players. That was my considered opinion. I ought not to have needed to remind Reid that I was only one of three selectors, and that they would not necessarily agree with me in every case. *C'est la vie*. As it happens, only three of those players – Cairns and Parore were two – were in the New Zealand team which was selected to tour Zimbabwe and Australia in 1997.

* * *

In mid-1996, mindful of the hiatus and the concerns of some players as to what was happening, I faxed John Reid a 'Draft Senior Squad Programme/Timetable' starting with a camp for a selected group (mainly batsmen) at the Lincoln academy from 17-21 June. I hoped to include sessions on spin with Australia's Terry Jenner and India's Bishen Bedi. I proposed a debrief from 15-19 July, a senior squad camp from 2-6 September, two two-day games prior to a trip to Queensland in late October, a two-day game and then two one-dayers before going to Sharjah, then Pakistan in November.

Reid decided that seeing I was still being paid I might as well do something constructive for cricket, so he got a few players together – Astle and Fleming among them – and I did some work with them in Christchurch. But he was non-committal about the rest of my proposed programme.

After working with Astle and Fleming I wrote down my thoughts on what they should look to work on in the off-season. NZC's office staff typed up my notes and they were given to the players. Here's what I suggested to them.

ASTLE

(A) *Area for Development* – learning to play the line

Preamble:

A line player is one who concentrates his strategies around the line of the ball rather than its length. Generally a line player is a good judge of where his off stump is, hence is able to let the ball go with more assurance. Often line players tend to be more restricted in their range of attacking options, although they are likely to be more compact and assured in defence. However, top players are able to combine the two strategies of applying line and length; it simply becomes a question of applying the correct strategy having assessed conditions, the opposition and team requirements. For example, facing Ambrose and Walsh with a new ball in the longer forms of the game you would look to let the ball go as often as possible, hence applying the line theory. Hooking short-pitched balls and driving at wide half volleys is unlikely to result in an extended stay at the crease. Nathan, if you can add the skill of line play to your already well developed ability to attack length, you will become a more complete player.

Method:

i) find out where your off stump is by letting the ball go as often as possible, even to the point of letting the ball hit your off stump (experiment).

ii) practise letting the very short ball go too.

iii) when the ball is short of a length and needs to be played, rely upon deflections to score, particularly on the on-side. Some balls will automatically slide off the face behind point.

(B) *Area for Development* – playing the ball which is pitched short of a length, with the line close in to the body (hip)

Method:

i) open up to play it into the leg-side.

ii) get over the top of the ball, allowing it to come onto the bat, playing it as late as possible.

NB Show the face of the bat to the ball as long as possible, rolling the wrists over the top of the ball, angling it down into the leg-side.

(C) *Area for Development* – attacking the ball with more control

Method:

i) hold position throughout the execution of the shot. Keep your head as still as possible.

ii) work on improving head position when attacking the ball into the off-side (off both feet) i.e. eyes level.

iii) I normally encourage players to *stroke* the ball, however, in your case I'm prepared to concede upwards to 'hit', but not *butcher.*

(D) *Area for Development* – look to get down to spinners allowing you to dominate

Method:

i) experiment by going down the pitch to every ball, to find out what is possible. Don't worry about being beaten occasionally. Perhaps spend half the batting session approaching it this way and the remainder of the session being more selective. However, only play back if forced to do so.

ii) when going down the pitch, move your rear (back) foot in behind your front foot, for balance and control.

iii) learn to cover the ball turning away from the bat, by planting your foot so as to give yourself at least the width of your bat to cover probable turn. Beware of closing the face (against the spin) and learn the percentage shots.

iv) with the ball turning into the bat adopt the same strategy of going down the pitch as stated above, but learn to go with the spin, playing the percentages. Learn to play balls which are not easily driven by going with the turn, rolling it down and away into the leg-side for possible runs.

NB Continue the good work making sure you don't compromise your strengths.

FLEMING

(A) *Area for Development* – driving the ball into the off-side off the front foot with improved precision

Method:

i) holding position throughout the execution of the stroke.

ii) being conscious of pointing your right shoulder more towards the direction in which you wih to propel the ball. i.e. *turn* your shoulder around more.

iii) more top hand dominance throughout the execution of the stroke and/or less bottom hand strength or shovelling.

(B) *Area for Development* – more control in hitting the ball along the ground or clearly over the top (on both sides of the pitch)

Method:

i) as for (A) iii) above.

ii) playing the ball a little later, allowing it to come onto the bat, particularly when hitting into the leg-side.

iii) stroke or clip the ball – control and placement are the likely outcomes.

iv) experiment and find out the length of the ball required for the ball to go along the ground, or over the top. Pace and bounce are obvious factors which will alter with conditions, but at least master what you have there.

(C) *Area for Development* – playing the ball down around the corner on the leg-side or letting it go

Method:

i) when the line of the ball is outside the line of your pads it is better to let it go.

ii) when the line of the ball is within the line of your pads, get over the top of the ball by allowing it to come onto the bat, playing it as late as possible. Roll it down around the corner rather than trying to hit it there.

(D) – spinners...same notes as for Astle above.

In 'The Best Interests of New Zealand Cricket'

On 17 June I received a copy of the advertisement calling for applications for the coach's job. Doig and Anderson were in Australia. Guess why? I wondered whether I should bother applying, then sent in my application on 3 July, the day I got another letter from Doig. In this letter (dated 2 July) he said that he'd 'become increasingly aware over recent weeks of your disaffection with my leadership of New Zealand Cricket,' and so on. He again says that it was the Board's decision to re-advertise the jobs, and that John Reid had told him that I felt I should have been allowed to see the McConnell report. At that time he didn't offer to let me see the report, but said that when he and Reid got back from a trip to London he'd be pleased to meet me and discuss it. He said that, 'You need to be aware that you have my support'. By now I felt he ought to have the courage to tell me what he really thought.

I decided to let Doig's letter sit on my desk for a few days and arranged to meet with Doig and Reid in Christchurch on 19 July. A day or two after I'd got Doig's letter of 2 July I wrote a letter to him, dated it 19 July but didn't post it. I took it with me and tabled it at the meeting with him and Reid. I didn't want to give him time beforehand to prepare an answer. In it I reminded him of matters I'd raised with him, to no avail, on previous occasions. I said that delays had undermined 'players' confidence in the administration', that the delays had inhibited 'their winter training programme and motivation', and had added, 'unwelcome stress to their lives'.

I reminded him of the previous administration's promise, which he had confirmed on more than one occasion, that everything would be sorted by the end of May ready for a new start on 1 June. I also said that 'some players returned to New Zealand on the assumption that they would receive retainers during the winter period, providing them with enough financial security to allow them to work on improving their game. Lucrative offers to play in the Northern Hemisphere were turned down on the basis of confidence and trust. Even a job arranged for the captain with the BNZ has been put on hold and thrown into doubt. Everyone has been left dangling, not knowing whether to accept other employment. They have been let down, the promises broken. Why?'

I wrote, 'The need and wisdom in choosing to readvertise the' manager, coach and physiotherapist's jobs 'is open to question. However, the decision is of little significance compared to the other issues raised in this letter.

'There is one question in particular remaining unanswered, one which more than any other is responsible for creating turmoil. Why was the incumbent selection panel not permitted to complete their work (within their period of office) by selecting the squad for winter training?'

When I gave this letter to Doig he couldn't or wouldn't answer the questions raised. It's clear why, now, but at the time he was uncharacteristically at a loss for words, for he hadn't had time to prepare an answer. This was the man who, in his 2 July letter to me, said he didn't 'have anything but the best interests of NZ Cricket at heart in every deliberation and change we are currently involved in.' When it became obvious that an answer wasn't coming from Doig, Reid stepped in, huffed a little and said it was the Board's insistence that things should have been happening this way.

It was pretty clear to me that Reid was no ally of mine. Having shifted down from Auckland expressly to take on the job of Operations Manager, one assumes he would not have wanted to be other than supportive of his boss, but from this moment on I concluded he was in no doubt as to what was going on.

Weeks before my interview I had let NZC know that in July I was required to go to Otaru in Japan with my wife. Otaru is a sister city to Dunedin, and Sukhi was going there as Dunedin's mayor.

Applications for the coach's job closed on 8 July and interviews were delayed until Doig and Anderson returned from an International Cricket Conference (ICC) meeting in London. (I'm sure I'm not the only one who thought it odd that both Doig and Anderson felt they knew enough about cricket to represent New Zealand at cricket's top international forum.) My interview this time was a lot different. On the previous occasion they put us through two to three hours of tests – IQ and personality tests – and two lengthy interviews with the selection panel. Two hours or more in the first instance and an hour or so second time round. I had also been sent in advance a whole host of questions intended to explore candidates' views on cricket generally.

Until I got to NZC's offices I was unaware of the make-up of the selection panel. When I saw who was on it, I thought, this is ludicrous, a farce. I was confronted with Doig, Reid, Martin Snedden and Ian Taylor. Board member Barry Dineen was meant to be there but didn't make it. Talk about a snarl of opposition, about conflict of interest and intimate connections. If NZC was serious about putting up an impartial panel to select the coach, how could they include Doig, knowing his opinion of me?

Taylor was a principal of NZC's consultant firm Sheffield Consultants and had put Doig forward for NZC's CEO's job. Reid, well, I knew his views and his relationship to his boss Doig. Then there was Snedden who acted as an agent for cricketers, among whom he listed Danny Morrison and Chris Pringle. I did not believe I could possibly receive a fair hearing from this panel.

This time my interview lasted about 45 minutes. I found the questions and questioning superficial, in the main, and answers were usually not followed by further questioning of a kind that often results in elaboration and/or clarification. The first half or more of my interview centred on selection issues. Snedden was particularly interested in talking about the need to get in behind bowlers – surprise surprise. After a while I said that 'I hadn't realised this was a selection meeting,' which steered them away from this preoccupation.

Taylor asked me only one question, which was about what type of team culture we were trying to develop. I thought that had been pretty obvious from the start. Taylor didn't pursue the matter.

There was no mention of job description, contracts or payments. Doig had begun proceedings by asking me to describe the process we had gone through with the players when establishing protocols. I'd detailed that in my reports so he knew it all anyway, and there was no further discussion about it during the interview.

I didn't know what to think after the interview. On the one hand I thought, maybe the paucity of questions and lack of in-depth discussion meant that as I was going to be reappointed there was little point in going further than a superficial tour of the territory. Either that or, let's not waste any more time than necessary on this guy because he's not a serious contender. I've been on enough interviewing panels to know how things work. Basically they weren't much interested.

I had taken a few papers along to the interview with me, as an example of the sort of work I was doing with some players, but due to the nature and length of the interview there was no time to talk about this and other matters. I left a couple of assessments on Astle and Fleming with the panel. I also gave them a copy of the game plan I had prepared for New Zealand's World Cup quarter-final against Australia.

It's fairly common knowledge in cricketing circles that NZC had a short-list of four applicants, and that apart from me the others were Steve Rixon, Warren Lees, and a former England player. Why they bothered to interview Warren I don't know because Don Cameron of the *New Zealand Herald* said Doig had told him a couple of months earlier that Lees didn't figure in NZC's plans. (Doig had made similar comments to me.) I travelled up from Dunedin in a plane with Lees and he said that he wasn't being interviewed for the coach's job; he was looking for a selector's job. He was after one or the other, or both actually.

* * *

I was in Otaru when I got a fax from Doig telling me that Rixon had been embraced. In his fax Doig said the decision 'should not be read as a sign of dissatisfaction by the Board in your contribution to the success of New Zealand Cricket over the past year. In fact, your contribution has been extremely valued by the Board and by me personally. We have made a point of stating that in the official announcement today.'

I actually received a phone call from Tim Murdoch of NZC who said to me that Doig had been trying to get hold of me to offer his condolences, etcetera. I said, 'Tell him not to bother. I've heard enough lies and deception.'

Back in New Zealand Doig and Reid performed a duet on prime time television. Doig told the populace that I had done a great job but it was just that the better man got the job. NZC had gone through an exhaustive, fair and transparent process, and Rixon would take New Zealand cricket forward. It was time, said Doig, to take our team to a 'new level'.

The reaction from a great many cricket followers was disbelief.

* * *

When I got back from Japan with Sukhi lots of letters and messages of support arrived from all over the country. This was gratifying, for I was feeling exasperated by the events – or non-events in some respects – since I'd returned from the West Indies. You see, some of the details as outlined in the previous pages were then unknown to me. I knew I'd been shafted, but was unaware of the extent of the besmirching of me that had gone on. But the number of letters, newspaper clippings, faxes and phone calls confirmed what many had been saying to me publicly and privately, that they had liked the direction we'd been taking, and progress that the national team had been making. New Zealand cricket was no longer a laughing stock, respect was coming back.

I had just about decided there was nothing more I could do, that I had been efficiently and finally eviscerated, when I received a letter from Mr H.C. (Peter) Hildreth, an agricultural consultant in the North Island. He sent me copies of recent correspondence he had had with NZC. He was one of many who said he felt I'd 'been handed a raw deal'.

Hildreth had written to Doig on 17 August and said that he was 'disturbed' that the Board had replaced me 'just when our sport seemed to have pulled itself out of the disgraceful state it was in.

'What concerns me now is that the egos of those guilty of forcing the change, might stand in the way of them ever admitting a mistake in the choice of Mr Rixon.' And so on.

Doig replied on 22 August saying that, 'I am sure you will understand that the decision was not arrived at lightly. Given a whole range of circumstances, none of which we are prepared to make public, there is no doubt in the minds of New Zealand Cricket that it has made not only a right decision but the only possible decision in the interests of advancing the fortunes of New Zealand Cricket in the future.'

Hildreth wrote back and said Doig's words weren't 'good enough. You have cast a shadow over everyone involved, but most particularly the reputation and character of Glenn Turner has been called into question.'

It was this correspondence that had made me decide it was time I took things further, made me want to find out more about what Doig and others had been saying about me behind the scenes.

Chapter 12

A 'People Person': the appointment of Steve Rixon

Why had I bothered re-applying for the coach's job? At one point I had jotted down some notes: '1) only part-way through a recovery plan; 2) a genuine desire to get things back on track and establish some ongoing protocols so that we don't return to previous depths; 3) if NZC's trying to stuff me, why make it easy?... new regime in NZC needs scrutiny... my strong desire for truth and justice... the need to keep faith with the large number of New Zealand cricket supporters who had been behind the initiatives taken in the previous year... NZC must not be allowed to treat employees like this in the future. Because cricket was one area in which I thought I might be able to make a difference.

'I don't like throwing in the towel and I don't like people walking all over the top of me.' Frankly, I couldn't think of any good reasons why I shouldn't apply.

* * *

Before I left for Japan I had rung NZC and spoken to Doig's personal secretary Stephanie Taylor and enquired about interviews for the new national team selection panel. A new panel had not been appointed and NZC had not raised the subject with me, even though I had applied to be a selector as well as the coach.

Stephanie said, 'Oh, I don't know. Just a moment.' She spoke to John Reid and came back to say, 'I've spoken to John and he says there's no need to interview you because they know the way that you think.'

Subsequently I learned that my name was not on the list of nominations received for the selection panel, and that the interview panel comprised Doig, Reid, and Don Neely. I had heard that Neely had been asked to make recommendations for the selection panel. Neely's aversion to me goes back 25 years or more. One of the nominees was Ross Dykes. His nomination was very interesting because he'd withdrawn 'due to philosophical differences' with me when I was appointed convenor. This time he must have heard that I was history. Another candidate was Rex Hooton. The day before Hooton got the plane in Auckland to go to Christchurch for an interview, Ross Dykes rang him and said 'Don't get a surprise when you see me on the plane with you.' On the flight down Hooton said that he told Dykes that 'obviously Glenn will continue to be coach', whereupon Dykes said 'well, not necessarily, I think they've got an Australian in mind.'

I spoke to Rick Pickard, and he said that he found his interview quite amazing. Pickard said Doig got up and left soon after his interview began and he felt the whole business was a *fait accompli*. Some time later, after the new panel of Dykes, Pickard and Shrimpton had selected their first team, I asked Rick if they had received or taken any notice of my, or Alabaster's, reports on players.

Rick said that he thought that he had been sent the reports, but that regardless NZC and Rixon had said that they were to start with a clean slate. Pickard said Rixon wanted everyone who was fit to be available for selection. Once again the past was past and bore no relevance...

Months later I learned that Sir John Anderson was unaware that I had expressed an interest in being considered for the selection panel. It can't have been documented.

In early August 1996 I received a letter from New Zealand Cricket Inc. It read:

> Dear Glenn
>
> A short note to express my thanks for your efforts with the New Zealand team since I arrived at New Zealand Cricket on 1 February. I enjoyed working with you and the frankness with which we could discuss issues was refreshing.
>
> You will of course be disappointed with the final decision on the team Coach. In terms of the process employed in reaching that decision I can only reassure you of its openness, fairness and democratic outcome. However, may I take this opportunity of wishing you well in the future and I hope that cricket will allow us to work together in some capacity in the future.
>
> Yours sincerely
> J F Reid
> Operations Manager

I drafted a reply to that letter but didn't send it.

In September I received a letter from another employee of NZC, John Howell. He expressed his 'big thanks' for all the work I'd done with him at the academy, and wrote that not once had he heard me 'promoting' my 'on the field successes'. He said he 'always found [me] most reliable and professional', that he 'enjoyed [my] sense of humour and modesty', and that at the academy I had 'added the necessary depth to the programmes, both men's and women's.' Etcetera.

Nice, but perplexing. Earlier in the year, prior to my sacking, a friend of mine had had dinner with Doig, Reid, Howell and others in NZC. My friend said he was astonished when Howell had engaged in a heated denunciation of me.

* * *

For the best part of two years after Rixon's appointment I refrained from commenting on his approach, performance or record. But due to what has transpired, and the fact that I was never seriously put up against him for the coach's job, I now feel more comfortable discussing it as I see it.

Soon after Rixon's appointment NZC sent Lee Germon to see him in Sydney. A 'getting to know each other' meeting. Germon was inclined to think that a principal part of the reason for his trip was so that Rixon could assess whether he felt he could work with Lee. Germon spent most of the time briefing Rixon on what was what, who was who, and what had been going on. Germ said Rixon's knowledge of New Zealand cricket and its players was barely perceptible.

But Rixon lost no time indicating that he was happy to be seen as one of the boys, as if it was an opportunity to re-live his playing days. As Germon put it, Steve was a bit of a 'Jack the Lad'. Rixon raised a few eyebrows during one of his first national squad meetings at the Lincoln academy by assuring the guys that he knew they all liked a drink and a root while on tour.

When Rixon took the team to Pakistan in 1996, Lee Germon introduced the on-field huddle when a wicket fell. Not really Lee. He said that one of the reasons for the huddle was to try to get some of those who weren't all that enamoured of others to bond together, if only for a few moments. In the radio commentary box Bryan Waddle was enraptured, told listeners in New Zealand that this was a wonderful thing to see, was indicative of a 'positive new approach'. The huddle is one way of trying to show a sceptical public that there is some truth in the catch-cries 'We're all working together now,' or 'We all like each other,' or 'We've got the right group,' and so on. Why do we persist in trying to run our national cricket team like a 1st XI school side? It's primitive to say the least.

Lee went out of his way to spend more time, not just huddling, but socialising with the players, getting 'close to them'. It didn't work.

By appointing Rixon NZC in effect downgraded the job, turned it into a part-time position. In 1996 the conditions for the coach's job were revamped. His 'Off Season Responsibilities' included meeting individually with national and emerging players, NZC's Operations Manager and the selection convenor and maintaining 'regular contact with all concerned'. The job description stated that the coach should, 'If New Zealand commitments allow,' '...assist in coaching at the National and Regional Academies.' The coach was supposed to visit other coaches around New Zealand. Hard to do if you live in Australia.

Immediately after his appointment Rixon said that he was happy not to be involved in selection. He didn't think, he said, the coach should be a selector because it upset the relationship between a coach and his players. It inhibited them, he asserted. As if we were really supposed to believe that selectors don't consult with a coach over the make-up of a team. It wasn't long before Rixon began to sing a different tune and in early 1998, when NZC renewed his contract, he was officially appointed to the selection panel. There are few who believe that Rixon had refrained from attempting to influence selections from early in the piece.

* * *

From the moment of Rixon's appointment NZC's promotional and marketing machine cranked up to sell a second-string Australian coach/player. Even Anderson went public saying they had the best man for the job. How would he know? Martin Crowe fronted on his Sky TV programme to say that Rixon was marvellous and just the sort of 'people-person' they needed, all of it thinly-veiled criticism of me.

The reaction from the sporting media was mixed. Many, including Peter Bidwell, Richard Boock, Don Cameron, Ron Palenski, Brent

Edwards and Jo Romanos, thought my sacking was a mistake, retrograde. John Dybvig said 'The cricket council's a pack of numb-nuts.' The whole business, and Rixon's credentials, might have received more scrutiny if it were not for the fact that several journalists and commentators were overseas covering the Atlanta Olympics at the time of the announcement.

I was surprised by the significance NZC placed upon Rixon's record with New South Wales and successes in Sydney grade cricket. NSW provided a large proportion of the Australian team. It would have been difficult to fail with them. And despite the supposed quality of Sydney grade cricket it's pretty irrelevant when compared to the nature and demands of international play. Rixon had not been one of Australia's more notable players – media magnate Kerry Packer's predations opened the door for him and even with Marsh out, during Rixon's career Australia used a bunch of other 'keepers – Robinson, McLean, Wright, Woolley and Phillips. Rixon hadn't toured to India, Pakistan, or New Zealand. He had applied for the job of coach of the Australian team but didn't get it. He didn't know New Zealand, the players or their backgrounds. So he was basically starting from scratch in important areas. He had no experience of coaching or preparing international teams. He'd captained New South Wales once as a stand-in when McCosker was injured, although it wasn't as if one captain dominated the period when Rixon played for NSW. In fact there were several captains: Colley, Simpson, Hilditch, Phillips and Welham.

I had little knowledge of Rixon's cricketing background until the puffery issued by NZC, but naturally I was curious. Although cricketing career records are just one aspect that needs to be taken into consideration, it's a pretty significant one. So it is interesting to look at Rixon's career record; 13 tests, total runs 394, average 18.76. In first-class cricket, 151 matches, runs 4303, average 23.13. One-day internationals: 6 innings, 40 runs, average 13.33. (Not a big enough sampling to tell you much except that he had no one-day international experience of consequence.)

At the time Rixon came along in 1996 Lee Germon had played 8 tests (13 innings) for a batting average of 26.80; 88 first-class matches for an average of 31.91; 19 one-day international innings at 25.06.

But NZC's promotional force presented Rixon as one of the wonders of cricket's coaching world, the Sydney Opera House of Australian cricketing knowledge, savvy and hard-headed and uncompromising in the style of those who, the spin-doctors asserted, came out of the world's greatest cricket-playing nation.

Rixon didn't claim to be a whizz when it came to the technical and tactical side of the game. At top level players don't need much technical help, he said. Really? Tell that to top golfers and tennis players and so on. It's all in the head he said, and his strengths were in the area of 'people skills' and 'man-management'.

My contention is that no one should be even considered for the job of coach of a national team unless they have considerable captaincy experience. Unless you have had to sit down and plan strategies and then apply them in a practical way on the field of play, how can you possibly be expected to have the knowledge, experience and expertise to produce game plans for an international side? What practice have you had at thinking on your feet and responding to changing circumstances?

Apropos of this, I should say that I saw part of my involvement with NZC as an opportunity to put forward some solid work on how to assess the knowledge of prospective coaches and captains, particularly through interviews. I am sure that many people find when applying for jobs that they know more about the subject than many of the interviewers.

Personally I'm not opposed to bringing in a coach from overseas, but it has to be someone at the top of his profession if that person's going to be in charge of a national team: for example, a Bob Simpson or a Bob Woolmer.

Doig and others in NZC are clearly enamoured of Australian cricket and cricketers. NZC has set about Australianizing the game here. We have Rixon as coach, Neil Maxwell as marketing manager, and Ashley Ross who is director of player development through the academy at Lincoln. It looks as if New Zealand cricket is becoming a training ground for emerging Australians. Can we imagine the Australian Cricket Board adopting a reciprocal arrangement? A New Zealand provincial coach, from Canterbury, say, becoming coach of the Australian team?

In cricket circles a few welcomed Rixon as just the man New Zealand needed. Others said, 'Ridiculous'; others said 'Wait and see'. A whole lot said, 'Wrong message to the wrong players, a victory for the egotists and troublemakers.'

Later in the year, in November, after New Zealand had snatched defeat from the jaws of near certain victory in a one-dayer in Sharjah, I received a letter which summed up my feelings and a lot of the comments I'd kept getting from people around the country. Molly Anderson, who is not known to me personally, wrote and said: 'As one of many who were outraged at your treatment by Christopher Doig and chorus, I can't resist writing to express a bit of *schadenfreude* at last night's Sharjah episode.

'It wasn't just what must be one of the most awful batting collapses in our cricketing history, it was having to sit and listen to all the back-slapping and hype – particularly from that manager – about how HAPPY and UNITED this team is now. Actually ever since the appointment of Steve Rixon, we have been fed this stuff. And for the first time in my LIFE of watching this great game, watching as wicket after wicket fell and the self congratulation swelled, I found myself last night almost wishing they would lose. And that is a terrible thing! And most unfair to the real cricketers in that side... who always try so hard.

'... So much for hugs and matiness.'

This was an example of the backlash that Murray Deaker had warned Doig about, and which has lingered.

Progress? No

I often think of where we'd come from when I took on the coach's job again in 1995, where we were when I got sacked, and what has happened since. To me it seems that since 1996 we have spent a lot of time going back over old, toxic ground. Partly it was because in my opinion the new regime run by Doig and Reid, and the Board led by Sir John Anderson, preferred to ignore salient aspects of the history of New Zealand cricket.

NZC has repeated old mistakes. Take the relationship and dealings between the media, NZC and the players. NZC has gone back to allowing media too much access to players, sometimes at inopportune times. This puts unwarranted, unhelpful pressure on players. It doesn't help a team's performance in the long run, and it doesn't make for better, more informed media coverage either.

NZC has adopted a near open-slather approach to media promotion. The object is to make as many players as possible into superstars. One problem, though, is that cameras in particular bring out the super-brat as well as the super-nice in the course of live coverage of games. Off-field, TV producers are pushing for access to players' dressing rooms; we have cameras on the drinks cart, and shots of twelfth men having fun on it prior to driving out onto the ground. TV employees are likely to say, apropos of all this, 'We might not know much about cricket but we know what makes good television.' So, increasingly, the media and cricket's administration is engaged in an elaborate, expensive, increasingly slick PR-exercise intended to persuade sponsors and the public that what they are seeing and hearing is the greatest. Commentators on both TV and radio, too, to an increasing extent, are exhorted to 'talk it up', 'be positive'. This is the Australian style of sports commentary, superlative after superlative, everything stunning, huge and sensational! This is cricket as rugby league. No point in letting the pictures and the action speak for themselves.

Most players are not naturally good, fluent, insightful talkers, which is hardly surprising. Why should they be? They do not usually, when put in front of a camera or brought to a microphone, have much to say of real consequence. With very few exceptions, what most people who have played any sport for New Zealand have shown, is that they are better at playing their code than they are at talking about it on air. Most of them know and accept that. They also quickly find out that the various media are voracious. One effect is to encourage some players to think that they are individually more important than they are, and to give them an inflated idea of their significance within the team.

Personally, I think we would all be better off if the focus was on the game of cricket: let the quality of the performance speak for itself. Admiration for the players is more likely to be sustained through their actions on the field than by allowing them to be used as pawns for media purposes. Players can be resolute and fiercely competitive without sacrificing their integrity and dignity, a respect for their opposition, and the paying public.

I think it is possible to argue that NZC's CEO Christopher Doig's own need for public attention is behind the enthusiasm to have players dance like bears to media tunes, and vice versa. What happens is that attention is drawn away from the quality of the cricket and focused on the personalities of the players.

Doig has often emphasised the importance of self-image, and

implied that I undervalued its importance. Nonsense. My concern is that NZC has been encouraging a style that conveys unacceptable, odious images. To me Doig has not taken a strong enough stand against behaviour and attitudes which bring the game into disrepute in the eyes of a large number of cricket's most loyal supporters, and the result is that the image presented in some quarters remains distasteful and unacceptable to many. Cricket-lovers look for players to admire, and those they admire most are those who speak loudest through the quality of their cricket, and the example they set by their conduct both on and off the field.

All along, as I see it, Doig seems to argue that in cricket as in most other areas, there are special, strange and gifted people who have to be handled as if they are Ming china. And, that we should be prepared to go the length of the Great Wall to condone what they do, how they behave and play.

None of us are saying that we were lily-white, nor that stupid and unacceptable cricketing behaviour is new. I remember when I was captaining Otago and there were a couple of games left in the season. There were some stroppy, vocal characters in our side, including the Blair brothers, Wayne and Bruce (one or other or both at the time), one of the Bracewells, John or Brendan (or was it both?), and Stephen Boock. They were noted for playing the game hard. That's okay, but at times they went over the top. I got sick of their niggling, their abuse of other players and chips at umpires. I called them together and told them if there was any more of it I'd send the offender off and bring on the twelfth man. I was taking a risk, for if they'd called my bluff and colluded we'd have been short of a player or two.

On another occasion, when I was captaining the University side in the Dunedin senior competition, we were playing against North East Valley in the last match of the season. NEV had a chance of winning the competition, if they bowled us out. The target was reachable but we lost wickets and eventually, when it became obvious we couldn't win, I told our guys to try and hold out. The weather was marginal, the light bad. It was seven o'clock or later when I told our guys to appeal the light and the players came off. We were about 8 down, were faced with about 25 runs to get off a couple of overs. That's a tall order for club tailenders. The NEV side included a few noted club sledgers, who shouted abuse at me, threw the ball into the creek alongside the ground at the University Oval, went into the changing rooms, turned on all the showers and left. Their ball had been lost earlier and we'd given them ours. Afterwards the former New Zealand player and first-class umpire Eric Dempster, himself a NEV member, apologised for their behaviour.

With the advent of Doig and Rixon, and under their tutelage, considerable effort has gone into trying to create new New Zealand cricketing heroes. But none of the players most indulged and pushed forward are truly great players, and none are in any way heroic in non-cricketing terms either. We have had a few true heros in New Zealand cricket – Bert Sutcliffe and Richard Hadlee for instance – who were exemplary when compared with those whom Doig deemed essential to the future of New Zealand cricket.

I want our cricketers to be household names. It is good when they attract attention and encourage youngsters to play cricket. Youngsters need role models, and NZC has a responsibility to ensure that its players set a good example. Over time, the way a team plays, its ability, behaviour and general tenor, will reflect the views, standards and skills – the collective cricketing savvy – of its captain, coach and manager. I don't think the New Zealand cricketing public expects us to win all the time, but what they do want to see is a side that's fully-committed, gives of its best, that doesn't have prima donnas in it, and a cackle of sledgers. Good teams provide the platform for the few genuine stars that shine now and then.

I am not opposed to players being made available and used to promote the game, but I do believe there needs to be more discrimination. Players can quickly become pop-in, pop-on, pop-off cliché-speaking marionettes, their remarks broadcast or written down and published by media people more interested in 'personalities' than in insightful, perceptive analysis of cricket.

NZC reacts sourly to any outside criticism, calls it 'negative'. Any criticism of the game, the players, or of NZC is deemed abominable, worse than mad cow's disease. Only blind men, said Doig in April 1998, can't see how much our cricket's improved. This kind of response from NZC has resulted in an antic insistence on the need to be 'positive'; for competitive commercial reasons and 'the good of the game', of course, and a promotion of the idea that nothing good can come of criticism.

Now the good of the game is best-served by selling TV rights to Sky so that large numbers of people will no longer be able to watch it.

We now get, or were getting, each morning, pre-match interviews with both coaches. 'The Coach's Word' is how it's billed. Monotonous and sometimes counter-productive. I think we have a surfeit of not very illuminating interviews, and it's actually not fair to the players. It's usually interesting to hear from Rixon, however, because he often changes his mind about things from one week to the next, and repeatedly says he's only interested in the 'positives' when, especially in Australia in 1997, he provided the players with lashings of negatives. With Rixon you start out for Ballarat and end up in Bundaberg.

During the New Zealand team's 1996 tour of Pakistan Mike Hosking interviewed Chris Harris on National Radio's 'Morning Report'. New Zealand had just lost a game. Harry's own low score hadn't helped and Hosking said so. Harry had to say something in reply, agree with Hosking's statement of the obvious. Hosking then said that Young had been brought in and he'd done worse than Harry had. So what do you think of that? Hosking asked. What, I thought, was the point of all this? I felt sorry for Harry and wondered why he'd agreed, or had been presented, to talk to Hosking, a point-scoring, take no prisoners interviewer. No one's interests are well-served by such interviews.

* * *

Before the 1996 tour to Pakistan, Doig must have been worried about whether Cairns and Parore were acceptable to other members of the New Zealand team because he asked some of them. The response of two of the more experienced players was that they would rather those two were not there. At a meeting before this tour Doig told a group of players that both Cairns and Parore would be in the team because they'd bring 20,000 people through the gate.

For the tour to Pakistan they reverted to a previous selection system, two players (one of whom was the captain, of course) and the coach. To me this is not the best arrangement, for that mix allows players too much power to limit other players' opportunities. A classic example was when the New Zealand team toured South Africa and India in early 1995. Lee Germon was given virtually no match cricket. One reason offered was that senior players, particularly Rutherford, weren't prepared to give him a chance to advance his claims for future selection as both a player and captain.

Practices also changed under the new coach Rixon. We had tried to make them fairly intense but not too long. Many players found that Rixon got them to practise for extended periods, both in the nets and at fielding, to the point whereby they thought it counter-productive. One player said he sometimes thought he'd left his best cricket at practice. Another said on one occasion in Pakistan they were forced to practise for over three hours in very hot conditions.

Under Rixon the length and severity of practices tended to be related to the nature of the most recent match performance. Players have seen these as punishment sessions. In Australia in 1997 some members of the touring party were made to go out and run around the ground after the team had put on an indifferent performance in a day-night game. There's no doubt many found Rixon's fondness for extended and intricate fielding sessions excessively long. (Former Australian coach Bob Simpson was wrily heard to say that some of Rixon's fielding routines 'he stole from me'.)

From the outset Rixon said that technical knowledge wasn't very important in coaching at top level. His approach and performance have illustrated this view. Many players generally concede that if they want technical help they need to go elsewhere. In Australia in 1997 some of the Canterbury players, for instance, frustrated by a lack of useful technical assistance from Rixon, started to look for advice from people at home.

Two players actually approached me early in 1998 and asked if I would have a look at their batting. I said that it was putting me in an awkward position, and that it would have to be done discreetly. As it happened we didn't manage to find the time to get together so nothing clandestine occurred. Pity.

* * *

What of New Zealand's tactical approach to cricket, and one-dayers particularly, since 1996? Who would know? Random is one word for it. Not very smart, either.

Although Doig, when announcing Rixon's appointment, said that New Zealand cricket would be taken to 'a new level', many were far from convinced. Someone in radio was alert to this, and in the second half of 1997 broadcasting journalist Stephen Hewson compiled and presented a documentary *Insight* programme on National Radio.

Lee Germon said some pertinent things. He said he'd personally felt, and still did, that NZC had a role in developing players as people, in developing the person as well as the player, and one of the reasons for that was that today's cricketers tended to live in 'a false world'. Some players, he said, behaved as if they were 'owed' things when they ought to see playing for New Zealand as a 'privilege'. He felt some of the current players had learnt their 'behaviour patterns' from the wrong models.

Germon felt that personalities do play a part in selections, that NZC had to be careful which players it marketed and how it marketed them. Some, he said, put themselves before the team.

Christopher Doig asserted that we, meaning New Zealand cricket teams, were judged 'wholly' by their success on the field. Not in my experience they're not. More is forgiven if they are winning, but that hasn't happened often enough anyway.

Germon's view was, and is, that the public wants a side it can be proud of – not just results.

Marketing manager Neil Maxwell said that one of the first things he noticed when he got here from Australia was that Cairns had a high profile but not the statistics to back it up. He also said that he was struck by a lack of professionalism from both administration and players, that we were amateurish. For how long had I and some others been saying this?

Maxwell said we couldn't afford to promote individuals because we didn't have the equivalent of a Shane Warne. He said stats showed that we didn't have any stars – which was when he cited Cairns as an example. Oh, Maxwell couldn't have been well-briefed by NZC. Maxwell also stated that New Zealand players needed to be paid much more (closer to what their Australian counterparts were getting) and that then, if they were asked to do something involving kids for a club, they wouldn't need to charge say $500. Which shower did he come down in? While contracted to Notts Cairns was getting more than twice as much as the New Zealand-based players, but still sold the exclusive rights to coverage of his wedding to a women's magazine. By contrast Chris Harris got married around the same time in the same church and allowed the media open access, and Lee Germon and Toni declined an offer for exclusive rights to their wedding.

Not long after Maxwell's remarks on the RNZ documentary the Australian cricketers were calling for strike action. Mark Taylor was said to be receiving close to half a million $Australian from the Australian Cricket Board alone, and that doesn't include endorsements. Warne was in a different league again. It's a pretty special individual who knows what enough is.

Accomplished former New Zealand and Wellington opening batsman Bruce Edgar said on the programme that in his view player-power was behind my removal and that proper boundaries hadn't been set.

Doig dismissed Edgar's views as being of no account. 'Full professionalism wasn't part of his era,' said Doig. No, but professional performance and conduct was very much part of Edgar's play and many of those who he played with. Patronisingly Doig went on to say Edgar was 'not close enough to the game to know what he's talking about.' At the time Edgar had just spent some months as part of a committee reviewing the state of Wellington cricket.

Bruce Edgar's test career spanned the years 1978-86. He will be 42 in November 1998, so he's no fossil. He played 39 tests, 68 innings, 1958 runs (3 centuries and 12 half-centuries) at 30.59. Only 16 New Zealanders have played more tests.

Compare Edgar's record and age with Doig's and decide for yourself who is 'close enough to the game to know what he's talking about.'

Chapter 13

Taking New Zealand Cricket to New Levels

One of the most disappointing things since I was dumped has been the continued negative behaviour and image of New Zealand players in the eyes of much of the public. Opinion is divided now as to whether things are again much the same as pre-1995, or worse. This is not only my opinion. Just before the end of the 1998 series against Zimbabwe a member of the TVNZ outside broadcasting team said to me, 'these New Zealand guys have got some serious attitude problems'. He said they were 'so arrogant' which was surprising, he added, coming from a group who weren't world-beaters. He'd spent the last few years covering rugby, and said to me that comparing the All Blacks and our cricketers was like comparing chalk and cheese. The All Blacks were cooperative, obliging, the cricketers far less so. It only takes a couple of bad apples in the box.

Others clearly felt standards had deteriorated again. Coaching New Zealand's (CNZ) president Nicki Turner (no relation) wrote in an editorial in CNZ's quarterly magazine that the New Zealand team's 'childish and inappropriate' behaviour compared unfavourably with the improvement in most other sports.

John Reid of NZC defended the cricketers and the approach encouraged by Rixon. He blamed the media for drawing attention to it. John, the cameras don't lie.

Recently, in 1998, Lee Germon, the Canterbury captain, was surprised when Stephen Fleming, just back from captaining New Zealand in Australia, sledged just about every batsman who came to the crease in a four-day Shell Trophy match. Fleming was not above sending a Zimbabwe batsman on his way back to the dressing room with a few words either. That sort of thing is unnecessary and regrettable, and something that would have been out of character for Fleming two to three years ago. I was told that Fleming was mercilessly sledged by the notorious former test player Greg Matthews while batting in Australia in 1997, and apparently that experience turned him into a committed convert himself.

In 1997 it became obvious that sledging of the opposition was openly encouraged. One player said that Rixon 'wanted the guys to be more confrontational on the park'. Rixon has said that cricket isn't a game for pussies. So.

In April, in an interview on New Zealand's sports radio station Radio Sport, the Australian wicketkeeper Ian Healy said that in 1997 the New Zealanders started it in Australia. He said our players were into it from the first day of the first test. I take an Australian arguing that others started the sledging with a grain of salt. But it was true that our guys were into it regularly, and there's something both ludicrous and pathetic about a New Zealand bowler mouthing off at batsmen when the opposition has a lead of over 200 runs on the first innings. Reports came back of players sitting around exchanging notes on who had come up with the best one-liners.

I remain convinced that most cricket supporters, and the sporting public generally, find sledging distasteful and unnecessary. My brother Greg, a pro golfer, raised the subject in his 'Chipping In' column in the New Zealand *Sunday Times* in March 1998. He wrote, 'Fortunately my game has largely avoided such puerile tactics. There has been the odd youngster come along thinking that intimidation, confrontation and emotion were the way forward. They tended to either disappear quickly or to work out they had better channel their energies into the more productive areas, such as technical improvement and emotion management, if they wanted to survive.

'As for... gamesmanship as a form of intimidation, I have always found such attempts as a great source of confidence. It was as though the opposition was admitting that to beat you by legitimate means was perhaps beyond them.'

I'll buy that.

Sledging doesn't seem to bother those at the top of NZC. In March 1998 Christopher Doig was interviewed by Brian Edwards on his National Radio 'Top of the Morning' show. Doig said sledging of a certain kind was justified as a means of getting a psychological edge over your opponent. His inference was that sledging could actually be skilful, and that sides actually planned it, used it as a tactic.

During my playing career I was part of teams that included some pretty rugged individuals, some of whom were mouthers, and I cannot recall one instance where sledging was planned. Generally sledging is practised by those who lack self-control, or who lapse into ratbag behaviour. But if, indeed, time is actually put into planning sledging, then this is scraping the bottom of the barrel. Why not spend that time on planning strategies to win games?

Take another instance of NZC's and some players' attitude to those who are critical of the 'game is not for pussies' approach. A couple of weeks before the end of the 1998 series of one-dayers against Australia in this country, John Morrison wrote in a column in the *New Zealand Herald* that there was a marked difference between the New Zealand and Australian players' attitude to autograph hunters. Morrison felt that if the attitude of one New Zealand player was in any way typical, improvement was called for.

He didn't want to mention names and this created a problem because the whole New Zealand team seemed to react as if he'd had a shot at them all.

What had happened was that Morrison took his nephews to the game in Wellington. As he left them he said, 'Have a good day, I'll see you here afterwards. Behave yourselves,' etcetera etcetera. When he picked them up and they were driving away from the ground, he asked them how things had gone. They said it was good, they'd got some Australians' autographs, 'Blocker' Wilson had offered to bowl to them on the ground, and one of the Waughs had asked them to give him a few throw-downs.

The boys said the New Zealanders' approach was rather different, and they specifically mentioned Adam Parore. According to the boys, he told them to 'fuck off'. All of us know that there are times when it is not convenient or appropriate to sign autographs, but there are ways of saying no.

So Morrison ('Mystery' to his friends, the nickname going back to his days as a player when he bowled slow left-armers that never spun and defied categorisation) alluded to this instance, without mentioning a name, in his column. My response if I had been manager or coach of the New Zealand team would have been to ask Morrison for more information. But the reaction from the New Zealand camp was, oh, it's just Morrison again getting stuck into us.

Morrison said to me and others, 'Here I am having to spend the whole week fielding flak from people in or associated with the team.

You'd think I was the one who had told the kids to fuck off.' When Morrison walked out on the park before the next game in the series he heard someone yelling at him. It was Chris Cairns. He was standing nearby signing autographs for kids. He said, 'See, I'm signing, will you go and write that?'

Doig complained about Morrison to the editor of the *New Zealand Herald* and to TVNZ Sport. Not for the first time. He'd done it before.

When Mystery told us about Cairns yelling at him it made me laugh. It reminded me of the season before, at the Basin Reserve in Wellington during a series against the Englishmen. One of the banners took the piss out of Cairns – clearly Cairns thought the owners were Turner supporters for as I passed by he broke off what he was doing, pointed at the banner, and yelled at me, 'You must have been up da da da early organising that.'

Cairnsie certainly has kept after me. More than once in the past two years or more Cairns has reminded the cricketing world how good the New Zealand team environment is now that there's a coach who recognises his right to express his individuality. This was the reason, said Cairns, dutifully reported by Geoff Longley in *The Press* in March 1998, why Rixon should be reappointed for another two years. Cairns has been nothing if not consistent and persistent in his attacks on me. One assumes he's been getting lots of praise and no dictation.

Whatever praise Cairns has been receiving hasn't improved his performance overall.

Out of curiosity I took out some statistics on Cairns's batting and bowling in order to compare his results while I was coach with his results since. During my term in 1995-96, Cairns had a test batting average of 36.22 (9 innings). Since then – all figures up until the end of June 1998 – he had a test batting average of 26.79 (29 innings). His test bowling average during 1995-96 was 25 (23 wickets, RPO 2.8); since then, 29.07 (52 wickets, RPO 3.25)

In one-day internationals in 1995-96 his batting average was 27 (19 innings). Since then, 24.64 (38 innings).

Bowling in one-dayers in 1995-96 his average was 37 (18 wickets, RPO 4.79); since then 29.65 (38 wickets, RPO 4.41).

What these stats show is that his performances overall were worse in 1996-98 in all but his bowling in one-day internationals. Unfortunately, Cairns's improved stats as a bowler in one-dayers hasn't resulted in more wins for the New Zealand team. Under the present regime he is more likely to be able to choose when he bowls. Good for Cairns, but not necessarily for the other bowlers or the team.

Incidently, it's interesting to look at Parore's stats too, just to see how he's got on under Rixon. When the Australian took over Parore had a test average of 26.80 (46 innings); in one-day internationals his average was 34.78 (50 innings). Two years later, at 30 June 1998, he was averaging 28.01 (77 innings) in tests and 29.32 (98 innings) in one-dayers.

* * *

John Graham's role as manager was unenviable. As a man he has a bit to him, is recognised as having integrity. At times he must have felt it was an uphill battle. Compared with Gren Alabaster, Graham's cricketing knowledge would barely have registered. I'm not saying it is essential that a manager have considerable cricketing knowledge, simply that when Gren was there it was very useful to have his informed input.

Graham had been principal of Auckland Grammar School when Doig taught there. When Doig was a schoolboy at Christchurch Boys' High Graham was there as a teacher. At times it has seemed as if NZC has been run by a cabal of old boys of Christchurch Boys' and Auckland Grammar. Dykes went to Auckland Grammar too. After his interview for the manager's job Graham is said to have remarked that he was a bit perplexed by the whole business, but that one thing he was sure of was that 'Turner's going to be the coach', for they kept asking him during the interview if he thought he could work with me. Graham is said to have replied that of course he could, why not?

Graham was left with some egg on his face soon after he took over during England's 1997 tour of New Zealand. A taxi driver potted Cairns, said he'd brought him back to the team's hotel around 4 a.m. in the morning. Graham wasn't prepared to take a hard line – not publicly anyway – and Doig barked at media correspondents. (For a comic account of Graham's and Doig's handling of this Cairns fiasco read Don Cameron's forthcoming book.) Lee Germon told the team and management that he felt Cairns ought to go. NZC wouldn't have it. In media interviews Doig blustered and wriggled, confirmed his reluctance to publicly admit to an error of judgement. Cairns again showed that as far as NZC was concerned he had total immunity. At the time New Zealand was performing badly on the field. People came up to me and smiled. Same old same old, they said.

I said nothing. I said nothing to the media either about Lee Germon's sacking although I was waiting for it to happen. I had told Lee in 1996 that Doig had said he was too much like me. I also told him he had one year to get himself sorted out for life after cricket – I was out by three weeks. What Lee didn't realise was that one or two of those in the team who he'd thought were allies had switched sides. It became clear after Fleming's ascension that he had been lukewarm in support of Lee. (Until then Flem had been viewed as sitting on the fence.) Writing in the *Otago Daily Times* soon after Fleming accepted the captaincy, Richard Boock reported Fleming as saying he wasn't 'prepared to treat his teammates as subordinates'. I thought this a cheap shot at Lee, and misrepresentative. Germon was not impressed, contacted NZC and said that he had refrained from taking shots at any in the team, and said that if there was any more of it he'd have something to say. Fleming backed off. Boock reported Fleming as saying of the team, 'The environment's right, and it hasn't been for a long time.' If Fleming thought that why had he not expressed his concerns beforehand?

Soon after my sacking and the return of Ross Dykes as convenor of selectors – hadn't he and Doig played club cricket together in Auckland? – the word went out that Dykes was keen to get Parore back behind the stumps. Bad news for Germon.

Meanwhile Germon's detractors within the team kept on pressing for his removal. For example, after an interview on TV at Napier, Chris Cairns turned to Ian Smith and said, 'The captain's got to go, hasn't he?' Smithy wasn't impressed. Lee was told that Cairns and Astle were two of a number of players in Napier who were heard to be discussing his future.

Germon said he'd been told that two weeks before he got dropped Martin Crowe was heard to say that the captain was going to go.

In Auckland at the penultimate one-day match against England, Doig told Germon that he understood the pressure he was under but that he could be assured he had his and Steve Rixon's total support. A few days later, after Germon had been dropped, Doig and Ross Dykes said to Lee it was because of poor form, decision-making, and that three or four senior players had questioned his captaincy. When Germon asked for specifics they declined to provide any. To the media Doig had said that the reason for Germon's demise was solely poor form.

The same day Rixon was saying publicly that it was Lee's poor decision-making and his captaincy as well as poor form.

Next morning Rixon told Germon he'd looked into Lee's captaincy and had spoken to four players who said they were struggling to communicate with him. When Germon asked him what he meant by that, Rixon said that maybe Lee didn't go out to dinner with them enough, but then he was only speculating. Lee suggested that Rixon should take into account the respective decision-making capabilities of those players.

Sacking Lee in 1997 cost NZC some money, for when he was reappointed captain in 1996 he was given a two-year contract. His contract still had a year to run, NZC had no intention of using him again, and Lee himself didn't want to have a bar of NZC ever again.

Not an Entirely Happy Family

One of the things that has characterised the current NZC administration is its determination to publicly declare that everything has never been better, that everything smells of roses. Radio Sport's Bryan Waddle, himself ticked off by NZC for some remarks he made about the crowd in Napier, usually looks to find good things to say about New Zealand cricket. But he has never been a fan of mine. He was quick to report evidence of player dissent in the West Indies but not so assiduous at delving into the causes of the problem. After we'd returned from the West Indies and I'd done several interviews on radio and TV, a journalist and a broadcaster told me, 'You've a real problem with Waddle. He's no mate of yours.' I've often heard Waddle talk of what a happy, united group the New Zealand side is under Rixon and Graham. In reality there has been quite a lot of strife and dissension.

After a match against England at Lancaster Park in 1997, the TV crew put on a barbecue for media people, players and others at the Russley Hotel. A group of New Zealand players and coach Rixon turned up. As they were leaving Rixon just happened to bump TVNZ Sport's then long-term unit manager Jimmy Biggam into the swimming pool. Biggam said that Rixon came up beside him, put his arm on him, said 'Thanks for everything, Jimmy,' and nudged him into the water.

Biggam, bespectacled, short, thickset and in his late fifties, was fully clothed – jacket and tie. He can't swim. He knocked his head. A TV employee, Warwick Larkins, reached into the pool and pulled Biggam out. Someone else recovered Biggam's glasses from the bottom of the pool. Biggam was shaken and, initially, distressed.

Rixon and the handful of New Zealand players didn't wait around long after Biggam surfaced. Biggam said Rixon 'did a runner'.

A day or so later, when out on the cricket ground at the next venue, Biggam said he asked the New Zealand captain what getting shoved into the pool was all about. Rixon was nearby and said that what he'd done was a 'sign of friendship in Australia'.

Jim Biggam, originally from Glasgow, said if Rixon had done that where he came from he wouldn't have got off with it. Biggam worked for TV for 23 years, the last 15 as unit manager for sports broadcasts, before he was made redundant after the 1997 Bledisloe Cup rugby test in Dunedin. After that match the All Black captain Sean Fitzpatrick called him into their dressing room and presented him with the match ball, signed by all team members. Biggam said, chuckling, 'it's still got blood stains on it.'

I had a lot of fun with Jimmy Biggam over the years. He never professed to know much about cricket, in fact virtually nothing, so it was easy to pull his leg. During one one-day series I went out with Jimmy and a cameraman to film the toss and briefly have a word to camera. It was the third game in a three-match series. The captains had each won a toss in the previous two games, so I told Jimmy that because of that, on this occasion they would toss three times. The captains tossed, one picked up the coin, then Jimmy stepped in and said, 'Now, for the second toss would you just move a bit closer together?' Everyone cracked up.

On another occasion, on day two of a test match, I said to Jimmy, 'Have you done the toss yet? It's getting close to the start.'

'Oh, shit,' he said, and rushed off to the dressing room to find the captains. People didn't let Jimmy forget that one.

* * *

NZC got former Australian leg-spinner Peter Philpott over to Christchurch for a few days prior to the New Zealand team's tour to

Australia in 1997. According to reports Rixon expressed the view that our guys would not score runs in Australia unless they could sweep, and sweep Warne in particular. So batsman after batsman attempted to sweep Philpott, some of them far from successfully. Rixon's response was to remark that we were going to be a failure and that we didn't have a batsman capable of succeeding in Australia. When a couple of the New Zealand players expressed their concerns about this to a former coach and player, and asked what they should do, the ex-coach, Warren Lees, told them to forget about it and play their own game.

On tour, after a succession of thrashings by state sides, Rixon admitted that he was at a loss to know where they could go next. After a poor effort against Queensland 'B' the team was subjected to a debunking tirade from Rixon, this a couple of days before a must-win one-dayer at the MCG. One player commented that this was not what they needed and that by then many players were sick of tantrums and negativity from the coach. Rixon was seen to rant and chuck items around in the dressing room when things weren't going well. He gained a reputation for being a very bad cricket watcher, unwilling to talk to people during the game and prone to kick chairs and throw cups around the room. Is that what Doig meant when he said that Steve tended to 'wear his heart on his sleeve'?

Rixon's habit of publicly criticising both the team and individual players when the team was losing was not welcomed. Some players detested it.

Rixon told players on tour that they were shaming him in front of his own people. So much for the vaunted 'people' and 'man-management' skills. What did NZC think? Who would know? But according to media reports, Doig publicly continued to praise Rixon for the job he was doing.

* * *

While the New Zealand team was struggling in Australia we kept being reminded how good the Australians were, and how we were on a steep learning curve. They – the Aussies – were 'the World Champions' said NZC and Rixon, so it's not reasonable to expect our 'inexperienced' boys to foot it with them. What rubbish. Many of our guys had played a lot of international cricket, and, further, some of the least experienced were performing best.

How did all this negativity, one wondered, square with Rixon's oft-uttered claim that he was only interested in 'the positives'?

Another tack NZC took was to remind us how few players we have compared with Australia. Yes, but numbers aren't everything. Look at how few rugby players Australia has, for example, compared to New Zealand's. And the West Indies only has a population of 4.5 to 5 million. Collectively the New Zealand cricketing public isn't stupid. They are tired of efforts to pull the wool over their eyes.

Reports had Rixon warning players that they'd better start performing quickly or they'd be replaced. More positives for the team. Rixon wasn't a national selector, and he hadn't yet said he wanted to be one, officially. 'I'm only interested in the positives.' This line came out again and again.

Sources within the team say that by the end of 1997 several players were uncomfortable about their coach, but that some, including Fleming, didn't want to see a new coach every year.

No one seemed to know what the game plan was most of the time. Often there didn't seem to be one. Seldom, if ever, were there targets, and usually it seemed as if tactics were left over to individuals, often individuals struggling for form.

Cairns remained a challenge. Early in the tour he was accorded the role of unofficial vice-captain and was involved in team selection, seemingly as part of a policy to make him feel valued and central to the action. This involvement was phased down. In the one-dayer against Australia in Adelaide, when the home side got up to win in the last over, reports came back that Cairns declined to bowl a second spell.

Once New Zealand dropped out of contention for the one-day finals Cairns wanted to come home even though there were two games left to play. (One player told me that in Pakistan, the season before, when New Zealand was 2-0 down in the one-dayers, Cairns said he'd rather not play the last game.)

There was pressure to keep him in Australia. Team management could see no reason why Cairns should not be able to play the remaining matches. Rixon's position was that Cairns could go home if he wanted to, but if he did he would never play again. John Graham and Cairns had a chat and Cairns stayed on.

Graham has gained a lot of respect for his efforts to hold the side together and set acceptable standards. Curfews were imposed in Australia and 'serious' fines introduced for breaking them. While the players accepted this curb, some felt that it was a pity they had to abide by restrictions imposed as a consequence of previous transgressions of a few. Graham also worked hard to mitigate the effects of Rixon's zealousness, what were referred to as punishment sessions. On the tour of Australia prior to Christmas there was hard training, nets and/or lengthy fielding sessions virtually every non-match day. Some of these fielding circus routines went on for an hour and a half – that's nothing but punishment – and sometimes after the end of a day's play. On some occasions there were lengthy sessions before play. The fielding didn't improve as a consequence. New Zealand was one of the best fielding sides when Rixon took over in 1996, and it still is at times, but the players haven't needed fielding sessions of the length and intensity applied since then.

The frustrating thing about the 1997 one-day series in Australia (South Africa was the other team in the competition) was that an average Australian side was there for the taking, but a poor tactical approach and absence of well-worked out game plans – if they existed at all – meant that Australia escaped and New Zealand underachieved. In an interview Fleming was asked about game plans and his answer suggested there weren't any.

Fleming found himself in an awkward situation in 1997. Prematurely made captain, inexperienced and, presumably, conscious of the fact that he was there partly as a result of a concerted campaign to undermine Germon, he was still feeling his way. At the time Fleming took over there was no way you could compare his experience of captaincy with Germon's. Rixon was largely running the show. But after the Christmas break in New Zealand, and, reportedly, John Graham's recommendations to NZC, Fleming started taking a more assertive role.

Two Years' Job Training: Re-appointing Rixon

Doig said early in 1998 that NZC was very pleased with the job Steve Rixon had been doing. Rixon, interviewed on Murray Deaker's radio programme, said he'd had no problems with Cairns or Parore, for instance, although he admitted that they'd known they'd been 'skating on skinny ice' when he came along. He also said it had been a steep learning curve for him, that he'd learnt a lot about New Zealand, New Zealanders and our cricket, and had had to change his ideas and approach. Lovely, two years of job training at NZC's expense. Fleming was upbeat about all the 'progress' that had been made. Martin Crowe's father, Dave, was singing Rixon's praises, too, in the business weekly *The Independent*. And Martin, after having had a sharp exchange with Rixon in the media over the coach's limitations, had been brought in to talk to the guys about their batting. All was well with the world. We had again turned the right corner.

* * *

After the conclusion of the one-day series in Australia early in 1998, a series which ended on a high note when Fleming played an excellent, reponsible innings that was the main reason why New Zealand won the last game against the home side, Steve Waugh, their one-day captain, said he didn't know why they were scheduled to come to New Zealand and play four one-dayers here. This was crazy, pointless, he said. Most of the Australians would rather not have to come over. Others hastily stepped in to say that this didn't mean that the Australians wouldn't be trying: of course they would, they were professionals, and so on.

But they didn't bring extra players and Paul Reiffel, Glen McGrath and Shane Warne (a late withdrawal) were unavailable through injury. In the end the Australians brought only 12 players to New Zealand. Wives and partners came as well. The Australians saw the trip as an opportunity for a bit of a holiday.

This is the sort of arrogance from the Australians which helps to motivate the opposition and its supporters, but not the Australians.

At the time I'd made a comment to our media about the Australianization, as I put it, of the game in New Zealand. As a result a couple of broadcasters on Aussie radio stations in Melbourne and Adelaide rang me for more. One of the radio hosts was part-way through discussing New Zealand cricket with a talkback caller as I waited on the phone. The host was saying that the New Zealand team should be in the second division of cricketing countries, and so on, and this wound me up sufficiently for me not to couch my views diplomatically. I said, 'Look, we don't appear to have a game plan but nor do you. Your team's brittle in the way it plays – you're trying to select a new team for one-dayers, which I think is the wrong thing to do, so your selection policy is up and down like a yo-yo. You could be knocked over easily. You could lose a couple of games.' The interviewer laughed at me, thought what I said was a joke. I meant it.

Predictably by now NZC had prepared the way in case of failure: the usual words to the effect 'don't expect too much from our lads, they're up against the World Champions.'

Australia won the first two games easily, looked in a different class. At this point some within the New Zealand sanctum felt that Rixon had just about given up on the side.

Then, the life-line. New Zealand played well in the last two games, Australia poorly, and the home side squared the series. In Napier Australia was heading for a large score then lost a bundle of wickets. New Zealand was within a whisker of going three down in the series, but it's amazing how things can turn around in cricket. Wickets tumbled, the Australians folded and left New Zealand with a modest total to chase. Our guys hardly had to play a shot in anger, went out and pushed the ball around sensibly and won easily.

In the last game, in Auckland, Australia had the wrong bowlers for the conditions. Because it was his turn they left out Moody, a big mistake. Steve Waugh got injured after colliding with Nash – or was it Nash colliding with him? Waugh admitted that their team selection policy, rotating the bowlers, and having insufficient players to choose from, hadn't helped. Irrespective, my pre-series prediction had been right. The result of the series was a fair reflection of the respective merits of the two sides.

New Zealand has a very good one-day side, potentially. The series over, out came the predictable rhetoric: New Zealand had turned the corner, had shown the benefit of the lessons learned in Australia beforehand, was developing consistency... Lessons learned. That sounds interesting, but no one spelled out precisely what it was we'd learned.

Zimbabwe arrived. Their captain Alistair Campbell said they had shown 'encouraging form' in Sri Lanka. They had had very much the better of a series against New Zealand in Zimbabwe in 1997. Hmmph. Here, in 1998, they played very badly, looked the equivalent of a side selected from Dunedin's senior club cricket competition. (Actually, it's said that that, numerically, is a fair comparison. There are very few first-class players in Zimbabwe.) That said, they underperformed dramatically. When they arrived, the statistics showed that the top three Zimbabwean batsmen – the Flowers, Grant and Andy, and Campbell – were on paper slightly better-performed than ours. Our bowlers' figures were more impressive than theirs and they confirmed it, took advantage of Zimbabwe's batsmen's failure to fire, and generally made them seem inept.

New Zealand had no trouble thrashing the visitors. This series did not prove, as NZC, Fleming and others asserted, that New Zealand had improved significantly in the past two years. Look at the facts.

Here are the results of New Zealand's internationals in recent years, up till 30 June 1998:

Tests

	P	W	L	D
1995-96	8	–	3	5
1996-97	9	3	4	2
1997-98	10	3	4	3

NB. In '96-'97, two of the wins were at home against Sri Lanka. In '97-'98 seven of the ten tests, and all wins, were against Zimbabwe and Sri Lanka.

ODIs

	P	W	L	T	NR	W%
1994-95	21	4	15	–	2	19
1995-96	23	11	12	–	–	48
1996-97	18	6	10	2	–	33
1997-98	28	10	15	1	2	36

NB. Stats for the '98 season include the Sharjah tournament in April. During '95-'96 New Zealand's games included 2 vs Zimbabwe, 1 vs Holland, 1 vs UAE. In '97-'98 our programme included 8 games against Zimbabwe.

The above statistics on the ODIs show that New Zealand's results improved significantly in 1995-96 but declined in the two years that followed.

ODIs are more popular and there are far more of them. As a result, in recent years New Zealand has played far fewer tests and a large proportion of them have been against the weaker cricketing nations. The wins against Zimbabwe and Sri Lanka shouldn't be ignored but until we begin to win more than the odd test against the recognised test-playing countries, we can't claim significant improvement in this area. In 1995-96 we lost to India, Pakistan and the West Indies 1-0. In 1996-97 we lost to England 2-0, and drew with Pakistan 1-1. In 1997-98 we lost to Australia 2-0.

During the two years from May 1996 till 30 June 1998, ten of the nineteen tests were against Zimbabwe and Sri Lanka.

* * *

The word after Zimbabwe's tour here in 1998 was that Rixon and Graham made a great team, the ideal team. The players were happy, everyone got on like a house on fire. TV cameras showed Cairns and Nash squabbling when it got tight towards the end of the last one-dayer against Zimbabwe. We had Parore mouthing off at length at the umpire for failing to give a batsman out caught off the glove when sweeping, then looking to set fields as if he and not Fleming was captain.

In May 1998 Martin Davidson wrote a piece for the New Zealand *Sunday Times* which, the sub-heading said, 'explores the rebirth' of Chris Cairns. The headline read 'Cairns earns back team respect'. When, I couldn't help thinking, was it ever admitted that he had lost it?

Davidson has Cairns contradicting himself and sniping at previous team management, again. Surprisingly John Graham seems to have bought into the myth concerning the nature of the team management of which I was a part. I was disappointed with Graham, would have expected more of a man of his background.

In the article Cairns says, 'It's not so much me who has changed; it's more the team environment.' But in the next paragraph Davidson reports Cairns as saying, 'There's no longer any scope for the way I used to carry on... if I want to be part of this environment I just don't behave that way.' Cairns is then reported as saying there's now 'enough rope' for players 'to be themselves with too' and that 'What's different from the past is that there is a total group involvement where everyone, from management to all the players, is involved in the decision making.'

This is a nasty misrepresentation of what pertained with the previous management, and the exasperating thing is that these sorts of remarks from Cairns keep being printed unchallenged.

Further, Davidson says that Cairns 'pulled out of a one-day international [in India in 1995] citing injury after team management fined him for what they believed to be inappropriate behaviour two nights before the game at a poolside function'. Davidson gets the first half of that right, but the second bit is wrong. And if that's what Cairns told him he's again loose with the truth. The true story is recounted earlier in this book.

Davidson writes that the current management 'consulted the players before revealing a set of guidelines that players had to follow.' Then he reports Graham, 'The rules you ask the guys to accept have to be fair and reasonable.' Exactly.

Davidson then reports Graham as saying of the rules imposed by him: 'Some may have appeared a little draconian to start with but they are now accepted as fair.' Graham was 'referring to rules such as 11 p.m. hotel curfews on match days and the requirment that the players are clean shaven on match days.'

We didn't have such requirements, mainly because the players didn't want them. And we're still accused of having been too rigid.

What is 'Man-management'?

The term 'man-management', presumably coined by someone in the social sciences about 30 years ago, has come to the fore in the nineties. It's chanted like a mantra and in New Zealand parallels the rise of increased player demands, increased player power – or increased player power for *some*, as most players don't abuse their position.

The term leadership is often mentioned in the same breath as man-management. But what I've come to notice is that increasingly people are accused of lacking leadership because they don't share their critic's views. It's the same with NZC and a few cricketers – play the game their way and you are a true leader, have the right man-management skills. Both catch-phrases – leadership and man-management – fit nicely into the era of the ten-second bite.

Let's look at man-management as it relates to coaching an international sports team, as opposed to running an office or business. My approach is this: be well-organised. Make sure that the rules and procedures to be followed are discussed and devised by the group so that they feel and know they have ownership of them. Put in place a system which ensures that where players break the rules natural justice prevails and they get a fair hearing. Essential to this is that a group of people makes decisions, not just one person. Make it clear how meetings will be run, and make sure that everyone knows how selections will be made. Explain tactics, invite input, and outline why a certain strategy is to be followed.

Have one-on-one sessions with players at which you discuss technique, thought-processes – how to bat or bowl for long periods in various conditions and circumstances, for instance, or where to hit the ball off certain bowlers – and specific approaches to a game. Talk about ways to improve a player's level of skill, ways to build on their strengths, ways to eradicate weaknesses.

Praise and confirmation of a good performance should be given in an adult way. Say, 'Well done.' Don't praise unexceptional performances, wait until players have lifted their game. Attempt to create a level, stable environment, which means you don't rage at players when they fail, nor make extravagant displays when they succeed. It should not be too hard for mature players to accept this. If some are not mature, help them to become so.

Discussions on management nowadays often centre on the need to complete the so-called 'management circle'. For this to happen, it is said, you need strong individuals who bring a variety of talents to the team. When you consider the differing ages, backgrounds, personalities and skills of Alabaster, Germon, Plummer and myself, that would appear to fit the management circle theory quite well. In terms of dispensing praise we were a balanced trio. Plums ladles on the praise, to the point of mollycoddling. He went out drinking and socialising with the players. Alabaster went out of his way to praise individuals. That's his way, as restraint is mine.

What Might Have Been

NZC has been down many 'right tracks' and 'turned' many corners since Germon, Alabaster and I returned home from the West Indies in 1996, a trifle apprehensive but hopeful and convinced that the national team was on the right path.

Here's what could and, in my view, ought to have happened. The first thing was a thorough debrief involving everyone concerned.

That would have been the time to discuss contentious issues, sort out our differences, make modifications after thorough analysis, plan ahead. I think it would have been best if a couple of current players had been taken out and given time for rehab and reflection.

Our plan was for Germon to remain as captain for another two to three years while another, probably Fleming, was groomed to take over in due course. At the time Fleming was appointed he just did not have the knowledge or experience required of an international captain.

If this scenario had run then we would have had little or no upheaval, none of the silliness, none of the cover-ups, and a better-informed, better-skilled, better-performed and more respected team.

Entertainment Packages: Cricket as a Product

NZC and administrators generally now talk of the need to market 'the product', cricket, especially the one-day game. Their 'entertainment package' appeals mainly to teenagers and those in their early twenties. The rest can like it or lump it. Pizazz, self-glorification and excessive behaviour; a high degree of extrovertism, petulance and rudeness is prominent. I wonder if NZC's present sponsors are happy with this development?

Commentators are moving towards hype-levels undreamed of ten years ago. Martin Crowe screaming as if calling a rugby league match. Hyperbole's in! Don't be surprised to find TV networks choosing commentators prepared to 'promote' the game in the interests of the administration, the sponsors and the networks. But aren't most of the cricket-watchers, still, people 35-plus, people with discrimination?

Many in cricket have been saying, 'Who decided on the nature and format of the entertainment packaging which now characterises international one-day matches here?' The thinking probably goes like this: tests are for the 'purists', one-dayers are for the non-serious, non-traditional cricket-goer, especially the young, those who are there for the occasion which must incorporate other 'entertainment'. But one-day internationals have been around for a long time now and many of the 'purists' quite like them.

One school of thought is that the package now provided for the one-dayers is best-suited to Cricket Max, which is backyard cricket. The greater fanfare surrounding one-day internationals here nowadays has come about since the advent of Neil Maxwell, another of Doig's finds from across the Tasman. The reason Maxwell is here is because Doig was impressed with the way a match he saw in Australia was promoted and presented. Maxwell was reported to be behind the promotion.

The break from tradition and intrinsic values has been swift and dramatic. Who decided the nature of this break? What breadth and depth of discussion took place within the game and among the cricketing public? I have no doubt that NZC will say the usual 'we have to move with the times' and it's 'essential to grow the game' stuff. But how many have been alienated in an effort to attract those whose interest is more in a social occasion than in cricket itself? When an invitation team which included Rodney Cass, an old friend and former 'keeper from Worcestershire, was here to play some cricket and watch a few of England's games against New Zealand in 1997, several members of the party said they found the off-field stuff associated with the one-dayers 'tacky'.

Nowadays the crowd is bombarded with blaring noise. Each player gets to choose a 'theme' or 'signature' song or tune to be played when they walk out to the wicket. Debate will rage over whether this adds or detracts. I suggest that more often than not it is thought to be absurd and intrusive rather than amusing or appealing.

In my view it is contrary to the essence of cricket. The true drama arises out of the cricket itself, as it always has and always will. All the sideshows do is invoke melodrama and serve to diminish the cricket, make it secondary. What is more, talking to your friends around you between overs is impossible without shouting.

NZC has said that it is looking to promote one-day games in particular as family-oriented entertainment. Many parents don't see it that way. I have spoken to a number who say that they refuse to take their young children along because of the low standard of crowd behaviour. At Napier in early 1998 one of our TV camera operators was hit on the head by a flying object and received a nasty gash. Steve Waugh, the Australian captain, reckoned the standard of crowd behaviour had dropped. If it concerns or offends Waugh it can't be overly savoury. Then you have older people like my father – he made a major contribution to the game as an umpire, and in other ways – who considers that it has 'ruined the game that I love.' At present NZC is trying to have it all ways in this regard, and the police are still grappling with how to deal with some of the crowd behaviour.

Former Central Districts player, now administrator, Blair Furlong, commented after a recent one-dayer in Napier that a great many of the people attending nowadays paid half price only. Why? Because they are still at school. They leave behind an awful mess and spend most of the time interacting with each other.

Before an administration decides to change the whole way the game is promoted and presented it ought to properly consult its traditional supporters. There are still people who subscribe to the sort of values that cricket, at its traditional best, embodies.

Many cricket-lovers are saying that NZC has virtually told them they can get lost. This process of alienation has been accelerated recently. NZC is paying lip service only to the traditions and history of a great game. Cricket's special dignity is under threat. The game is being cheapened. I think that's regrettable and unnecessary.

Will this new very young audience for one-day matches as they are promoted now come through for cricket in the long-term? That's a big question and I'm not sure of the answer. It is a question that needs to be brainstormed, to be talked through. But I do not believe that such a democratic, consultative approach is possible with NZC as it is run at present.

The Corporate Model in Cricket

Cricketing decisions need to be made by knowledgeable, astute, respected cricketing people. NZC has gone down a certain corporate road, which means you give a CEO his or her head. The Board members can easily become mere rubber stampers because it is assumed, often wrongly, that success in their own fields automatically ensures that they will make sound decisions in others. An interest in cricket does not mean a person has a deep knowledge and expertise in matters pertaining to it. Also, highly successful people in other fields often do not have the time to properly examine the issues. I have found claims of generic skills a load of nonsense when it comes to administering cricket.

I don't like the corporate model. A great many New Zealanders don't. The Deputy Editor of the New Zealand *Listener* summed it up well when he wrote in the issue of 2 May 1998 that, 'One really surprising thing is the level of blind faith that true believers have in the corporate model's ability to produce accountability. The modern corporation is many things, but open and democratic are not among its most obvious qualities. Authoritarian, secretive, intensely political, adventure playgrounds for the ambitious and obsequious would be closer to the mark.'

A few years ago NZC had what was called a cricket committee. It comprised people with impressive cricketing pedigrees. Such a group is needed as an ongoing think tank, and it needs to be given real power.

Previously all the authority lay with the Board. Under the present system what use is the Board? NZC would be better off if a cricket committee made the important cricket decisions and the CEO implemented them. That would avoid the Il Duce situation which is common in organisations where CEOs are given so much power that they succumb to megalomania.

The cricket committee as a whole should determine the approach to and culture of New Zealand cricket. If the committee decided, for instance, that the national side should not indulge in sledging, then the coach would have to instruct the players accordingly. The cricket committee would decide on the best policy in respect to player availability to the media, and so on. In such an environment the CEO would be more of a servant, less of a policy libertine. The CEO and Board would remain in control of the wider 'business' of NZC, but the cricket matters would be over to the cricket committee. The CEO, coach and other employees would, of course, be expected and encouraged to bring their ideas on these matters to the cricket committee. To me the system NZC has now is flawed and too much power is in the hands of a CEO with a limited, amateur's knowledge of cricket. I suppose it could be workable if the CEO kept out of the cricket side of things and acted solely as a facilitator, but why risk it?

A question that immediately arises is, 'Who selects the members of the cricket committee? And how?' Let's leave that aside for now and just say that a cricket committee of six very knowledgeable and preferably former international cricketers would give stable, informed direction, more consistency and continuity of policy direction. The core of such a committee is likely to stay together for many years, far longer than the customary tenure of managers, coaches and some CEOs. Co-opting others from time to time to assist in some areas is to be expected; those brought in would add to the core of knowledge.

There remains a lack of trust in NZC. It permeates the scene. To those players who say they now have faith and trust in NZC I say, Beware of Greeks bearing gifts. If you've got this far reading this book you'll know what I mean.

Cricket supporters find it hard to know what to believe of messages issuing from NZC. In the business world there are often good reasons for maintaining confidentiality. But that's seldom the case in cricket where the paying supporters – shareholders if you like – have a right to be told the truth. The public expects higher standards of sport, and of those involved in it.

Soon after I was sacked I was reported in the media as saying my demise had a great deal to do with a desire for 'power and control'. That's become even more evident.

A friend of mine from Napier, Brian Talbot, a graduate of Otago, unbeknown to me rang Doig soon after I'd been removed and expressed his displeasure. Doig's reply was to ask, 'Will you be as quick to ring me up and congratulate me when I bring the World Cup to New Zealand in two years' time?'

Talbot's reply was, 'Actually, the World Cup's in three years' time, not two. You can't even get that right.'

Recently, radio commentators and talkback callers have been saying that, 'Perhaps it's simply that New Zealanders aren't very good at playing cricket, and never will be.' It's not that simple. I don't agree with that at all.

That will be obvious to readers of this book. No one has all the answers on how best to play the great game of cricket. It's too complex, unpredictable, and fascinating a game for that. But I am certain that there is a sickness at the heart of New Zealand cricket, and that many of those who have been running the game here have not been good at recruiting and retaining those with most knowledge of it.

The deeper-seated problems in our cricket have still not been addressed. Until they are the sporting public will continue to view New Zealand cricket with amusement, bemusement, exasperation, and disappointment.

APPENDIX

GLENN MAITLAND TURNER

Playing Record

First Class Career: 1964/65 – 1982/83
Test Career: 1968/69 – 1982/83
Worcestershire: 1967 – 1982
Otago: 1964/65 – 1975/76; 1979/80; 1982/83
Northern Districts: 1976/77

	Mtchs	*Inngs*	*NO*	*HS*	*Agg*	*Ave*	*100s*	*50s*	*Ctchs*
First Class Career	455	792	101	311*	34,346	49.70	103	148	410
Test Career	41	73	6	259	2,991	44.64	7	14	42
One-Day Internationals	41	40	6	171*	1,598	47.00	3	9	13
Limited-Overs Matches for Worcestershire	195	195	12	147	6,958	38.02	8	47	82

International Tours

1969; 1973 New Zealand in the United Kingdom
1969; 1976 New Zealand in India
1969; 1976 New Zealand in Pakistan
1969/70; 1973/74 New Zealand in Australia
1972 New Zealand in the West Indies
1972; 1974; 1975 International Wanderers in Rhodesia
1976 International Wanderers in South Africa
1975; 1979; 1983 World Cup in England

Also played in Ireland, Holland, Germany, Switzerland, USA, Canada, Bermuda, Singapore and Hong Kong.

Coaching Positions

1971/72 – 1975/76; 1979/80; 1982/83	**Otago Cricket Association**
1976/77	**Northern Districts Cricket Association**
	New Zealand Cricket Team (Cricket Manager)
1985/86	New Zealand in Australia
1986	New Zealand in Australia (Benson & Hedges Cup)
1985/86	Australia in New Zealand
1986	New Zealand in England
1986/87	West Indies in New Zealand
1987	New Zealand in India (World Cup)
	New Zealand Cricket Team (Coach)
1995/96	New Zealand in Darwin
1995/96	New Zealand in India
1995/96	Pakistan in New Zealand
1995/96	Zimbabwe in New Zealand
1996	New Zealand in India/Pakistan (World Cup)
1996	New Zealand in the West Indies
	New Zealand Cricket Academy
1991	Youth XI, Emerging Players Squad, World Cup Squad
1992	Youth XI, Emerging Players Squad
1993	NZ Women's Squad
1994	NZ Women's Squad

Coaching Record

1985/86	New Zealand in Australia	*(Tests: NZ 2, Aust 1)*
1986	New Zealand in Australia	*(B&H Cup: W3, L6)*
1986	Australia in New Zealand	*(Tests: NZ 1, Aust 0)* *(ODI: NZ 2, Aust 2)*
1986	New Zealand in England	*(Tests: NZ 1, Eng 0)* *(ODI: NZ 1, Eng 1)*
1987	West Indies in New Zealand	*(Tests: NZ 1, WI 1)* *(ODI: NZ 0, WI 3)*
1987	New Zealand in India	*(World Cup: W2, L4)*
1995/96	New Zealand in Darwin	*(W5, L1)*
1995/96	New Zealand in India	*(Tests: NZ 0, India 1, drawn 2)* *(ODI: NZ 2, India 3)*
1995/96	Pakistan in New Zealand	*(Tests: NZ 0, Pak 1)* *(ODI: NZ 2, Pak 2)*
1995/96	Zimbabwe in New Zealand	*(Tests: NZ 0, Zim 0, drawn 2)* *(ODI: NZ 2, Zim 1)*
1996	New Zealand in India/Pak.	*(World Cup: W3, L3)*
1996	New Zealand in West Indies	*(Tests: NZ 0, WI 1, drawn 1)* *(ODI: NZ 2, WI 3)*

Captaincy

1974/75; 1975/76	**Otago**	
1976/77	**Northern Districts**	
1975/76	**New Zealand**	*(India in New Zealand)*
1976	**New Zealand**	*(NZ in India & Pakistan)*
1976/77	**New Zealand**	*(Australia in New Zealand)*
1981	**Worcestershire**	

Captaincy Record

1974/75	**Otago**	*(Winners Plunket Shield)*
1975/76	**Otago**	*(Second, Shell Cup)* *(Second, Shell Trophy)*
1976/77	**Northern Districts**	*(Winners, Shell Cup)*
1975/76	**New Zealand** India in New Zealand	 *(Tests: NZ 1, India 1)* *(ODI: NZ 2, India 0)*
	New Zealand in Pakistan	*(Tests: NZ 0, Pak 2)* *(ODI: NZ 1, Pak 0)*
	New Zealand in India	*(Tests: NZ 0, India 2)*
	Australia in New Zealand	*(Tests: NZ 0, Aust 1)*

Selector

1974/75; 1975/76	**Otago**
1973 –	**New Zealand** (whilst on tours from 1973 on)
1995 – 1996	**New Zealand**